Elements of Literature

First Course

Holt Assessment: Literature, Reading, and Vocabulary

- Entry-Level Test and End-of-Year Test
- Collection Diagnostic Tests
- Selection Tests
- Collection Summative Tests
- Answer Key

HOLT, RINEHART AND WINSTON

A Harcourt Education Company

Orlando • **Austin** • New York • San Diego • Toronto • London

STAFF CREDITS

Editorial Staff: Thomas Browne, e2 Publishing Services, llc, *Writers and Editors;* Lanie Lee, Shelley Hoyt, *Text Editors*

Copyediting: Michael Neibergall, *Copyediting Manager;* Kristen Azzara, Mary Malone, *Copyediting Supervisors;* Christine Altgelt, Elizabeth Dickson, Leora Harris, Anne Heausler, Kathleen Scheiner, *Senior Copyeditors;* Emily Force, Julia Thomas Hu, Nancy Shore, *Copyeditors*

Project Administration: Marie Price, *Managing Editor;* Elizabeth LaManna, *Associate Managing Editor;* Janet Jenkins, *Senior Editorial Coordinator;* Christine Degollado, Betty Gabriel, Mark Koenig, Erik Netcher, *Editorial Coordinators*

Permissions: Ann Farrar, *Senior Permissions Editor;* Sally Garland, Susan Lowrance, *Permissions Editors*

Design: Betty Mintz, Richard Metzger, *Design Directors;* Chris Smith, *Senior Designer*

Production: Beth Prevelige, *Senior Production Manager;* Carol Trammel, *Production Manager;* Myles Gorospe, *Production Assistant*

Manufacturing: Shirley Cantrell, *Manufacturing Supervisor;* Mark McDonald, *Inventory Analyst;* Amy Borseth, *Manufacturing Coordinator*

Printed in the United States of America

ISBN 0-03-068518-4

1 2 3 4 5 6 179 06 05 04 03

Table of Contents

Collection 4 Point of View: Can You See It My Way?

Collection 5 Worlds of Words: Prose and Poetry

Collection 6   Our Literary Heritage: Greek Myths and World Folk Tales

Collection 7 Literary Criticism: Where I Stand

Collection 8 Reading for Life

Overview of ELEMENTS OF LITERATURE Assessment Program

Two assessment booklets have been developed for ELEMENTS OF LITERATURE.

(1) Assessment of student mastery of selections and specific literary, reading, and vocabulary skills in the **Student Edition:**

- *Holt Assessment: Literature, Reading, and Vocabulary*

(2) Assessment of student mastery of writing workshops and specific media, writing, listening, and speaking skills and assignments in the **Student Edition:**

- *Holt Assessment: Writing, Listening, and Speaking*

Holt Assessment: Literature, Reading, and Vocabulary contains two types of diagnostic tests:

- The Entry-Level Test is a diagnostic tool that helps you determine (1) how well students have mastered essential prerequisite skills needed for the year and (2) to what degree students understand the concepts that will be taught during the current year. This test uses multiple tasks to assess mastery of literary, reading, and vocabulary skills.

- The Collection Diagnostic Tests help you determine the extent of students' prior knowledge of literary, reading, and vocabulary skills taught in each collection. These tests provide vital information that will assist you in helping students master collection skills.

Holt Online Essay Scoring can be used as a diagnostic tool to evaluate students' writing proficiency:

- For each essay, the online scoring system delivers a holistic score and analytic feedback related to five writing traits. These two scoring methods will enable you to pinpoint the strengths of your students' writing as well as skills that need improvement.

Diagnostic Assessment

NOTE: You may wish to address the needs of students who are reading below grade level. If so, you can administer the Diagnostic Assessment for Reading Intervention, found in the front of *Holt Reading Solutions.* This assessment is designed to identify a student's reading level and to diagnose the specific reading comprehension skills that need instructional attention.

Ongoing, Informal Assessment

The **Student Edition** offers systematic opportunities for ongoing, informal assessment and immediate instructional follow-up. Students' responses to their reading; their writing, listening, and speaking projects; and their work with vocabulary skills all serve as both instructional and ongoing assessment tasks.

Overview of ELEMENTS OF LITERATURE
Assessment Program *(continued)*

- Throughout the **Student Edition,** practice and assessment are immediate and occur at the point where skills are taught.

- In order for assessment to inform instruction on an ongoing basis, related material repeats instruction and then offers new opportunities for informal assessment.

- Skills Reviews at the end of each collection offer a quick evaluation of how well students have mastered the collection skills.

Progress Assessment

Students' mastery of the content of the **Student Edition** is systematically assessed in two test booklets:

- *Holt Assessment: Literature, Reading, and Vocabulary* offers a test for every selection. Multiple-choice questions focus on comprehension, the selected skills, and vocabulary development. In addition, students write answers to constructed-response prompts that test their understanding of the skills.

- *Holt Assessment: Writing, Listening, and Speaking* provides both multiple-choice questions for writing and analytical scales and rubrics for assignments in the writing and media workshops. In addition, scales and rubrics are included for the speaking and listening skills and assignments in the Speaking and Listening Handbook in the **Student Edition**. These instruments assess proficiency in all the writing applications appropriate for each grade level.

Summative Assessment

Holt Assessment: Literature, Reading, and Vocabulary contains two types of summative tests:

- The Collection Summative Tests, which appear at the end of every collection, ask students to apply their recently acquired skills to a new literary selection. These tests contain both multiple-choice questions and constructed-response prompts.

- The End-of-Year Test helps you determine how well students have mastered the skills and concepts taught during the year. This test mirrors the Entry-Level Test and uses multiple tasks to assess mastery of literary, reading, and vocabulary skills.

Holt Online Essay Scoring can be used as an end-of-year assessment tool:

- You can use *Holt Online Essay Scoring* to evaluate how well students have mastered the writing skills taught during the year. You will be able to assess student mastery using a holistic score as well as analytic feedback based on five writing traits.

Monitoring Student Progress

Both *Holt Assessment: Literature, Reading, and Vocabulary* and *Holt Assessment: Writing, Listening, and Speaking* include skills profiles that record progress toward the mastery of skills. Students and teachers can use the profiles to monitor student progress.

***One-Stop Planner*® CD-ROM with ExamView® Test Generator**

All of the questions in this booklet are available on the *One-Stop Planner*® **CD-ROM with ExamView® Test Generator.** Use the ExamView Test Generator to customize any of the tests in this booklet and create a test unique to your classroom situation. You can then print a test or post it to the *Holt Online Assessment* area at www.myhrw.com.

Holt Online Assessment

Holt Online Assessment provides an easy way to administer tests to your students online. Students can log on to www.myhrw.com to take a test that you have created using the ExamView Test Generator, or you can assign one of the tests already available on the site: the Entry-Level, End-of-Year, and Collection Diagnostic Tests from *Holt Assessment: Literature, Reading, and Vocabulary* and the Writing Workshop Tests from *Holt Assessment: Writing, Listening, and Speaking*.

About This Book

Holt Assessment: Literature, Reading, and Vocabulary accompanies ELEMENTS OF LITERATURE. The booklet includes copying masters for diagnostic tests, selection tests, and summative tests to assess students' knowledge of prerequisite skills, their comprehension of the readings in the **Student Edition,** and their mastery of the skills covered in each collection.

Entry-Level Test

The **Entry-Level Test** is a diagnostic tool that enables you to evaluate your students' mastery of essential skills at the start of the year. This objective, multiple-choice test contains several reading selections followed by questions assessing students' comprehension of their reading and their knowledge of select literary skills. Other sections of the test evaluate students' command of vocabulary skills.

Collection Tests

The copying masters in *Holt Assessment: Literature, Reading, and Vocabulary* are organized by collection. There are three types of tests for each collection:

- A **Collection Diagnostic Test** is included for every collection. These multiple-choice tests cover literary terms and devices as well as reading and vocabulary skills. These tests will enable you to assess students' prior knowledge of the skills taught in each collection.

- A **Selection Test** accompanies every major selection in the **Student Edition.** Each Selection Test includes objective questions that assess students' comprehension of the selection, mastery of literary skills as they apply to the selection, and acquisition of vocabulary words. In addition, students write a brief essay in response to a constructed-response prompt that asks them to formulate answers independently using their newly acquired skills.

- A **Collection Summative Test** follows the selection tests for each collection. This test asks students to apply their new skills to a selection that does not appear in the **Student Edition.** Students are asked to read a brief selection and then respond to multiple-choice questions and constructed-response prompts that assess their comprehension of the selection and vocabulary, reading, and literary skills.

End-of-Year Test

The **End-of-Year Test** is a summative tool that assesses students' mastery of the skills and concepts taught during the year. Like the Entry-Level Test, this test uses a multiple-choice format to assess students' comprehension of several reading selections and their mastery of literary and vocabulary skills.

About This Book *(continued)*

Answer Sheets and Answer Key

Answer Sheets are provided for the Entry-Level Test and the End-of-Year Test. If you prefer, students may mark their answers on the tests themselves. For all collection tests, students should write their answers on the tests. The **Answer Key** provides answers to objective questions. It also provides model responses to constructed-response prompts.

Skills Profile

The **Skills Profile** lists the skills assessed by the tests in this booklet. You can use the Skills Profile to create a developmental record of your students' progress as they master each skill.

Administering the Tests

The format of the Entry-Level Test and the End-of-Year Test, with their accompanying answer sheets, replicates that of most standardized tests. You can use these tests to help familiarize your students with the types of standardized tests they will take in the future.

To administer these tests, prepare a copy of the appropriate test and answer sheet for each student. Some sections of the tests have sample items. Before students begin these sections, you may want to select the correct answer for the sample items with the class. Then, answer any questions students have about the samples. When students demonstrate that they understand how to do the items, have them begin these sections. Students may record their answers on the answer sheets or on the tests.

To administer the collection tests, prepare a copy of each test for your students. Students should mark their answers on the tests themselves. When administering Selection Tests that cover poetry, you may want to allow students to use the textbook, since these tests often require a response to the precise wording, rhythm, or meter of a particular poem. You also have the option of making any Selection Test an open-book test.

***One-Stop Planner*® CD-ROM with ExamView® Test Generator**

The tests in this booklet are included on the ***One-Stop Planner*® CD-ROM with ExamView® Test Generator.** Use the ExamView Test Generator to customize and print a test tailored to the needs of your students. You can also post the test to the *Holt Online Assessment* area at www.myhrw.com.

Holt Online Assessment

Using *Holt Online Assessment,* students can log on to www.myhrw.com to take a test that you have customized using the ExamView Test Generator. They can also take the Entry-Level Test, End-of-Year Test, and Collection Diagnostic Tests, which are already available on the site.

Entry-Level Test

Reading and Literary Analysis

DIRECTIONS: Read each selection. Then, read each question about the selection. Decide which is the best answer to the question. Mark the space for the answer you have chosen.

SAMPLE

> Two tools can make your computer screen more exciting to look at. One tool is a background image that covers your screen but does not move. This image is called wallpaper. Wallpaper may be a photograph of a mountain, an abstract painting, or a geometric design.
>
> Another tool is called a screen saver. Screen savers are like wallpaper but with motion. For example, a screen saver may show colorful balls bouncing around the screen. Some screen savers even produce sound effects.

A   What is the *main* difference between wallpaper and screen savers?

    A Color
    B Size
    C Motion
    D Shape

B   A person would *most* likely use wallpaper and screen savers to —

    F make the screen last longer
    G create a more attractive screen
    H help a viewer see the screen
    J make the computer easier to use

Reading and Literary Analysis

from Black Beauty

by Anna Sewell

In this selection a horse named Black Beauty describes an adventure he has while pulling a carriage toward home on a blustery day. Black Beauty's master and the driver, John, ride in the carriage.

1   The wind was then much higher, and I heard the master say to John, he had never been out in such a storm. . . .

2   [Suddenly] there was a groan, and a crack, and a splitting sound, and tearing, crashing down among the other trees came an oak, torn up by the roots, and it fell right across the road just before us. I will never say I was not frightened, for I was. I stopped still, and I believe I trembled. . . . John jumped out and was in a moment at my head.

3   "That was a very near touch," said my master. "What's to be done now?"

4   "Well, sir, we can't drive over that tree nor yet get round it; there will be nothing for it, but to go back to the four crossways, and . . . round to the wooden bridge. . . ."

5   So back we went and round by the crossroads; but by the time we got to the bridge, it was very nearly dark. We could just see that the water was over the middle of it; but as that happened sometimes when the floods were out, master did not stop. We were going along at a good pace, but the moment my feet touched the first part of the bridge I felt sure there was something wrong. I dare not go forward, and I made a dead stop. "Go on, Beauty," said my master, and he gave me a touch of the whip, but I dare not stir; he gave me a sharp cut, I jumped, but I dare not go forward.

6   "There's something wrong, sir," said John, and he sprang out of the *dogcart* and came to my head and looked all about. He tried to lead me forward. "Come on, Beauty, what's the matter?" Of course I could not tell him, but I knew very well that the bridge was not safe.

7   Just then the man at the tollgate on the other side ran out of the house, tossing a torch like one mad.

8   "Hoy, hoy, hoy, halloo, stop!" he cried.

9   "What's the matter?" shouted my master.

10   "The bridge is broken in the middle, and part of it is carried away; if you come on you'll be in the river."

Reading and Literary Analysis

11   "Thank God!" said my master. "You Beauty!" said John, and took the bridle and gently turned me round to the right-hand road by the riverside. The sun had set some time, the wind seemed to have lulled off after that furious *blast* which tore up the tree. It grew darker and darker, stiller and stiller. I trotted quietly along, the wheels hardly making a sound on the soft road.

1. **Which words help the reader *hear* the action in the story?**

    A "he gave me a touch of the whip"
    B "It grew darker and darker, stiller and stiller."
    C "there was a groan, and a crack, and a splitting sound"
    D "I will never say I was not frightened, for I was."

2. **In paragraph 5, the phrase "made a dead stop" is —**

    F an analogy
    G an idiom
    H a metaphor
    J a simile

3. **What does Beauty's master mean when he says, "That was a very near touch"?**

    A That was an enormous tree.
    B The tree almost fell.
    C The tree almost hit us.
    D That tree blocked our path home.

4. **In this story, the reader learns about Beauty's character *mostly* through —**

    F Beauty's thoughts and actions
    G the way that John treats Beauty
    H the words and actions of Beauty's master
    J how Beauty reacts to John

5. **In the story, Beauty says, ". . . the moment my feet touched the first part of the bridge I felt sure there was something wrong." The author *most* likely included this detail to —**

    A suggest that the story is fictional
    B establish point of view
    C identify characters
    D create suspense

6. **In paragraphs 5 through 11, the master's feelings about the horse's actions change from —**

    F frustrated to thankful and proud
    G angry to confused
    H frustrated to angry
    J proud and happy to frustrated

Reading and Literary Analysis

7. The author organized this story by —

    A listing a series of people and events
    B presenting causes and effects
    C comparing and contrasting
    D describing events in the order they happened

8. Which of Beauty's character traits helps him solve the problem at the bridge?

    F Great strength
    G Ability to trust his instincts
    H Ability to learn from mistakes
    J Gentle nature

9. How does Beauty save his master and John from danger?

    A He pulls the carriage to the toll gate.
    B He goes around the fallen oak tree.
    C He pulls the carriage onto the bridge.
    D He refuses to step further onto the bridge.

10. In paragraph 11, the word *blast* means —

    F an explosion
    G the blowing of a horn
    H a strong gust of wind
    J a fun time

11. There is enough information in the story to suggest that a *dogcart* is a type of —

    A carriage
    B darkness
    C tree
    D raincoat

12. Which phrase *best* describes one of the topics of this story?

    F Safety during storms
    G Travel by carriage
    H The power of nature
    J The loneliness of travel

GO ON

Holt Assessment: Literature, Reading, and Vocabulary

Reading and Literary Analysis

Stars
by Sara Teasdale

Alone in the night
On a dark hill
With pines around me
Spicy and still,

5   And a heaven full of stars
Over my head
White and *topaz*
And misty red;

Myriads[1] with beating
10 Hearts of fire
The aeons[2]
Cannot *vex* or tire;

Up the dome of heaven
Like a *great* hill
15 I watch them marching
Stately and still.

And I know that I
Am honored to be
Witness
20 Of so much majesty.

1. myriads (mir′ē·ədz) *n. pl.*: many; large numbers.
2. aeons (ē′ənz) *n. pl.*: ages; long periods of time.

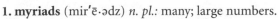
GO ON

Reading and Literary Analysis

13. Which line from the poem gives stars human traits?

    A Line 3—With pines around me
    B Line 14—Like a great hill
    C Line 15—I watch them marching
    D Line 20—Of so much majesty

14. In line 4, the poet uses the word *Spicy* to describe the —

    F darkness all around
    G chill in the air
    H smell of the pines
    J sparkle of the stars

15. Which word helps the poet create a quiet tone?

    A Still
    B Beating
    C Honored
    D Majesty

16. The phrase "beating/Hearts of fire" helps the reader to picture the —

    F milky white light of the moon
    G dark background of the night sky
    H towering pine trees
    J flickering light of the stars

17. In line 12, the word *vex* means —

    A bother
    B soar
    C love
    D chase

18. The setting of this poem is *most* likely —

    F near a fire
    G in a forest
    H on another planet
    J in outer space

GO ON

Reading and Literary Analysis

19. **In line 7, the word *topaz* means —**

    A yellow

    B enormous

    C moving

    D bright

20. **This poem is *mainly* about —**

    F a person's fear of nature

    G feelings of loneliness

    H the importance of color

    J the beauty of the stars

21. **The first stanza of the poem —**

    A establishes the setting

    B states the main idea or theme

    C uses a metaphor

    D uses a simile

22. **In line 16, what does *Stately* mean?**

    F Sorrowful

    G Grand

    H Alone

    J Bright

23. **Which line from the poem contains a metaphor?**

    A Line 6—Over my head

    B Line 8—And misty red

    C Line 13—Up the dome of heaven

    D Line 19—Witness

24. **The poet's attitude could be described as —**

    F full of awe

    G disappointed

    H somewhat nervous

    J marked by sadness

GO ON

Reading and Literary Analysis

Click, Click . . . Click

1   Mary Hagedorn places a bicycle helmet on her head and wades silently into the murky Amazon River. Then she bends over and puts the tip of a wire attached to the helmet into the water. The wire is part of an electronic device that *registers* sounds. Hagedorn doesn't notice the typical sounds of the rain forest—the shrill call of birds and the buzzing of mosquitoes. Instead, she concentrates on the noises coming from a speaker attached to the wire.

2   Hagedorn is a biologist who studies fish that emit electrical pulses. The pulses travel from these "electric fish" through the water. The end of the wire Hagedorn has placed in the water has a microphone designed to pick up the pulses. The pulses travel from the microphone to the speaker near Hagedorn's ear. To Hagedorn, the pulses sound like clicking noises or notes from a flute.

3   There are more than 100 kinds of electric fish, and each makes a different signal. Because Hagedorn has learned to recognize the sounds made by different types of electric fish, she can tell what type of fish made a particular sound. She can even tell if a male or female fish made the sound.

4   Working with other scientists, Hagedorn has learned that some of the fish use the signals to communicate with one another. The fish also use the electrical charges to protect themselves and to detect objects as they swim.

5   Some electric fish are called "strongly electric fish." These fish use electric signals to stun their prey. One strongly electric fish, the electric eel, can grow to be nine feet in length and can generate enough electricity to power three refrigerators! This monster fish can even stun large animals, such as deer, that wade into a river. It's no wonder that Hagedorn quickly leaves the river if she hears the slow, irregular clicks made by an electric eel, sounds she calls "creepy."

6   Hagedorn doesn't spend all of her time wading in the Amazon River. She also studies fish that she captures from the river and keeps in tanks at a lab located in Manu Park, Peru. One type of fish kept at the lab is the knife fish, so named because its body looks like the blade of a knife. Knife fish use electrical signals as a kind of radar to locate insects to eat.

Reading and Literary Analysis

7   Hagedorn's work adds to our knowledge of the world. It also helps the people who live near the Amazon River. Hagedorn and other scientists keep track of the number of electric fish that live in different parts of the river. They listen to the sounds made by the fish. Then they record the types of fish they hear and note where the fish are located. They use this information as an *indicator* of the river's health. If the number of a certain type of fish drops suddenly, the scientists know that something is wrong.

8   Hagedorn enjoys studying electric fish and sharing her knowledge with others. She hopes her discoveries about electric fish help people around the world better understand Earth's animals.

GO ON

Reading and Literary Analysis

25. **This article is *mainly* about —**

    A   how animals communicate
    B   the health of the Amazon River
    C   a woman who listens to fish
    D   the dangerous knife fish

26. **There is enough information in the article to show that —**

    F   only male knife fish make clicks
    G   knife fish are shaped like the blade of a knife
    H   knife fish do not emit much electricity
    J   the clicks made by knife fish can be very loud

27. **In paragraph 7 of this article, the word *indicator* means —**

    A   sound
    B   microphone
    C   improvement
    D   measurement

28. **Why does Hagedorn place the microphone in water?**

    F   If the microphone is not wet, it will not work properly.
    G   She needs to rinse off the microphone before she records observations.
    H   She wants to pick up electrical pulses from fish in the river.
    J   The microphone is powered by electricity in the water.

29. **From this article, you could conclude that —**

    A   studies of fish in the river are more valuable than studies of fish in the lab
    B   Mary Hagedorn's work disturbs the fish in the Amazon River
    C   Mary Hagedorn contributes in important ways to the field of biology
    D   Mary Hagedorn's studies mostly help people who live along the Amazon River

Reading and Literary Analysis

30. **Which of these sentences gives the *best* summary of the selection?**

    F Mary Hagedorn is a biologist who studies electric fish in the Amazon.

    G Mary Hagedorn hates to hear slow, irregular clicks.

    H Mary Hagedorn studies fish at a lab located at Manu Park, Peru.

    J Mary Hagedorn uses a microphone in the water.

31. **In the article, an electric eel is described as a —**

    A monster

    B deer

    C refrigerator

    D microphone

32. **The author *most* likely wrote this article to —**

    F tell a frightening story about electricity

    G describe the wildlife of the Amazon rain forest

    H explain how to convert a helmet into an electronic device

    J describe the exciting work of Mary Hagedorn

33. **Which sentence states the *main* idea of paragraph 6?**

    A Hagedorn studies fish in her lab.

    B Hagedorn captures fish and puts them in tanks at a lab.

    C The knife fish is named for its shape.

    D Knife fish use electrical signals to locate insects to eat.

GO ON

Reading and Literary Analysis

34. This article would *most* likely be found in —

  F an autobiography

  G a math book

  H a short story collection

  J a science magazine

35. The author of the article uses the first paragraph to —

  A describe how Hagedorn does her work

  B explain why Hagedorn's work is important

  C provide information about the Amazon River

  D explain how electric fish send pulses through water

36. "Strongly electric fish" are electric fish that —

  F are very large

  G use electricity to stun prey

  H swim very fast

  J send out loud electrical pulses

37. In paragraph 1 of this article, the word *registers* means —

  A picks up

  B sends out

  C carries across

  D signs up

38. There is enough information in this article to show that an electric eel could —

  F make sounds like a flute

  G swim rapidly

  H crawl onto land

  J harm a person

39. When Hagedorn is listening for fish sounds, which event happens last?

  A Hagedorn hears electrical pulses as clicks.

  B An electric fish emits an electrical pulse.

  C An electrical pulse travels through the water.

  D A microphone picks up the sound of an electrical pulse.

40. Why does Mary Hagedorn get out of the water when she hears a slow, irregular clicking noise?

  F The speaker's battery may be running low.

  G A knife fish is about to attack.

  H An electric eel may be nearby.

  J The noise is a signal from camp.

Vocabulary

DIRECTIONS: Choose a word or group of words that has the same, or about the same, meaning as the underlined word. Mark the space for the answer you have chosen.

SAMPLE   A

Please <u>delete</u> the messages after you read them.

A remove
B re-read
C sign
D open

---

41. The snowstorm <u>obscured</u> the hiker's tracks.

A melted
B covered
C created
D froze

42. The bakery provided an <u>assortment</u> of muffins.

F order
G shipment
H basket
J variety

43. The <u>tenants</u> of the apartment building wanted better service.

A leaders
B managers
C children
D residents

44. The store will <u>discount</u> all its shoes on Saturday.

F rearrange
G move to another spot
H lower the price of
J get rid of

45. The book tells about Jane Goodall's <u>notable</u> work with apes.

A important
B difficult
C pleasant
D future

46. The fruit salad looked too <u>irresistible</u> to pass up.

F unappetizing
G alluring
H tasteless
J aromatic

GO ON

NAME _____ CLASS _____ DATE _____

Vocabulary

DIRECTIONS: Read each sentence in the box. Then, choose the answer in which the underlined word is used in the same way. Mark the space for the answer you have chosen.

SAMPLE   B

> **Alaska is the largest state.**
>
> A He will state his reason for missing the meeting.
> B The chemical was not in a stable state.
> C The state of his health was fair.
> D We have visited every state in the West.

47. **We must seek harbor from the wind.**

    A The cave may harbor many pests.
    B He didn't harbor any bad feelings after the incident.
    C The island provided us harbor during the storm.
    D The enormous ship pulled safely into the harbor.

48. **We waited for two hours at the railroad station.**

    F He will station himself near the store to watch for you.
    G We hurried into the crowded station.
    H He was unhappy with his station in life.
    J The weather station was equipped with radar.

49. **The frame of the house had been damaged by the storm.**

    A The expensive painting had a beautiful frame.
    B The window frame needs to be repaired.
    C I will frame my answer in simple terms.
    D The boat's frame was made of wood.

50. **My grandmother shared her formula for treating colds.**

    F Give the baby her formula at noon.
    G The formula for making soap was more than 100 years old.
    H He wrote the chemical formula very carefully.
    J The formula for settling the argument begins with good communication.

STOP

Holt Assessment: Literature, Reading, and Vocabulary

COLLECTION 1 DIAGNOSTIC TEST

Facing Danger

On the line provided, write the letter of the *best* answer to each of the following items.
(100 points; 10 points each)

_____ **1.** The **plot** of a story is —

    A a series of related events

    B an idea about life

    C the place where the story occurs

    D the writer's attitude toward the subject

_____ **2.** Which of the following sentences contains an example of a **conflict**?

    F While Nicole played the piano, her brother played the violin.

    G Mitch and Robby went to the same school for many years.

    H At the campsite that night, the family was threatened by a hungry bear.

    J Nina was elected class president two years in a row.

_____ **3.** When **complications** arise in a story, —

    A actions and events do not seem logical

    B the characters face new problems

    C the events make the story as long as a novel

    D there is more than one main character

_____ **4.** A story's most exciting moment is called —

    F the main idea

    G its subject

    H foreshadowing

    J the climax

_____ **5.** In the **resolution** of a story, —

    A new characters are introduced

    B mysterious events occur

    C information about the author is presented

    D all the loose ends of the story are tied up

_____ **6.** When people read a **suspenseful** story, they feel —

    F happy because events in the story are funny

    G disappointed because the story is not believable

    H disturbed by the frightening, bloody details in the story

    J uncertainty or anxiety about what will happen next in the story

_____ **7.** The **table of contents** of a textbook tells you the —

    A year the book was published

    B topics covered in the book

    C reference books the author used to write the book

    D definitions of key terms covered in the book

_____ **8.** In nonfiction books, **captions** are used to —

    F explain the subject of pictures

    G provide directions for completing a task

    H highlight important ideas

    J divide the text into sections

_____ **9.** Which of the following words or phrases would be a clue indicating that a writer is contrasting two items?

    A in addition to

    B therefore

    C although

    D finally

_____ **10.** Which of the following words or phrases signals that a writer is presenting an example?

    F next to

    G such as

    H meanwhile

    J because

SELECTION TEST *Student Edition page 14*

Rikki-tikki-tavi Rudyard Kipling

COMPREHENSION *(40 points; 4 points each)*

On the line provided, write the letter of the *best* answer to each of the following items.

_____ 1. According to this story, what two animals is a mongoose like?

    A A tailorbird and a rabbit

    B A cat and a weasel

    C A rabbit and a weasel

    D A muskrat and a cat

_____ 2. Which event directly leads up to Rikki-tikki's living in the house with Teddy and his parents?

    F A snake attacks Teddy.

    G Rikki eats a banana on the veranda.

    H A summer flood washes Rikki out of his burrow.

    J Darzee tells Rikki about his lost baby.

_____ 3. Why is Rikki-tikki not afraid of fighting the snakes?

    A He instinctively knows how to fight them.

    B His mother taught him how to fight cobras.

    C Many of his childhood friends were snakes.

    D Darzee and his wife tell him how to fight.

_____ 4. Why does Nag hide in the bathroom?

    F He wants to surprise the mongoose by attacking him in the house.

    G He is angry at his wife and wants to get away from her.

    H He wants to kill Teddy's father when he comes to the bathroom in the morning.

    J He is lost and wants to wait until daylight to find his way out of the house.

_____ 5. Which of the following events causes the war in this story?

    A The cobras want to kill Rikki-tikki before he kills them.

    B The cobras killed Darzee, and the other animals want revenge.

    C The family decides to rid the garden of all the snakes.

    D Nag and Nagaina fight with each other about their eggs.

_____ 6. The narrator makes the animal characters seem human by —

    F telling how the animals have strong loyalties and conflicts

    G explaining that Rikki-tikki's eyes grow red when he is angry

    H explaining where the animals live in the garden

    J showing how Rikki-tikki lives in the bungalow

_____ **7.** If Teddy's father had not used his _____, Rikki-tikki might have _____.

    A wits, laughed

    B gun, been killed

    C common sense, stayed inside

    D stick, given up

_____ **8.** Why is it unwise for a mongoose to follow a cobra into a hole?

    F A mongoose is frightened of dark places.

    G The hole might open up or widen, allowing the cobra to turn and strike.

    H The red ants that live in the hole might attack the mongoose.

    J The earth in the hole is dark and moist.

_____ **9.** Darzee's wife and Nagaina are similar because they both —

    A stay in their nests and care for their young

    B plot with their husbands to kill Rikki-tikki

    C take action when their husbands fail

    D worry about the presence of humans in the bungalow

_____ **10.** The birds and frogs in the garden rejoice at the end of the story because they are —

    F afraid that Rikki-tikki might be killed

    G overjoyed that the snakes are dead

    H trying to wake Rikki-tikki from his long nap

    J attempting to communicate with Teddy's mother and father

LITERARY FOCUS (20 points; 5 points each)

On the line provided, write the letter of the *best* answer to each of the following items.

_____ **11.** Which of the following is not a conflict or source of conflict in the story?

    A Teddy's parents argue about keeping Rikki-tikki.

    B The cobras eat one of Darzee's eggs.

    C The cobras plot to kill the family.

    D Darzee builds his nest high up in the tree.

_____ **12.** Which of the following statements about conflict is *true* about the story?

    F Conflict cannot be avoided.

    G Conflict is caused by lack of communication.

    H Conflict is healthy for everyone.

    J Conflict is caused by hurt feelings.

_____ **13.** The climax of this story occurs when —

    A Nag hides in the bathroom

    B Teddy's parents praise Rikki-tikki for saving Teddy's life

    C Rikki-tikki smashes two eggs

    D Rikki-tikki follows Nagaina into the hole

_____ **14.** All of the following events help resolve the conflicts in the story *except* —

    F Darzee sings a mournful song when he thinks Rikki-tikki is dead

    G Rikki-tikki kills Nagaina after he follows her into the hole

    H Teddy's father shoots Nag in the bathroom

    J Rikki-tikki destroys Nagaina's eggs

VOCABULARY DEVELOPMENT *(20 points; 4 points each)*

Match the definition on the left with the Vocabulary word on the right.
Write the letter of the Vocabulary word on the line provided.

_____ **15.** comfort   **a.** valiant

_____ **16.** crouched and trembled with fear   **b.** consolation

_____ **17.** brave and determined   **c.** impotent

_____ **18.** powerless   **d.** immensely

_____ **19.** enormously   **e.** cowered

CONSTRUCTED RESPONSE *(20 points)*

20. Rikki-tikki destroys all of the cobra eggs, save one. This last egg is important for Nagaina because it represents her family's survival. In the final conflict between Rikki-tikki and Nagaina, the cobra grabs the egg and carries it to her underground nest. How did Rikki-tikki's actions foreshadow his final conflict with Nagaina? On a separate piece of paper, write a paragraph that explains your answer. Support your ideas with details from the story.

SELECTION TEST *Student Edition page 32*

from People, Places, and Change

COMPREHENSION *(100 points; 10 points each)*

On the line provided, write the letter of the *best* answer to each of the following items.

_____ **1.** In this textbook, you will find information on India's history in the unit titled —

    A India

    B The Indian Perimeter

    C South Asia

    D East and Southeast Asia

_____ **2.** The Reading Focus sums up the main points of each chapter by telling you what questions —

    F will be answered in the section

    G will be answered in the unit

    H appear in the Section Review

    J give students the most difficulty

_____ **3.** Why is very little known about the Harappan civilization?

    A It existed long ago.

    B Scholars are unable to read the Harappans' writing system.

    C The Mesopotamians destroyed all the records.

    D Present-day Pakistan now controls this region.

_____ **4.** The English East India Company had its own army made up mostly of sepoys. Sepoys are —

    F British troops controlled by British officers

    G British troops controlled by Indian officers

    H Indian troops controlled by British officers

    J Indian troops controlled by Indian officers

_____ **5.** The inset map on page 34 shows that the Harappan city called Mohenjo Daro was located in present-day —

    A Pakistan

    B India

    C Afghanistan

    D China

_____ **6.** A key place discussed in this section is Mumbai. A former name for Mumbai is —

    F India

    G Calcutta

    H Delhi

    J Bombay

_____ **7.** Gandhi believed in nonviolent protests, such as a boycott. A boycott is —

    A a club made up entirely of boys

    B a refusal to buy goods

    C a refusal to carry weapons

    D a type of bed used in the Indian army

_____ **8.** In a caption on page 35, you learn about a battle where British and Sikh troops fought with rebel sepoys. This battle occurred in —

    F Bombay

    G Calcutta

    H Delhi

    J Mohenjo Daro

_____ **9.** In this section, you would expect to find all of the following information *except* —

    A India's plans for the future

    B the role of the East India Company in the 1600s

    C how India won its independence

    D the history of early Indian civilizations

_____ **10.** The Reading Checks help you to —

    F review what you have learned

    G learn about the next section

    H provide a list of key terms and key places

    J check that you have read all of the captions

People, Places, and Change

SELECTION TEST *Student Edition page 38*

Three Skeleton Key George G. Toudouze

COMPREHENSION *(40 points; 4 points each)*

On the line provided, write the letter of the *best* answer to each of the following items.

_____ 1. Why does the narrator take the job at Three Skeleton Key?

    A He wants to set aside some money before he gets married.

    B He wants to protect the lighthouse.

    C He wants to watch the ships sail in the nighttime.

    D He is sent there to find three escaped convicts.

_____ 2. Why is it unusual for the lighthouse keepers to see a ship in their waters?

    F Sailors are afraid of the *Flying Dutchman*.

    G Sailors know that there are many rats on the island.

    H The waters are treacherous.

    J The island is off-limits to sailors.

_____ 3. Why does the narrator watch the *Cornelius de Witt* with tears in his eyes?

    A He knows that all the men on board the ship are dead.

    B He knows that the ship is about to be wrecked.

    C He knows that the rats are on board the ship.

    D He had once served on the ship.

_____ 4. How does the narrator convince us that the sea rats in this story are of the worst possible sort?

    F He tells of the two terrier dogs on a Dutch ship that were eaten by sea rats.

    G He says that sea rats are worse than land rats.

    H He says that the rats are able to scratch and tear through wood, metal, and glass.

    J He says that Dutch sea rats eat dogs, cats, men, sharks, and one another.

_____ 5. The narrator's descriptions of the window in the lantern room imply that the —

    A thick glass will keep the rats out

    B skeletons will open the window

    C window will collapse

    D rats will eat the glass

_____ 6. How do the rats first get inside the lighthouse?

    F They dig a tunnel under the lighthouse.

    G They eat a hole through the door.

    H The metal sheeting that was sealing the window gives way.

    J Crazed by the sight of the rats, Le Gleo opens the door.

_____ **7.** Why do the officers and crew of the first patrol boat look at the lighthouse with a horrified expression?

    A Sharks are circling the island.

    B The light is completely covered by a seething mass of rats.

    C Sharks are hungrily devouring the rats.

    D They see the skeletons of the three lighthouse keepers.

_____ **8.** When some rats return defeated from the attack on the patrol boat, the narrator says that the other rats greeted them with "shrill cries … with … a derisive note … ." The author is showing that the rats —

    F can laugh

    G have humanlike qualities

    H do not like each other

    J have begun to attack each other

_____ **9.** All of the following strategies are used to rescue the three men from the island *except* —

    A the crew tempt the rats onto a barge filled with meat

    B the lighthouse keepers set fire to the island

    C the crew drench the barge with gasoline and then set it on fire

    D the crew shoot any escaping rats and leave the rest to be eaten by the sharks

_____ **10.** What becomes of the three lighthouse attendants?

    F One man returns to the key; two refuse to go back to the lighthouse.

    G Two men return to Three Skeleton Key; the third man dies.

    H One man returns to the key; one goes insane; one dies.

    J Two men return to the island; the third man is too frightened to return.

LITERARY FOCUS *(20 points; 5 points each)*

On the line provided, write the letter of the *best* answer to each of the following items.

_____ **11.** Which of the following is an example of foreshadowing?

    A A man dreams of the three convicts' skeletons.

    B Some of the rats fall into the ocean and are eaten by the sharks.

    C The narrator sees the Dutch ship heading for the island.

    D The narrator sees a tug pulling a barge covered with raw meat.

Three Skeleton Key

_____ **12.** Which of the following details found early in the story enables you to predict that "Three Skeleton Key" will be a frightening tale?

    F The history of the rock

    G The narrator's history

    H The work that had to be done at the lighthouse

    J The revolving beam of light

_____ **13.** In a story filled with suspense, the reader feels —

    A sadness about the fate of the characters

    B anxious curiosity

    C overwhelming joy

    D sure about the outcome

_____ **14.** Which of the following details is *not* intended to create suspense?

    F The waters around the key swarm with hungry sharks.

    G The framework of one window is eaten away and sags inward.

    H Through their glasses, the men see a barge.

    J The men watch the abandoned Dutch ship sail straight toward them.

VOCABULARY DEVELOPMENT *(20 points; 4 points each)*

Match the definition on the left with the Vocabulary word on the right. Write the letter of the Vocabulary word on the line provided.

_____ **15.** understand		**a.** derisive
_____ **16.** large, moving crowds		**b.** receding
_____ **17.** fit to be eaten		**c.** fathom
_____ **18.** scornful and ridiculing		**d.** hordes
_____ **19.** moving back		**e.** edible

CONSTRUCTED RESPONSE *(20 points)*

20. Why does Le Gleo's explanation of the *Flying Dutchman* myth increase suspense in the story? On a separate sheet of paper, write a paragraph that explains your answer. Support your ideas with details from the story.

Holt Assessment: Literature, Reading, and Vocabulary

Eeking Out a Life Matt Surman

COMPREHENSION *(50 points; 10 points each)*

On the line provided, write the letter of the *best* answer to each of the following items.

_____ 1. Why did Hayley Huttenmaier and Nashshun Rose welcome an abandoned pet rat into their home?

    A They were paid to do so by the hospital.

    B They were concerned for his safety.

    C They knew the former owner was a little boy.

    D They wanted to find its original owner.

_____ 2. Why did Rose conclude that the rat had been a pet?

    F The rat was wearing tags.

    G They saw a "lost pet" ad in the paper.

    H There were remnants of a leash.

    J His behavior was docile and his fur was clean.

_____ 3. Experts compare rats like Sunny Jim to which of the following?

    A Cats

    B Wild rats

    C Hamsters

    D Dogs

_____ 4. What is the author's main purpose for writing this newspaper article?

    F To tell how cats, dogs, and rats can live happily together

    G To persuade you to go out and buy a pet rat

    H To tell about a couple who rescued a rat and welcomed it into their home

    J To persuade you to become a rat's best friend

_____ 5. "They can sit on your shoulder and watch TV with you" implies that rats —

    A have the potential to become pets

    B also like to watch TV

    C are clean enough to sit on your shoulder

    D can be trained to watch TV

VOCABULARY DEVELOPMENT (50 points; 10 points each)

On the line provided, write the word that *best* completes each sentence.

> **voracious**   **marauding**   **docile**
>
> **extolling**   **diminutive**

6. The wild and _____ rats roamed the streets and rummaged through the town's garbage site.

7. Huttenmaier and Rose were _____ Sunny Jim for his manners and cleanliness.

8. Huttenmaier and Rose saved Sunny Jim from _____ creatures that would have probably eaten him.

9. The couple was able to offer Sunny Jim a comfortable home because of his

_____ size.

10. Sunny Jim's _____ behavior made it easy for the couple to care for and love him.

SELECTION TEST *Student Edition page 57*

The Monsters Are Due on Maple Street Rod Serling

COMPREHENSION *(40 points; 4 points each)*

On the line provided, write the letter of the *best* answer to each of the following items.

_____ **1.** Why do you think the writer made the events occur on Maple Street, U.S.A.?

   A   The aliens were told to find this street.

   B   The setting indicates that small towns are filled with superstitious people.

   C   The main characters live on this street.

   D   The setting suggests that the events could happen anywhere.

_____ **2.** All of the following events make the residents nervous and arouse their suspicions *except* —

   F   one man's power mower stops working

   G   Tommy's computer starts displaying strange messages

   H   a screeching roar is heard overhead

   J   Mrs. Brand's stove stops working

_____ **3.** Right after the power failure, Charlie says, "A little power failure and right away we get all flustered and everything." Why is this statement significant?

   A   It suggests that there will be a greater power failure later in the story.

   B   It suggests that the residents will discover the reason behind the power failure.

   C   It is similar to what the creatures later say about the humans.

   D   It shows that Charlie will overcome his fear and save the town.

_____ **4.** When Tommy tells Mr. Brand not to go downtown, he says, "They don't want you to." To whom is he referring?

   F   Aliens from outer space

   G   The residents of Maple Street

   H   The wives

   J   His parents

_____ **5.** Why do the residents start to believe Tommy's story?

   A   They had read similar stories in books.

   B   Tommy has always told the truth before.

   C   Fear overtakes their good sense.

   D   They think it is wise to consider every possibility.

_____ **6.** Which statement *best* describes a mob scene?

    F Individual voices are drowned out, and fear and anger take over.

    G Everyone works together to reach an agreement.

    H Individual voices are heard, and everyone tries to act together.

    J No one person is important, and each individual is respected.

_____ **7.** The residents turn against Les Goodman because they —

    A like fifth columnists

    B don't like people with foreign cars

    C distrust anyone who is different

    D know the Goodman family owns a ham radio

_____ **8.** When Charlie sees all of Maple Street lit by candles, he says, "Why, it's like goin' back into the dark ages or somethin'." Considering what happens in the play, what second meaning could this statement have?

    F The space creatures may take the townspeople to a different time period.

    G The residents have let their fear, rather than their reason, take over.

    H The creatures causing the power failure are from the Dark Ages.

    J People used candles during the Dark Ages.

_____ **9.** Why does Charlie shoot Pete Van Horn?

    A He thinks Pete caused the power failure.

    B He believes Pete is making ham radios.

    C He has seen Pete gazing at the night sky.

    D He sees a dark figure approaching and thinks it is the monster.

_____ **10.** At the end of the play, it turns out that the *real* monster is —

    F Tommy's mind

    G the fear and prejudice of human minds

    H Charlie's behavior

    J Steve's mind

LITERARY FOCUS (20 points; 5 points each)

On the line provided, write the letter of the *best* answer to each of the following items.

_____ **11.** In a play or a story, *complications* —

    A are the most exciting moments in the story

    B are the sequence of events in the story

    C are the solutions to the problems

    D make it hard for the characters to get what they want

_____ **12.** At the opening of the play, the camera pans down to show Maple Street. At this point, the residents seem —

    F friendly with each other

    G like a violent mob

    H suspicious of one another

    J like aliens from outer space

_____ **13.** At first, the residents do not believe Tommy's tale. A complication arises when —

    A the lights suddenly go on at Steve's house

    B Les Goodman's car suddenly starts up

    C the neighbors find out that Les Goodman is an alien

    D the aliens send four creatures to earth to prepare for the landing

_____ **14.** At the end of the play, the residents of Maple Street are —

    F resolving their problems

    G meeting with the aliens

    H turning on one another

    J moving to another town

VOCABULARY DEVELOPMENT *(20 points; 4 points each)*

On the line provided, write the word that *best* completes each sentence.

transfixed	**intelligible**	**assent**	**intimidated**
converging	**defiant**	**idiosyncrasy**	**menace**
variations	**explicit**		

15. Everybody's eyes were _____ on the sky. All were in

_____ that something was terribly wrong.

16. Although there was no _____ danger, the residents believed there

was a real _____ threatening their safety.

17. Tommy was not _____ when the adults told him he was being foolish;

instead he felt _____.

18. As the mob began _____ on the house, their cries blended together and

were no longer _____.

The Monsters Are Due on Maple Street

19. The mob did not like _____ in behavior; they feared anyone who showed

an _____ .

CONSTRUCTED RESPONSE *(20 points)*

20. At the end of Act I, Les Goodman says, "As God is my witness…you're letting
something begin here that's a nightmare!" What is the nightmare that this
statement foreshadows? On a separate piece of paper, write a paragraph
that explains your answer. Support your ideas with details from the story.

SELECTION TEST *Student Edition page 81*

**INFORMATIONAL
READING**

Cellular Telephone Owner's Manual

COMPREHENSION *(100 points; 10 points each)*
On the line provided, write the letter of the *best* answer to each of the following items.

_____ 1. The purpose of an instructional manual is —

    A to inform you about the design of a product

    B to persuade you to buy a product

    C to help you operate and care for a specific device

    D to compare and contrast different types of products

_____ 2. All of the following items tell you where to get additional help from the manufacturer *except* the —

    F index

    G Web site

    H e-mail address

    J customer service phone number

_____ 3. Instructional manuals usually contain diagrams showing —

    A where to go to buy other products

    B important parts of the device and their functions

    C the people who designed the product

    D other products available for sale

_____ 4. In an instructional manual, the glossary provides —

    F an alphabetical list of special terms and their definitions

    G a list of all the topics covered in the manual

    H e-mail addresses and Web sites

    J directions telling you how to use the device

_____ 5. This instructional manual helps you understand how to change batteries by providing —

    A only steps

    B only diagrams

    C both steps and diagrams

    D important abbreviations

_____ 6. Use the standard method to change the battery when you —

    F are talking on the phone to someone important

    G want to take half the time as the quick-change method

    H can turn off your phone

    J have only one extra battery

_____ **7.** Use the quick-change method to change the battery when you —

  A receive the "low battery" message during a call

  B want to take half the time as the standard method

  C can turn off your phone

  D have only one extra battery

_____ **8.** Which step is the same for the standard method and the quick-change method?

  F Turn off your phone.

  G Change the battery.

  H Press PWR.

  J Advise the party on the other line that you are going to change batteries.

_____ **9.** Why would you press PWR?

  A To put in the new battery

  B To return to your telephone call

  C To make another call

  D To remove the old battery

_____ **10.** How do you know it is time to change the battery?

  F You receive a "low battery" message or an audible tone during a call.

  G One month has passed since you last changed the battery.

  H You have a spare battery.

  J The person you are calling tells you that there is interference.

Facing Danger

This test asks you to use the skills and strategies you have learned in this collection.
Read this passage from "Seventh Grade," and then answer the questions that follow it.

from **Seventh Grade**
by Gary Soto

They were among the last students to arrive in class, so all the good desks in the back had already been taken. Victor was forced to sit near the front, a few desks away from Teresa, while Mr. Bueller wrote French words on the chalkboard. The bell rang, and Mr. Bueller wiped his hands, turned to the class, and said, "*Bonjour.*"

"*Bonjour,*" braved a few students.

"*Bonjour,*" Victor whispered. He wondered if Teresa heard him.

Mr. Bueller said that if the students studied hard, at the end of the year they could go to France and be understood by the populace.

One kid raised his hand and asked, "What's 'populace'?"

"The people, the people of France."

Mr. Bueller asked if anyone knew French. Victor raised his hand, wanting to impress Teresa. The teacher beamed and said, "*Très bien. Parlez-vous français?*"

Victor didn't know what to say. The teacher wet his lips and asked something else in French. The room grew silent. Victor felt all eyes staring at him. He tried to bluff his way out by making noises that sounded French.

"La me vava me con le grandma," he said uncertainly.

Mr. Bueller, wrinkling his face in curiosity, asked him to speak up.

Great rosebushes of red bloomed on Victor's checks. A river of nervous sweat ran down his palms. He felt awful. Teresa sat a few desks away, no doubt thinking he was a fool. Without looking at Mr. Bueller, Victor mumbled, "Frenchie oh wewe gee in September."

Mr. Bueller asked Victor to repeat what he had said.

"Frenchie oh wewe gee in September," Victor repeated.

Mr. Bueller understood that the boy didn't know French and turned away. He walked to the blackboard and pointed to the words on the board with his steel-edged ruler.

"*Le bateau,*" he sang.

"*Le bateau,*" the students repeated.

"*Le bateau est sur l'eau,*" he sang.

"*Le bateau est sur l'eau.*"

Victor was too weak from failure to join the class. He stared at the board and wished he had taken Spanish, not French. Better yet, he wished he could start his life over. He had never been so embarrassed. He bit his thumb until he tore off a sliver of skin.

The bell sounded for fifth period, and Victor shot out of the room, avoiding the stares of the other kids, but had to return for his math book. He looked sheepishly at the teacher, who was erasing the board, then widened his eyes in terror at Teresa who stood in front of him. "I didn't know you knew French," she said. "That was good."

Mr. Bueller looked at Victor, and Victor looked back. Oh please, don't say anything, Victor pleaded with his eyes. I'll wash your car, mow your lawn, walk your dog—anything! I'll be your best student, and I'll clean your erasers after school.

Mr. Bueller shuffled through the papers on his desk. He smiled and hummed as he sat down to work. He remembered his college years when he dated a girlfriend in borrowed cars. She thought he was rich because each time he picked her up he had a different car. It was fun until he spent all his money on her and had to write home to his parents because he was broke.

Victor couldn't stand to look at Teresa. He was sweaty with shame. "Yeah, well, I picked up a few things from movies and books and stuff like that." They left the class together. Teresa asked him if he would help her with her French.

"Sure, anytime," Victor said.

"I won't be bothering you, will I?"

"Oh, no, I like being bothered."

"Bonjour," Teresa said, leaving him outside her next class. She smiled and pushed wisps of hair from her face.

"Yeah, right, *bonjour,*" Victor said. He turned and headed to his class. The rosebushes of shame on his face became bouquets of love. Teresa is a great girl, he thought. And Mr. Bueller is a good guy.

He raced to the metal shop. After metal shop there was biology, and after biology a long sprint to the public library, where he checked out three French textbooks.

He was going to like seventh grade.

VOCABULARY SKILLS *(25 points; 5 points each)*

Each of the underlined words below has also been underlined in the selection. Re-read those passages in which the underlined words appear, and then use context clues and your prior knowledge to help you select an answer. On the line provided, write the letter of the word or words that *best* complete each sentence.

_____ 1. If you get to know the populace of a country, you become familiar with the _____.

    A plant life

    B language

    C wildlife

    D people who live there

_____ 2. Mr. Bueller beamed at the class because they did well on the quiz; he could not stop _____.

    F smiling

    G frowning

    H crying

    J yelling

From "Seventh Grade" from *Baseball in April and Other Stories* by Gary Soto. Copyright © 1990 by Gary Soto. Reprinted by permission of **Harcourt, Inc.**

_____ **3.** He tried to <u>bluff</u> his way out of an awkward situation by _____.

    A sitting down

    B whispering

    C sobbing loudly

    D misleading others

_____ **4.** As Victor walked <u>sheepishly</u> toward the girl, the teacher knew Victor felt _____.

    F content

    G angry

    H afraid

    J embarrassed

_____ **5.** If the <u>sprint</u> from the library to the gym only took three minutes, Victor must have been _____.

    A walking slowly

    B running at top speed

    C skipping lightheartedly

    D traveling in one direction

COMPREHENSION *(25 points; 5 points each)*

On the line provided, write the letter of the *best* answer to each of the following items.

_____ **6.** When Mr. Bueller has a curious expression on his face and asks Victor to speak louder, the reader can predict that —

    F Mr. Bueller will be curious about Victor's interest in Teresa

    G Victor does not know French

    H Teresa will be interested in Victor

    J Mr. Bueller will give a difficult homework assignment

_____ **7.** How do Victor's efforts at speaking French affect Teresa?

    A She believes his act and asks him to help her with French.

    B She finds him ridiculous and laughs at him.

    C She is upset that he has pretended.

    D She feels sorry for him and promises to tutor him.

_____ **8.** Victor pretends to understand and speak French because he wants to —

    F impress Teresa

    G show the teacher how smart he is

    H be a role model for other seventh-graders

    J show how much French he has learned from movies and books

9. It is reasonable to assume that Mr. Bueller does not expose Victor in front of Teresa because he —

    A knows that Victor will flunk French

    B was involved in a similar situation when he was a college student

    C does not realize that Victor is inventing words

    D thinks that Victor did the right thing

10. Why do you think Victor checks out French textbooks from the library?

    F He wants to be able to go to France and be understood.

    G He plans to do extra credit to obtain a good grade.

    H He wants to learn more so that he can tutor Teresa.

    J He wants to get an early start on his report.

READING SKILLS AND STRATEGIES: CONSTRUCTED RESPONSE *(30 points; 10 points each)*
Making Inferences

11. Why does Victor know after the first day that he is going to like seventh grade? From the following options, choose the one you think is the *best* response to this question. On the lines provided, write the letter of the answer you chose, and briefly defend your choice. Use at least one example from the selection to support your ideas.

    A He is looking forward to earning extra money by doing chores for Mr. Bueller.

    B He realizes that he has become the class clown, a role he always wanted to play.

    C He thinks he can go through French class without learning the language.

    D He is happy about having an understanding teacher and perhaps a new girlfriend.

Holt Assessment: Literature, Reading, and Vocabulary

Retelling

12. In your own words, retell what happens after Victor returns to the classroom to pick up his math book.

_____

_____

_____

_____

_____

Making Predictions

13. Do you think Teresa will become Victor's girlfriend? Write a paragraph explaining your prediction. Use details from the selection to support your response.

_____

_____

_____

_____

_____

LITERARY FOCUS: CONSTRUCTED RESPONSE *(20 points)*

14. Conflict is a struggle between opposing characters or forces. As you read a story, you learn how the conflict is resolved. In the left-hand side of the following chart, identify Victor's conflict as either internal or external, and explain with whom or with what he is struggling. Then, in the right-hand side, explain how Victor's conflict is resolved.

▶ Description of Conflict	▶ Resolution

Characters: Living Many Lives

On the line provided, write the letter of the *best* answer to each of the following items.
(100 points; 10 points each)

_____ 1. **Character traits** refer to —

    A a character's experiences in a story

    B the characteristics shared by members of a family

    C the qualities that make up the personality of a character

    D the author's opinion of a particular character in a story

_____ 2. If a **character** takes risks in a story, the character's actions would *most likely* reveal that he or she is —

    F bold

    G social

    H athletic

    J competitive

_____ 3. To show what a **character** is like, a writer would *most likely* use all of the following strategies *except* —

    A describing the character's appearance

    B explaining the character's feelings

    C indicating how others react to the character

    D revealing the character's date of birth

_____ 4. The reason for a character's actions is called —

    F theme

    G biography

    H resolution

    J motivation

_____ 5. When a writer uses a **first-person narrator,** the story —

    A does not contain dialogue between the characters

    B is told by one of the characters

    C does not contain a main character

    D has only one character

6. Using an **omniscient,** or **third-person, narrator,** instead of another type of narrator, enables a writer to —

 F tell a story that is set in the past

 G reveal the thoughts of all the characters in a story

 H describe events that actually took place

 J express all of his or her opinions

7. When authors use the **block method** to compare and contrast two subjects, they —

 A do not use a separate paragraph for each idea in their work

 B write about either the similarities between the two subjects or their differences

 C describe one aspect of subject 1 and subject 2 and then a second aspect of both subjects

 D first discuss all the features of subject 1 and then all the features of subject 2

8. To determine the **main idea** of an informational text, you should first —

 F identify the most important details in the work

 G read other works by the author on the same subject

 H place the events described in the text in chronological order

 J review the illustrations and photographs in the work

9. Which of the following words contains a **prefix**?

 A dinner

 B revise

 C star

 D angle

10. A **suffix** is a(n) —

 F word that has a similar meaning to another word

 G clue planted by a writer to explain a word's meaning

 H word part added to the end of a word

 J expression unique to a language

SELECTION TEST   *Student Edition page 136*

Mother and Daughter   Gary Soto

COMPREHENSION *(40 points; 4 points each)*
On the line provided, write the letter of the *best* answer to each of the following items.

_____ **1.** Which word describes Mrs. Moreno's sense of humor?

   A Conventional

   B Ordinary

   C Strange

   D Cruel

_____ **2.** Why does Mrs. Moreno leave Yollie on the couch after the movie?

   F Yollie asked to sleep on the couch.

   G Yollie is too heavy for her to lift.

   H She forgot to wake Yollie.

   J She wants to play a joke on Yollie.

_____ **3.** Why does Yollie leave a glass of water on her mother's nightstand?

   A Yollie wants to play a prank on her.

   B Mrs. Moreno gets thirsty at night.

   C Yollie wants to help her mother water the plants.

   D Mrs. Moreno asked her to.

_____ **4.** Mrs. Moreno is proud of Yollie because she —

   F looks and acts like her

   G is smart and hardworking

   H has many boyfriends

   J has already gotten a good job

_____ **5.** Why doesn't Mrs. Moreno buy Yollie a new dress for the dance?

   A She doesn't approve of dances.

   B She cannot afford it.

   C Yollie doesn't need another dress.

   D Mrs. Moreno is selfish and miserly.

_____ **6.** Yollie is surprised that the dyed dress looks good because —

   F she had never seen a dyed dress before

   G she had heard that dyed dresses look second-hand

   H her mother's projects usually fail

   J the dress was in very bad shape already

7. For Yollie, the dance is magical because —

    A she just met Ernie, and they fall in love

    B all her friends are there

    C she gets to see the nuns dancing

    D she likes Ernie and he likes her

8. How does Yollie feel about the family's poverty?

    F She is bitterly ashamed.

    G She blames her mother for being lazy.

    H She is sad because she cannot help relieve it.

    J She feels sympathy for her mother's difficult life.

9. Mrs. Moreno decides that the best way to make money is to —

    A get an education

    B work at the county fair

    C invent a screwdriver with two heads

    D cook tortillas and *chile verde* for other families

10. Mrs. Moreno and Yollie are happy at the end of the story because —

    F they earn enough money to buy Yollie a new outfit

    G Mrs. Moreno uses her savings to buy Yollie a new outfit

    H Yollie gets a new outfit from Janice

    J Yollie has a date with Ernie

LITERARY FOCUS *(20 points; 5 points each)*

On the line provided, write the letter of the *best* answer to each of the following items.

11. The low-riders think Mrs. Moreno is —

    A admirable

    B amusing

    C beautiful

    D intelligent

12. Based on the description of the homemade candy apples and dyed dress, you can infer that Mrs. Moreno is —

    F skilled at cooking and other home skills

    G creative and clever with her hands

    H always looking for shortcuts

    J well-meaning but not good with homemade projects

_____ **13.** The author uses indirect characterization to show that Ernie considers Yollie —

   A well-meaning, kind, and intelligent

   B a laugh riot

   C beautiful and desirable

   D poor and dominated by her mother

_____ **14.** The author makes Mrs. Moreno's character sympathetic by —

   F describing her hairstyle

   G explaining how her sister feels about her

   H showing how much she loves Yollie

   J giving examples of her work history

VOCABULARY DEVELOPMENT *(20 points; 4 points each)*

On the line provided, write the Vocabulary word that *best* completes each sentence.

sophisticated   meager   tirade   matinees   antics

15. On Saturday afternoons, Yollie and her mother enjoyed going to _____ at the movies.

16. They watched comedies because they liked to see the actors' ridiculous

_____.

17. They also liked _____ dramas with worldly actors and cultured behavior.

18. Since Mrs. Moreno had only _____ funds to spend on pleasure, she and Yollie did not go to the movies often.

19. Once at a matinee, Mrs. Moreno delivered a _____ against another movie-goer because he talked throughout the movie.

CONSTRUCTED RESPONSE *(20 points)*

20. Mrs. Moreno is fictional, yet she seems like a real person because her character is fully developed. Explain how Gary Soto made Mrs. Moreno so lifelike. On a separate sheet of paper, write a paragraph that explains your answer. Support your ideas with details from the story.

SELECTION TEST *Student Edition page 146*

LITERARY RESPONSE AND ANALYSIS

The Smallest Dragonboy Anne McCaffrey

COMPREHENSION *(40 points; 4 points each)*

On the line provided, write the letter of the *best* answer to each of the following items.

_____ **1.** The great winged dragons were created to —

   A protect the planet from outside attacks

   B provide practice for warriors

   C prevent internal conflicts

   D prevent accidents

_____ **2.** How are riders chosen for each dragon?

   F The riders select their own dragons.

   G Riders and dragons are matched, based on their size.

   H Dragons select their own riders.

   J The Weyrwoman Lessa makes the selection.

_____ **3.** Why does Keevan fear that he won't get a dragon?

   A The Weyrwoman Lessa does not like him.

   B He is very small.

   C He has a history of fighting with other boys.

   D He is a foster child.

_____ **4.** The most impressive and important dragons are the —

   F blue dragons

   G newborn dragons

   H green dragons

   J bronze dragons

_____ **5.** Impression time takes place when the —

   A sands get hot

   B boys and girls reach age sixteen

   C dragons learn to fly

   D dragons are hatched

_____ **6.** At an Impression the dragon selects a rider by —

   F asking Lessa

   G using telepathic communication

   H guessing the candidate's age

   J challenging the candidate's strength

_____ **7.** When Beterli attacks Keevan, Beterli —

    A is not allowed to participate in the Impression

    B blames Keevan for the attack

    C is punished by Mende

    D is forced to accept a green dragon

_____ **8.** What special power does Lessa have?

    F She can tame dragons.

    G She can predict which dragon will select which candidate.

    H She can hear each dragon's thoughts.

    J She can ride with the queen dragon.

_____ **9.** Why can Keevan be considered the underdog in the story?

    A He has already been to several hatchings.

    B His father was never chosen to be a dragonrider.

    C There are seventy-two candidates and only forty eggs.

    D He is the smallest candidate for dragonrider.

_____ **10.** What is the lesson we can learn from "The Smallest Dragonboy"?

    F Some people are born lucky.

    G Self-serving people are always punished.

    H In spite of obstacles, people can realize their dreams.

    J Some people suffer more than others.

LITERARY FOCUS *(20 points; 5 points each)*

On the line provided, write the letter of the *best* answer to each of the following items.

_____ **11.** You can infer that Keevan wants to prove himself because he —

    A has already failed before

    B has many enemies among teens as well as adults

    C is short and young

    D comes from a famous and well-respected family

_____ **12.** Because of Keevan's character and his attitude, readers can predict that he will —

    F be picked by a strong dragon

    G not attend the Impression

    H fight Beterli and defeat him

    J not be picked by a dragon

_____ **13.** What is the most important difference between Keevan's character and Beterli's character?

    A Beterli is not certain that he wants to be a dragonboy, while Keevan is sure.

    B Keevan is determined, but Beterli is stubborn as well as smart.

    C Beterli is selfish and mean, while Keevan is fair and good-hearted.

    D Keevan is weak, while Beterli is more powerful.

_____ **14.** Heth chooses Keevan as his dragonrider because —

    F he knows how badly Keevan wants to be a dragonrider

    G Keevan is the smallest boy so he is the lightest

    H Keevan's father was a dragonrider

    J Keevan is gentle, kind, and courageous

VOCABULARY DEVELOPMENT *(20 points; 4 points each)*

On the line before each sentence, write the Vocabulary word that is a synonym for the italicized word or phrase in the sentence.

      confrontation   **alleviate**   **imminent**

      perturbed   **goaded**

_____ **15.** Keevan was *pushed* into walking faster by the pace Beterli set.

_____ **16.** The hatching of forty eggs was *about to happen*.

_____ **17.** His foster mother seemed *disturbed* by his clumsiness.

_____ **18.** Numbweed was used to *relieve* the pain.

_____ **19.** Keevan found himself in a *face-to-face argument* with Beterli.

CONSTRUCTED RESPONSE *(20 points)*

20. How does the author make the underdog come out on top? Identify two obstacles that Keevan faces, and explain how they are overcome or removed. In your answer, include specific references to the author's use of characterization. On a separate piece of paper, write a paragraph that explains your answer. Support your ideas with details from the story.

SELECTION TEST *Student Edition page 164*

Here Be Dragons Flo Ota De Lange

COMPREHENSION *(50 points; 10 points each)*

On the line provided, write the letter of the *best* answer to each of the following items.

_____ 1. How are the characters of dragons in Asia and Europe different?

    A In Asia, they are wise and help people; in Europe, they are evil and harm people.

    B In Europe, they are wise and help people; in Asia, they are evil and harm people.

    C There are no differences; they are wise and help people.

    D There are no differences; they are evil and harm people.

_____ 2. It is said in Asia that if a person met a dragon on the road of life it would give that person —

    F fire and brimstone

    G advice

    H a gift

    J an honor guard

_____ 3. How are Eastern and Western dragons the same?

    A Both shoot fire and brimstone.

    B Both are genuine.

    C Both are feared as foes of civilization.

    D Both are mythical.

_____ 4. In many Western dragon tales, the hero often must —

    F ride a dragon

    G create a dragon

    H find a dragon and tame it

    J slay a dragon

_____ 5. Which is the most suitable title for this selection?

    A Beware of Dragons!

    B Dragons: Your Friends

    C Dragons in Eastern and Western Cultures

    D Searching for Dragons

VOCABULARY DEVELOPMENT *(50 points; 10 points each)*

Match the Vocabulary word on the left with its synonym or antonym on the right. Write the letter of the synonym or antonym on the line provided. In this section, one word has both a synonym and an antonym listed.

_____ **6.** synonym for *primal*

_____ **7.** antonym for *seething*

_____ **8.** synonym for *cosmos*

_____ **9.** synonym for *seething*

_____ **10.** antonym for *primordial*

a. violently agitated

b. orderly and harmonious universe

c. basic or fundamental

d. last

e. calm

Holt Assessment: Literature, Reading, and Vocabulary

SELECTION TEST *Student Edition page 168*

A Rice Sandwich Sandra Cisneros

COMPREHENSION *(40 points; 4 points each)*

On the line provided, write the letter of the *best* answer to each of the following items.

_____ 1. What reason does Esperanza's mother give for refusing to let her eat in the canteen?

    A It will make more work for her.

    B She knows that the canteen food isn't good.

    C The family can't afford to pay for lunch.

    D Esperanza is a very picky eater.

_____ 2. The narrator creates humor by —

    F describing Esperanza's appearance

    G providing Esperanza's reasons for wanting to eat in the canteen

    H having the nun point out Esperanza's house

    J describing the rice sandwich

_____ 3. Why does Esperanza ask her mother to allow her to eat at the canteen?

    A Her mother works so Esperanza can't go home for lunch.

    B Esperanza lives too far away from home and gets tired.

    C Esperanza wants to eat with the kids in the canteen.

    D Esperanza is very skinny and often faints.

_____ 4. Why does Esperanza take a rice sandwich to school?

    F Esperanza's mother is punishing her for defying the nuns.

    G Rice is the only lunch food she will eat.

    H They do not have any lunch meat.

    J Esperanza's mother is playing a joke on her.

_____ 5. Why is Esperanza sent to the Sister Superior?

    A She started crying in the lunch line.

    B She needs permission to eat in the canteen.

    C She cut school to spend the day with Kiki and Carlos.

    D The nun knows that she doesn't have money for a school lunch.

_____ 6. What does Sister Superior discover when she reads the note?

    F Esperanza is not well.

    G All the kids dislike the canteen.

    H Esperanza's family has moved.

    J Esperanza cannot afford to buy lunch.

_____ **7.** How does Sister Superior react to the note?

    A She calls Esperanza's mother.

    B She visits Esperanza's apartment.

    C She sends Esperanza to the nurse's office.

    D She confronts Esperanza about where she lives.

_____ **8.** What can you infer about Sister Superior?

    F She has just started teaching.

    G She is cruel to the children.

    H She does not like Esperanza.

    J She is clever and experienced.

_____ **9.** The story's narrator is about —

    A four years old

    B seven years old

    C twelve years old

    D fifteen years old

_____ **10.** The story's theme can be expressed as —

    F it is important to demand your rights

    G eating lunch in school is better than eating lunch at home

    H things are not always as wonderful as they seem

    J parents always know what's best for their children

LITERARY FOCUS (20 points; 5 points each)

On the line provided, write the letter of the *best* answer to each of the following items.

_____ **11.** The author selected the first-person point of view to —

    A help readers experience Esperanza's thoughts more fully

    B persuade parents to be less strict

    C show what Esperanza's mother feels

    D explain the advantages and disadvantages of eating in the school canteen

_____ **12.** Which phrase *best* describes Esperanza's character?

    F Weak and easily swayed

    G Cynical and suspicious

    H Experienced and sophisticated

    J Strong-willed and determined

_____ **13.** Esperanza's mother is characterized as —

    A lazy and foolish

    B close to the nuns

    C harsh and unyielding

    D hard-working and loving

_____ **14.** Esperanza emerges from her experience —

    F unchanged

    G sadder but wiser

    H very bitter

    J determined to succeed

VOCABULARY DEVELOPMENT *(20 points; 4 points each)*

Match the definition on the left with the Vocabulary word on the right. Write the letter of the Vocabulary word on the line provided.

_____ **15.** hardy, disciplined person   **a.** canteen

_____ **16.** pale and weak   **b.** triangle

_____ **17.** cafeteria   **c.** suffering

_____ **18.** a three-sided object   **d.** Spartan

_____ **19.** experiencing pain   **e.** anemic

CONSTRUCTED RESPONSE *(20 points)*

20. Would you like Esperanza as a friend? Why or why not? What aspects of Esperanza's character do you find appealing? What aspects of her character do not appeal to you? On a separate piece of paper, write a paragraph that explains your answer. Support your ideas with details from the story.

SELECTION TEST *Student Edition page 174*

Antaeus Borden Deal

COMPREHENSION *(40 points; 4 points each)*

On the line provided, write the letter of the *best* answer to each of the following items.

_____ 1. Why do T. J.'s parents move their family to the North?

    A To meet people with similar interests

    B To find jobs in a factory or war industry

    C To give their children more freedom

    D To escape the boredom of life on a farm

_____ 2. How does T. J. meet the boys in the gang?

    F The boys greet him when his family first arrives in an old car.

    G T. J. approaches the boys on his own and introduces himself.

    H The narrator introduces T. J. to his other friends in the building.

    J His parents are friends with the narrator's parents.

_____ 3. T. J. notes that in the South, unlike in his new neighborhood, —

    A people's lives are connected to the land

    B everyone uses initials in place of a full name

    C there are no grocery stores

    D spring weather lasts all year

_____ 4. T. J. becomes part of the gang because the boys are impressed by his —

    F white hair

    G physical strength

    H family

    J ideas

_____ 5. Why don't the boys give up the difficult task of carrying dirt to the roof?

    A Being competitive, none of the boys wants to be viewed as lazy.

    B They feel satisfied when they complete a large project.

    C They enjoy working outside in the warm weather.

    D T. J. keeps them focused on their goal.

_____ 6. T. J. agrees to plant grass on the roof because —

    F he just wants to grow something

    G raising grass reminds him of his home in Alabama

    H he does not have any cotton seeds to plant

    J he knows that nothing else will grow in the garden

Holt Assessment: Literature, Reading, and Vocabulary

_____ **7.** How do the boys feel about the grass that they have planted?

    A Ashamed

    B Disappointed

    C Proud

    D Unconcerned

_____ **8.** T. J. is angry at the owner of the building because —

    F the owner does not believe that the boys planted the grass themselves

    G the owner thinks that the grass is ugly

    H T. J. feels that the garden belongs to the gang

    J T. J. thinks that the owner is rude to them

_____ **9.** Why do T. J. and the boys destroy the garden?

    A T. J. does not want anyone else to touch what they have created.

    B Respectful of authority, the boys are following the rules.

    C Now that the garden has been discovered, the boys no longer enjoy it.

    D They are afraid that they will be arrested for planting the garden.

_____ **10.** What happens to T. J. at the end of the story?

    F He is reunited with the gang.

    G He is stopped by the police while trying to run away.

    H He disappears, and no one ever learns what happens to him.

    J He moves back to his home in the South.

LITERARY FOCUS _(20 points; 5 points each)_

On the line provided, write the letter of the *best* answer to each of the following items.

_____ **11.** What is an allusion?

    A A figure of speech in which an object or animal is given human qualities

    B The author's attitude toward the audience, a subject, or a character

    C A brief story that teaches a moral or a practical lesson about life

    D A reference to a person, place, or an event from literature, mythology, or history

_____ **12.** What motivates the boys to plant a garden on the roof of the factory?

    F They have always been interested in farming.

    G They are bored and are seeking a hobby.

    H They want to have their own private space.

    J They want to prove to their parents that they can be successful.

_____ **13.** Which adjective *best* describes T. J.'s character?

    A Practical

    B Determined

    C Cowardly

    D Disloyal

_____ **14.** The author uses all of the following strategies to characterize T. J. *except* —

    F having T. J. state his feelings about himself

    G describing T. J.'s appearance

    H telling what T. J. says and does

    J showing how other characters view him

VOCABULARY DEVELOPMENT   *(20 points; 4 points each)*

Match the definition on the left with the Vocabulary word on the right. Write the letter of the Vocabulary word on the line provided.

_____ **15.** look at or think about carefully   **a.** resolute

_____ **16.** barren; lacking interest or vitality   **b.** domain

_____ **17.** territory   **c.** contemplate

_____ **18.** clever   **d.** shrewd

_____ **19.** firm and purposeful; determined   **e.** sterile

CONSTRUCTED RESPONSE   *(20 points)*

20. In the myth of Antaeus, Hercules easily defeats Antaeus by removing him from his source of strength, the earth. How does the owner of the building resemble Hercules? In what ways are T. J. and the rest of the boys like Antaeus? On a separate piece of paper, write a paragraph that explains your answer. Support your ideas with details from the selection.

SELECTION TEST *Student Edition page 187*   INFORMATIONAL
                                                                                READING

In a Mix of Cultures, an Olio of Plantings Anne Raver

COMPREHENSION *(100 points; 10 points each)*

On the line provided, write the letter of the *best* answer to each of the following items.

_____ **1.** Juan Guerrero's tomatillo garden is referred to as "his little piece of Mexico" because —

    A he loves to grow things

    B his neighbors are from Mexico

    C growing tomatillos is a reminder of life in Mexico

    D he has not adopted any American habits

_____ **2.** Why does Mr. Garcia speak on behalf of Mr. Guerrero?

    F The two men have been good friends for many years.

    G Mr. Garcia, like Mr. Guerrero, is from Mexico.

    H Mr. Guerrero is too shy to speak to the reporter.

    J Mr. Garcia is translating for Mr. Guerrero, who speaks little English.

_____ **3.** Mr. Guerrero uses tomatillos to make —

    A soup

    B salsa

    C tomatoes

    D tortillas

_____ **4.** As Mr. Guerrero peels the fruit, he explains to Mr. Garcia —

    F how the fruit can be dried and the seeds removed

    G why the fruit is green and hard

    H how easy it is to prepare tomatillos for cooking

    J that they both like the taste of tomatillos

_____ **5.** Which of the following statements about the strip of land used for the garden is *true*?

    A It was once a much larger garden.

    B It is used mostly by professional gardeners.

    C It used to be filled with garbage and stolen items.

    D It is shared by ten people in the neighborhood.

_____ **6.** The gardeners call the strip of land "The Garden of Happiness" because —

    F the flowers are unusually beautiful

    G they have grown wealthy from selling tomatillos

    H everyone who works in the garden gets along very well

    J the garden reminds them of their family roots

_____ **7.** Community groups can garden in city-owned lots thanks to —

    A Operation Green Thumb

    B private funding from local residents

    C the mayor of the city

    D the efforts of Juan Guerrero

_____ **8.** Which of the following sentences *best* states the main idea of the article?

    F When people cooperate, they can be successful.

    G Gardening can help people feel a connection to their cultural backgrounds.

    H Crime can be overcome with determination, goodwill, and hard work.

    J Gardening is a pastime that everyone enjoys.

_____ **9.** What idea is emphasized by the title of the article?

    A The world is made up of many cultures.

    B Different kinds of people are growing a variety of plants.

    C Diverse people have distinct needs and opinions.

    D People are more similar than different.

_____ **10.** The purpose of this article is to —

    F spark debate

    G instruct

    H inform

    J describe a person

COLLECTION 2 SUMMATIVE TEST

Characters: Living Many Lives

This test asks you to use the skills and strategies you have learned in this collection. Read "Mercury and the Woodman" by Aesop, and then answer the questions that follow.

Mercury and the Woodman
by Aesop

A poor Woodman was cutting down a tree near the edge of a deep pool in the forest. It was late in the day and the Woodman was tired. He had been working since sunrise and his strokes were not so sure as they had been early that morning. Thus it happened that the axe slipped and flew out of his hands into the pool.

The Woodman was in despair. The axe was all he possessed with which to make a living, and he had not enough money to buy a new one. As he stood wringing his hands and weeping, the god Mercury suddenly appeared and asked what the trouble was. The Woodman told what had happened, and straightaway the kind Mercury dived into the pool. When he came up again, he held a wonderful golden axe.

"Is this your axe?" Mercury asked the Woodman.

"No," answered the virtuous Woodman, "that is not my axe."

Mercury laid the golden axe on the bank and sprang back into the pool. This time he brought up an axe with a silver handle, but the Woodman declared again that his axe was just an ordinary one with a wooden handle.

Mercury dived down for a third time, and when he came up again he had the very axe that had been lost.

The poor Woodman was very glad that his axe had been found and he could not thank the kind god enough. Mercury was greatly pleased with the Woodman's honesty.

"I admire your honesty," he said, "and as a reward you may have all three axes, the gold and the silver as well as your own."

The happy Woodman returned to his home with his treasures, and soon the story of his good fortune was known to everyone in the village. Now there were several Woodmen in the village who believed they could easily win the same good fortune. They hurried into the woods, one here, one there, and hiding their axes in the bushes, pretended they had lost them. Then they wept and wailed, and called on Mercury to help them.

And indeed, Mercury did appear, first to this one, and then to that one. To each one he showed the axe of gold, and each one eagerly claimed it to be the one he had lost. But Mercury did not give them the golden axe. Oh no! Instead he gave them each a hard whack over the head with it and sent them home. And when they returned the next day to look for their own axes, they were no longer to be found.

Honesty is the best policy.

VOCABULARY SKILLS *(25 points; 5 points each)*

Each of the underlined words below has also been underlined in the selection.
Re-read those passages in which the underlined words appear, and then
use context clues and your prior knowledge to help you select an answer.
On the line provided, write the letter of the word that *best* completes
each sentence.

_____ **1.** The Woodman is in despair when he _____ his axe.

    A loses

    B uses

    C regains

    D grips

_____ **2.** Wringing one's hands is a sign of _____.

    F cheer

    G joy

    H distress

    J cleanliness

_____ **3.** To dive straightaway is to dive _____.

    A gradually

    B obediently

    C immediately

    D unwillingly

_____ **4.** The Woodman was virtuous because he was _____.

    F poor

    G clever

    H sneaky

    J honest

_____ **5.** The other Woodmen wailed to pretend they were _____.

    A angry

    B sorrowful

    C trapped

    D content

COMPREHENSION *(25 points; 5 points each)*

On the line provided, write the letter of the *best* answer to each of the following items.

_____ **6.** Which of the following events happens first in the story?

     F The Woodman loses his axe.

     G Others hear about the Woodman's problem.

     H Mercury appears to the Woodman.

     J The Woodman works all day.

_____ **7.** The Woodman becomes frantic about his axe because it —

     A is broken

     B belongs to the god Mercury

     C is made of gold

     D is the only one he has

_____ **8.** Mercury brings up different axes from the water because —

     F there are many axes at the bottom of the pool

     G he wants to test the Woodman's honesty

     H the Woodman is confused about which axe is his

     J he wants to show that plain axes are the best

_____ **9.** The other Woodmen hide their axes in an attempt to —

     A show their sympathy for the first Woodman

     B prove that they are also honest

     C receive a valuable axe from Mercury

     D show that they are poor

_____ **10.** At the end of the story, the other Woodmen cannot find their axes because —

     F Mercury has punished the Woodmen

     G they forget where they have put them

     H the axes are in the pool

     J the first Woodman has taken them

READING SKILLS AND STRATEGIES: CONSTRUCTED RESPONSE *(30 points; 15 points each)*

Making Inferences

11. In this tale, why does the author have Mercury give the Woodman all the axes? From the following options, choose the one you think is the best response to this question. On the lines provided, write the letter of the answer you chose, and briefly defend your choice. Use at least one example from the selection to support your ideas.

A To teach readers about gods and their powers

B To show people that honesty is its own reward

C To suggest that hardworking people are honest

D To describe how one man outwits a god

_____

_____

_____

_____

_____

Understanding Motivation

12. What motivated the other Woodmen to pretend to lose their axes? Write a paragraph explaining their motivation. How does understanding their motivation help you understand what kind of characters they are?

_____

_____

_____

_____

_____

LITERARY FOCUS: CONSTRUCTED RESPONSE *(20 points)*

13. Authors describe their characters through both direct and indirect characterization. As you read the story, you see how Aesop makes these characters seem like real people. Complete the following chart by describing the characters' traits. Give examples from the story. Include at least two traits for each character.

Character	Trait	Example
The Poor Woodman	_____	_____
		_____
		_____
	_____	_____
Mercury	_____	_____
		_____
		_____
	_____	_____
		_____
The Other Woodmen	_____	_____
		_____
		_____
	_____	_____

COLLECTION 3 DIAGNOSTIC TEST

Living in the Heart

On the line provided, write the letter of the *best* answer to each of the following items.
(100 points; 10 points each)

_____ **1.** Unlike a theme, the **topic** of a work of literature —

    A relates to the characters' lives

    B can be expressed in one word

    C may be stated indirectly by the author

    D is central to the work

_____ **2.** One way a reader can identify a story's **theme** is by —

    F creating a list of the major characters in the story

    G summarizing the plot of the story

    H analyzing the meaning of the story's title

    J predicting the outcome of the story

_____ **3.** Which of the following statements about **themes** is *true*?

    A Literary works by different authors may share the same themes.

    B Themes describe the lives of authors.

    C Authors add themes to their works to make them more suspenseful.

    D Poems, unlike short stories, do not have themes.

_____ **4.** If a writer sets a story in an old house near the ocean, which details would be the *most* useful in helping you picture the **setting**?

    F A FOR SALE sign on a lawn; cars moving slowly in a rain storm

    G A garden filled with blooming flowers; shoes drying on a sunny porch

    H Stars sparkling at night; a long, curving driveway

    J Peeling paint; birds circling over an empty beach

_____ **5.** Which of the following phrases contains **alliteration**?

    A friendly fox

    B lost dog

    C pale moon

    D green seeds

Holt Assessment: Literature, Reading, and Vocabulary

_____ **6. Myths** *most* frequently describe —

    F animals that seem human

    G characters who are lost

    H the origin of something

    J true historical events

_____ **7.** Which of the following words or phrases would be used in an article to show a **cause-and-effect** relationship?

    A for instance

    B similarly

    C as a result

    D during

_____ **8.** An **outline** of an article should include —

    F a biography of the author

    G the main ideas and supporting details

    H a list of sources

    J a retelling of the text

_____ **9.** What is a **word root**?

    A The dictionary definition of a word

    B A word with several meanings

    C The feeling suggested by a word

    D A word from which other words are formed

_____ **10.** A commonly used expression that is not literally true is called a(n) —

    F idiom

    G synonym

    H prefix

    J antonym

SELECTION TEST *Student Edition page 246*

The Highwayman Alfred Noyes

COMPREHENSION (60 points; 6 points each)

On the line provided, write the letter of the *best* answer to each of the following items.

_____ **1.** In Part 1, we learn that —

    A the highwayman and Bess are secretly married

    B Tim the ostler loves the landlord's daughter, Bess

    C the highwayman is not really a thief

    D Bess loves Tim the ostler, but he does not love her

_____ **2.** In Part 1, the highwayman plans to return to Bess before daylight unless the —

    F stagecoach is late

    G horse goes lame

    H redcoats harass him

    J stagecoach is not carrying gold

_____ **3.** The redcoats probably learn of the highwayman's plans from —

    A Bess

    B King George

    C the innkeeper

    D Tim the ostler

_____ **4.** In Part 2, the redcoats —

    F tie Bess up and place a musket by her chest

    G torture Bess into giving up the highwayman

    H take Bess away to use as bait

    J show her the highwayman's lifeless body

_____ **5.** Bess is being used as —

    A a reward for a successful robbery

    B punishment for a crime

    C bait for a trap

    D revenge for betrayal

_____ **6.** How does Bess warn the highwayman in Part 2?

    F She sends him a letter.

    G She tells the innkeeper.

    H She yells out his name.

    J She shoots herself.

Holt Assessment: Literature, Reading, and Vocabulary

_____ **7.** In Part 2, the reader is primarily concerned with the fate of —

    A the innkeeper

    B the redcoats

    C Bess

    D the innkeeper's wife

_____ **8.** Bess can be described as —

    F cowardly

    G self-sacrificing

    H greedy

    J selfish

_____ **9.** The poet uses a strong rhythm to capture the beat of the —

    A pounding rain

    B the blazing sun

    C rat-a-tat of gunfire

    D horse's hooves

_____ **10.** Which of the following lines *best* illustrates the poem's setting?

    F "His eyes were hollows of madness, his hair like moldy hay."

    G "He'd a French cocked hat on his forehead, a bunch of lace at his chin."

    H "Plaiting a dark red love knot into her long black hair."

    J "The road was a ribbon of moonlight over the purple moor."

LITERARY FOCUS *(20 points; 5 points each)*

On the line provided, write the letter of the *best* answer to each of the following items.

_____ **11.** Which statement below is *true* about the theme of a work?

    A No two works of literature can have the same theme.

    B The theme of a work expresses a universal truth about life.

    C Theme is the same as the plot of a work.

    D Authors always express the theme directly.

_____ **12.** Which of the stories below would most likely have a theme similar to that of "The Highwayman"?

    F A woman faces the danger of the wilderness alone.

    G Two brothers compete against each other in a football game.

    H A man becomes a spy to protect himself and betrays his friends.

    J A man puts himself in danger to protect his family from enemy forces.

_____ **13.** The sacrifice a woman makes for love is the poem's —

    A topic

    B plot

    C setting

    D theme

_____ **14.** Which of the following alternative titles would *best* suit this poem's theme?

    F What I Did for Love

    G What's Love Got to Do with It?

    H Love Never Lasts

    J Love Betrayed

CONSTRUCTED RESPONSE *(20 points)*

15. Writers develop their themes through plot, characters, and setting. Explain how the author uses plot to convey his theme in "The Highwayman." On a separate piece of paper, write a paragraph that explains your answer. Support your ideas with details from the poem.

Gentlemen of the Road Mara Rockliff

COMPREHENSION *(100 points; 10 points each)*

On the line provided, write the letter of the *best* answer to each of the following items.

_____ **1.** What caused the poor to live in filthy slums?

    A They refused to work hard.

    B There were too many rich people.

    C Government officials did not care about the poor.

    D There was not enough land for everyone.

_____ **2.** What was one effect of the miserable living conditions of the poor?

    F More babies were born.

    G Fewer babies were born.

    H Fewer babies died.

    J More babies died.

_____ **3.** What was one effect of worsening social conditions in seventeenth- and eighteenth-century England?

    A Robberies on the highways increased.

    B The gap between the "haves" and the "have-nots" narrowed.

    C Many people got very rich.

    D The highwaymen had few victims.

_____ **4.** Travel increased due in part to —

    F imports and exports

    G better roads

    H more inns being built

    J highwaymen

_____ **5.** What inference can you make about Robin Hood and the typical highwayman?

    A Both were hated as terrible criminals.

    B Neither was well-known in his own day or now.

    C Neither was admired for his actions.

    D Both were admired for helping the poor.

_____ **6.** What caused highwaymen to be mistaken for aristocrats?

    F They spent their time with upper-class people.

    G They dressed in beautiful clothing and acted like gentlemen.

    H They had beautiful stagecoaches.

    J They used the names of upper-class people.

_____ **7.** What was one positive effect of the highwaymen's upper-class manners?

    A People had less to carry.

    B People were rarely injured during robberies.

    C Many rich people and poor people became close friends.

    D The highwaymen gave all their money away.

_____ **8.** How were captured highwaymen usually punished?

    F They were hanged.

    G They were shot.

    H They were sent to prison.

    J They were deported to America.

_____ **9.** You can infer from the article's tone that the author —

    A believes that all highwaymen were vicious criminals

    B hopes that highwaymen return someday

    C has met several highwaymen

    D admires some highwaymen

_____ **10.** What was one long-term effect of the highwaymen's actions?

    F The government built safer roads.

    G A fair system of taxation was created.

    H The highwaymen became romanticized in poems and songs.

    J Poor people received good medical care.

SELECTION TEST *Student Edition page 260*

Annabel Lee Edgar Allan Poe

COMPREHENSION *(60 points; 6 points each)*

On the line provided, write the letter of the *best* answer to each of the following items.

_____ **1.** The poem is set —

    A on the moon

    B by the sea

    C in the ocean

    D in heaven

_____ **2.** The narrator's feelings for Annabel Lee can *best* be described as —

    F immature

    G fleeting

    H casual

    J intense

_____ **3.** According to the narrator, how did Annabel Lee die?

    A Strangers attacked her by the ocean.

    B She froze to death in a high wind.

    C The jealous angels sent a wind to chill her.

    D Her jealous relatives killed her.

_____ **4.** By referring to Annabel Lee's kinsmen as "highborn," the speaker implies that —

    F he is also "highborn" and deserves the reader's admiration

    G Annabel Lee should have married him

    H he is "lowborn" and deserves the reader's sympathy

    J Annabel was queen of the kingdom

_____ **5.** After her death, Annabel Lee is shut into a tomb by —

    A her husband

    B the angels

    C the demons

    D her kinsmen

_____ **6.** Dreams are brought to the narrator by the —

    F moon

    G stars

    H earth

    J sea

_____ **7.** Which of the following phrases is repeated throughout the poem?

    A "Kingdom by the sea"

    B "I and my Annabel Lee"

    C "Of many far wiser than we"

    D "In the sepulcher there by the sea"

_____ **8.** You can infer that after Annabel Lee's death the speaker feels —

    F more removed from Annabel Lee

    G thankful to Annabel Lee's relatives

    H great relief that his problems are over

    J resentment against Annabel Lee's relatives

_____ **9.** The speaker is most likely —

    A a young child

    B in his early twenties

    C a contemporary teenager

    D an old man

_____ **10.** Readers of this poem are *most likely* to associate it with —

    F an autobiography

    G a fairy tale

    H a letter

    J a detective story

LITERARY FOCUS *(20 points; 5 points each)*

On the line provided, write the letter of the *best* answer to each of the following items.

_____ **11.** Which of the following statements *best* describes the poem's narrator?

    A Mentally unbalanced by the death of his loved one

    B Overwhelmed by his life by the sea

    C Content with his life by the sea

    D Relieved by the death of his loved one

_____ **12.** What is the poem's topic?

    F The danger of living too close to the ocean

    G The problems of getting along with your in-laws

    H Love that can never be returned

    J The death of a loved one

_____ **13.** The poem's theme concerns feelings of —

    A delight

    B love and loss

    C pity

    D regret

_____ **14.** Which statement would the narrator *most likely* agree with?

    F Love ends with death.

    G We each have only one special love in our life.

    H You can never trust someone you love.

    J Only the good die young.

CONSTRUCTED RESPONSE *(20 points)*

15. Describe how the narrator reacts to the death of Annabel Lee. Then, explain how his reaction reinforces the poem's theme. On a separate piece of paper, write a paragraph that explains your answer. Support your ideas with details from the story.

SELECTION TEST *Student Edition page 266*

The Fall of the House of Poe? Mara Rockliff

COMPREHENSION *(50 points; 10 points each)*

On the line provided, write the letter of the *best* answer to each of the following items.

_____ **1.** Why did preservationists want to save the building?

    A It is a priceless storehouse of Poe's letters and poems.

    B It is an excellent site for classrooms and offices.

    C Poe wrote "The Raven" there.

    D They believe it is a genuine literary landmark.

_____ **2.** Preservationists studied all of the following sources *except* —

    F their own personal interviews with Poe

    G letters of people who knew Poe

    H documents of people who knew Poe

    J public records showing the neighborhood's history

_____ **3.** NYU officials believe the building should be demolished because —

    A many of the buildings in which Poe lived are still standing

    B Poe's relatives agreed to the demolition

    C Poe only lived there a short time and had not written important works there

    D according to city records the building wasn't even built when Poe lived in Manhattan

_____ **4.** Which of the following phrases would *most likely* be a heading in an outline of this essay?

    F Maps division of the New York Public Library

    G Washington Square Park

    H "The Tell-Tale Heart"

    J Judge's decision

_____ **5.** How did the judge rule in this case?

    A He dismissed the case.

    B He ruled in favor of the preservationists.

    C He appealed the decision.

    D He directed NYU to destroy the house.

Holt Assessment: Literature, Reading, and Vocabulary

VOCABULARY DEVELOPMENT *(50 points; 10 points each)*
Think about the relationship between the first pair of words in each item.
Then, choose the word for the second pair that *best* matches that relationship.
Choose the word from the Vocabulary words listed below, and write it on
the line provided.

circulated   **petitions**   **representatives**   **absorbed**   **demolish**

6. *disregarded* is to *consumed* as *ignored* is to _____

7. *hired* is to *teachers* as *elected* is to _____

8. *tourists* is to *traveled* as *news* is to _____

9. *read* is to *newspapers* as *sign* is to _____

10. *build* is to *construct* as *smash* is to _____

The Fall of the House of Poe?

User Friendly T. Ernesto Bethancourt

COMPREHENSION *(40 points; 4 points each)*

On the line provided, write the letter of the *best* answer to each of the following items.

_____ **1.** Where does the story take place?

    A Chicago, Illinois

    B Washington, D. C.

    C Santa Rosario, California

    D San Diego, California

_____ **2.** Kevin's father works as a —

    F computer designer

    G computer operator

    H traveling salesman

    J teacher

_____ **3.** Kevin is worried about all of the following problems *except* —

    A his reputation as a nerd

    B his father's business trip

    C Chuck's threats to beat him up

    D the fact that Louis is operating independently

_____ **4.** Which of the following words *best* describes Kevin's character?

    F Outgoing

    G Insensitive

    H Intelligent

    J Carefree

_____ **5.** How does Ginny Linke react to Kevin?

    A She makes fun of him.

    B She returns his love.

    C She ignores him.

    D She asks her brother to beat him up.

_____ **6.** What is one effect of Louis's acts of revenge?

    F Kevin's father is fired.

    G Louis is permanently disconnected.

    H Chuck Linke is arrested.

    J Kevin is suspended from school.

_____ **7.** What is the effect of patching Louis to a new modem?

    A Louis can communicate only with computers owned by Kevin's friends.

    B Louis can access and learn from computers all over the globe.

    C Louis can become Kevin.

    D Louis can give orders to the Secret Service.

_____ **8.** After Kevin's father returns home and works on the computer, he —

    F wonders how the computer got disconnected

    G is puzzled by Louis's final message

    H suspects that Kevin and Louis have become friends

    J decides to rebuild the other computers in the house

_____ **9.** How did Kevin's father change Louis?

    A He disconnected the printer and changed the modem.

    B He added a logic/growth program.

    C He gave Louis a personality and changed the modem.

    D He erased the entire program and set up Louis as a normal computer.

_____ **10.** What caused Louis to act as he did?

    F A modem error

    G A computer error

    H He liked practical jokes

    J His affection for Kevin

LITERARY FOCUS *(20 points; 5 points each)*

On the line provided, write the letter of the *best* answer to each of the following items.

_____ **11.** The story describes a computer named Louis that —

    A develops human feelings

    B does not follow directions

    C stops working

    D seeks revenge on people who have harmed it

_____ **12.** The printout that Kevin's father shows him at the end of the story probably expresses Louis's —

    F confusion about the computer's name

    G plans for keeping Chuck in prison

    H passion for Ginny

    J affection for Kevin

User Friendly

_____ **13.** The computer's character is revealed to Kevin by its —

    A fondness for binary code

    B negative feelings toward Kevin's father

    C messages and actions

    D tone of voice and vocabulary

_____ **14.** How does the title reinforce the story's theme?

    F It is ironic because Louis hates Kevin.

    G It reinforces Louis's feelings for Kevin.

    H It is sad because Louis is not user friendly.

    J It shows that computers can never be human.

VOCABULARY DEVELOPMENT (20 points; 4 points each)

Match each idiom on the left with its definition on the right. Write the letter of the definition on the line provided.

_____ **15.** great weight taken off one's shoulders   **a.** going crazy

_____ **16.** miss the boat   **b.** left out

_____ **17.** losing one's mind   **c.** got relief

_____ **18.** pull the plug   **d.** miss an opportunity

_____ **19.** out in the cold   **e.** let die

CONSTRUCTED RESPONSE (20 points)

20. A unique friendship is formed between a boy and his computer. How are Louis's and Kevin's characters similar? How are they different? Compare and contrast their personalities. On a separate piece of paper, write a paragraph that explains your answer. Support your ideas with details from the story.

It Just Keeps Going and Going… Joan Burditt

COMPREHENSION *(100 points; 10 points each)*
On the line provided, write the letter of the *best* answer to each of the following items.

_____ **1.** The title "It Just Keeps Going and Going…" refers to —

    A a computer virus

    B a specific computer

    C the Internet

    D a science-fiction monster

_____ **2.** The opening paragraph is designed to —

    F define a computer virus

    G explain in detail how a computer virus works

    H attract the reader's attention

    J describe a creature from science fiction and fantasy

_____ **3.** What is *not* an effect of a computer virus?

    A A person's computer can shut down.

    B Entire computer networks can crash.

    C A life-threatening situation can arise.

    D A person can catch the virus and become ill.

_____ **4.** A computer virus can cause problems in each of the following *except* the —

    F basic software program

    G computer case

    H hardware system

    J operating system

_____ **5.** What causes a computer virus?

    A A systems crash

    B A self-replicating computer program

    C An error in the operating system

    D A faulty piece of hardware

_____ **6.** The writer provides an analogy between a test answer key and a computer virus to —

    F persuade people to buy more computers

    G show how computer viruses are spread

    H argue that computers are dangerous

    J explain how teachers make answer keys

It Just Keeps Going and Going …

_____ **7.** "He finds mistakes in the midterm answer key, so he tosses it in the trash." This sentence contains —

    A a cause and an effect

    B neither a cause nor an effect

    C a cause

    D an effect

_____ **8.** "The next day the teacher stays home because he has the flu." Which transition shows effect?

    F Because

    G Next

    H Stays

    J Flu

_____ **9.** What effect does the substitute teacher's action have on the other teachers?

    A They have correct copies of the answer key.

    B They are allowed to use computers.

    C They have incorrect copies of the answer key.

    D They are not allowed to make copies of the answer key.

_____ **10.** What is the writer's attitude toward computer viruses?

    F She admires their strength.

    G She finds them boring.

    H She thinks they can be helpful.

    J She thinks they are dangerous.

SELECTION TEST *Student Edition page 289*

Echo and Narcissus *retold by* Roger Lancelyn Green

COMPREHENSION (40 points; 4 points each)

On the line provided, write the letter of the *best* answer to each of the following items.

_____ **1.** What is Echo's biggest problem at the beginning of the myth?

  A She is invisible.

  B She talks too much.

  C She is too beautiful.

  D She falls in love too easily.

_____ **2.** How does Hera punish Echo?

  F She makes her fall in love with Narcissus.

  G She transforms her into a flower.

  H From now on, she can only repeat what other people say.

  J She is thrown out of Olympus.

_____ **3.** Narcissus calls out for help when —

  A Aphrodite confronts him

  B he realizes that he is lost

  C he sees a nymph in the water

  D Echo throws her arms around him

_____ **4.** Which sentence *best* explains why Narcissus rejects Echo?

  F Narcissus is capable only of loving himself.

  G Echo is too greedy and pushy.

  H Narcissus thinks she is ugly and clumsy.

  J Echo annoys him by repeating his words.

_____ **5.** What happens to Echo after Narcissus rejects her?

  A She pines in grief and dies.

  B She begs Aphrodite to punish Narcissus.

  C She kisses Narcissus and dies.

  D She throws herself on the rocks.

_____ **6.** What causes Aphrodite to punish Narcissus?

  F He hunts in the forbidden northern mountains.

  G He mistreats Echo.

  H He falls in love with his own reflection.

  J He wanders away from his Theban friends.

_____ **7.** Narcissus spends his remaining days —

    A feeling sorry for rejecting Echo

    B picking flowers in the valley

    C growing weaker as he looks at his own reflection

    D playing jokes on the nymphs

_____ **8.** Narcissus's character is *best* described as —

    F arrogant and self-absorbed

    G selfless and kind

    H misunderstood and loyal

    J tender and sensitive

_____ **9.** After his death, Narcissus turns into a —

    A pool of water

    B flower

    C mountain

    D voice

_____ **10.** Echo <u>pines</u> away with grief because her love is not returned. What is the meaning of *pines* in this sentence?

    F Blooms

    G Expands

    H Remains

    J Wastes away

LITERARY FOCUS *(20 points; 5 points each)*

On the line provided, write the letter of the *best* answer to each of the following items.

_____ **11.** The subject of this myth is the origin of —

    A gods and goddesses

    B water nymphs

    C echoes and the narcissus flower

    D love and grief

_____ **12.** Both Echo and Narcissus die —

    F in a flood

    G because of Hera's jealousy

    H in each other's arms

    J because of a love they could not have

_____ **13.** Another good title for this myth would be —

    A Love and Jealousy

    B Power and Glory

    C War and Peace

    D Mistaken Identity

_____ **14.** That self-love and love for others can be equally painful is the myth's —

    F topic

    G plot

    H theme

    J setting

VOCABULARY DEVELOPMENT *(20 points; 4 points each)*

On the line provided, write the Vocabulary word that is *closest* in meaning to the word or phrase in italics.

detain   vainly   unrequited   parched   intently

_____ **15.** Hera tries *uselessly* to escape Echo's chatter.

_____ **16.** Echo manages to *delay* travelers with her long stories.

_____ **17.** He is *very hot and dry* from wandering all day, so he rests awhile by the cool pool.

_____ **18.** He stares *with great concentration* at the face in the pool.

_____ **19.** Both Narcissus and Echo are doomed to a love that is *not returned*.

CONSTRUCTED RESPONSE *(20 points)*

20. Hera and Aphrodite have different attitudes toward Echo. Describe how Hera and Aphrodite treat Echo, and explain how they affect Echo's fate. On a separate piece of paper, write a paragraph that explains your answer. Support your ideas with details from the story.

COLLECTION 3 SUMMATIVE TEST

Living in the Heart

This test asks you to use the skills and strategies you have learned in this collection.
Read "Anansi's Riding Horse," and then answer the questions that follow it.

Anansi's Riding Horse
by Marian E. Barnes

Linda was the most beautiful girl in ten villages. Brer Tiger and Anansi were
both in love with her. For Linda there was nothing whatsoever to think about.
Anansi was puny and weak, and not at all good-looking. Nobody glanced around
when he entered a room. His limbs were spindly like a spider. His voice was like a
thin reed. He was very stupid to think she would ever look his way. Linda laughed
at him.

Tiger was strong and handsome with brilliant burning eyes. His velvet black
stripes were bold and beautiful against his orange hide. Brer Tiger was powerful.
When he roared, the ground shook and the trees trembled. Linda was in love with
him. Poor Anansi! When Brer Tiger came into a room, Anansi was left out in the
cold!

But then the forest began to buzz with a most peculiar rumor: Anansi claimed
that Brer Tiger was his riding horse. How Linda laughed when she heard that
ridiculous story! Her friends repeated it over and over. Soon, it wasn't funny any-
more; indeed, it had become so annoying that Linda got hot under the collar. It was
all she could think about the day Tiger's eyes burned into hers and his mighty voice
rumbled, "I love you, Linda. Let's we two get married."

"Well, I certainly will not marry Anansi's riding horse," Linda pouted. "That's
what Anansi is telling everyone you are!" Brer Tiger raced over to Anansi's house
and shouted at the top of his lungs, "ANANSI, YOU ARE A DIRTY LIAR! COME
ON OUT HERE!" Anansi's little house quaked and wobbled and seemed to fall but
didn't. The door opened slowly and there stood Brer Rabbit. He pleaded with Tiger
to be quiet. He said Anansi was ready to kick the bucket.

"He *can't* die *now,*" Brer Tiger shrieked, and he bounded in the door. Sure
enough, there was Anansi covered up in bed, only his weak eyes showing. When
Brer Tiger asked him about the dirty lie he had told, tears clouded Anansi's eyes.

"I never said that," he said weakly. "Please, Brer Tiger, let me die in peace."

"NO SIREE," Brer Tiger roared. "You have to come with me to tell Linda the
truth."

"Well, all right," Anansi said reluctantly. "Hand me my fly whisk." His voice was
tired and thin.

"What do you want with a fly whisk?" Tiger asked in surprise.

"Those nasty insects in the forest will eat me alive if I don't have my fly whisk to
chase them away," panted Anansi, pointing to his oxtail fly whisk, which Tiger then
handed him. "Help me, please, Brer Rabbit," Anansi pleaded. "Put the blanket on
Brer Tiger's back and help me up."

"How come you need a blanket?" Brer Tiger wondered irritably.

"My body is very sore. The ride would be too painful for me without the blanket," Anansi grunted softly. "I couldn't stand it."

"All right, all right. Hurry up, Brer Rabbit," Tiger said. He was terribly afraid that Anansi would die before they could get back to Linda and clear his name.

After Brer Rabbit had saddled Brer Tiger and placed Anansi on the blanket, Anansi kept slipping down. "Oh, how weak and sick I feel!" Anansi said. "Everything is whirling around. Bring me a rope, Brer Rabbit. Please, bring me a rope."

"Why do you need a rope?" Brer Tiger asked.

"I must have a rope to hold on to, or else I shall fall off," Anansi replied, coming dangerously close to falling off as he spoke.

"Give Anansi a rope, Brer Rabbit!" Tiger ordered. "Why are you taking so long?" he roared.

But at last they moved off with much pleading from Anansi to Tiger to slow down because he couldn't stand the pace and was fainting. When they reached the clearing before Linda's cabin, she was standing on the porch with her friends. Her eyes grew wider and wider as Tiger approached, Anansi riding arrow-straight on his back. Suddenly Anansi plunged his heels deeper into Brer Tiger's sides and shouted, "Giddyap, Tiger! Giddyap!" He whacked Brer Tiger with the fly whisk.

Tiger yelled with pain and leaped forward; Anansi jerked the rein back, shouting gleefully as he dismounted, "See, gal, didn't I tell ya he was my riding horse!"

Brer Tiger, embarrassed to his back teeth, dashed into the forest. He hasn't been seen in those parts from that day until this.

VOCABULARY SKILLS *(25 points; 5 points each)*

Each of the underlined words below has also been underlined in the selection. Re-read those passages in which the underlined words appear, and then use context clues and your prior knowledge to help you select an answer. On the line provided, write the letter of the word that *best* completes each sentence.

_____ **1.** The phrase <u>spindly like a spider</u> is *best* described as a(n) _____.

     A metaphor

     B idiom

     C analogy

     D simile

_____ **2.** The phrase <u>his voice was like a thin reed</u> is *best* described as a(n) _____.

     F metaphor

     G simile

     H idiom

     J analogy

_____ **3.** The phrase <u>left out in the cold</u> is a(n) _____.

    A metaphor

    B analogy

    C idiom

    D simile

_____ **4.** Linda got hot under the collar because she is _____.

    F angry

    G confused

    H pleased

    J delighted

_____ **5.** The phrase <u>to kick the bucket</u> is a(n) _____.

    A idiom

    B metaphor

    C analogy

    D simile

COMPREHENSION (25 points; 5 points each)

On the line provided, write the letter of the *best* answer to each of the following items.

_____ **6.** The quality that Anansi and Brer Tiger have in common in this story is —

    F good looks

    G physical strength

    H love for Linda

    J the ability to trick each other

_____ **7.** Linda's attraction to Brer Tiger is based on his —

    A good looks and strength

    B cleverness

    C loyalty

    D kindness to her

_____ **8.** Which of the following events happens first in the story?

    F Brer Tiger comes to Anansi's house.

    G Brer Rabbit saddles Brer Tiger for Anansi.

    H Brer Rabbit tells Brer Tiger that Anansi is going to die.

    J Brer Tiger proposes to Linda.

_____ **9.** Why does Brer Tiger agree to let Anansi ride on his back?

    A He is afraid of Anansi.

    B He agrees to play a trick on Linda.

    C He wants to take Anansi to Linda to tell her the truth.

    D Linda asks Brer Tiger to carry Anansi to her.

_____ **10.** What happens to Brer Tiger at the end of the story?

    F He challenges Anansi to a fight.

    G He runs away from Linda in shame.

    H He pleads with Linda to believe him.

    J He discovers what Anansi is doing before it is too late.

READING SKILLS AND STRATEGIES: CONSTRUCTED RESPONSE *(30 points; 10 points each)*
Understanding Cause and Effect

11. What causes Brer Tiger to fall for Anansi's trick?

_____

_____

_____

_____

_____

12. List two effects of the trick.

_____

_____

_____

_____

_____

13. What causes Linda to believe that Brer Tiger was Anansi's horse?

_____

_____

_____

_____

_____

_____

LITERARY FOCUS: CONSTRUCTED RESPONSE (20 points)

14. Theme is the writer's central idea about human experience. As you read
a story, you infer the theme from clues the writer provides in the title,
characters, and plot. Complete the following chart to identify the theme
of "Anansi's Riding Horse" by inferring from clues in the text.

Story Clues	Inference About Theme
Title: _____	_____
	_____
	_____
Linda's Character: _____	_____
_____	_____
_____	_____
_____	
_____	
_____	
_____	
_____	

Story Clues	Inference About Theme
Plot: _____ _____ _____ _____ _____ _____ _____ _____ _____ _____ _____ _____ _____ _____ _____ _____ _____ Theme: _____ _____	_____ _____ _____ _____ _____ _____ _____ _____

Point of View: Can You See It My Way?

On the line provided, write the letter of the *best* answer to each of the following items.
(100 points; 10 points each)

_____ 1. The **third-person point of view** is used —

    A only in short stories

    B in both fiction and nonfiction

    C only in newspapers and magazine articles

    D in both personal essays and plays

_____ 2. When a story is told from the **first-person point of view,** the reader —

    F knows only what the narrator knows

    G must guess who the narrator is

    H does not learn about the characters in the story

    J views the characters as friends

_____ 3. What is an **autobiography**?

    A A short story that focuses on one main character

    B A book in which the writer presents his or her opinions about a subject

    C The story of a person's life written by that person

    D An analysis of a character in a story

_____ 4. Which of the following works is an example of a **biography**?

    F A report called "The History of Montana"

    G An essay about the impact of a factory on the local community

    H A book, written by a professor, that describes the life of a local hero

    J A newspaper article about current trends in England

_____ 5. **Historical fiction** is based on —

    A the experiences of several generations of a family

    B real people and events from the past

    C situations and ideas that seem outdated today

    D stories that have been told throughout the ages

_____ 6. The **theme** of a literary work is *best* described as —

    F what happens in the work

    G the truth or insight the writer reveals about life

    H the topic or subject

    J the time and place of the action

_____ **7.** The purpose of an **argument** is to —

    A persuade the reader to think or act in a certain way

    B provide instructions for completing a task

    C present rules that people must obey

    D advertise a product or service

_____ **8.** A statement that can be proved true is called —

    F prior knowledge

    G an assertion

    H a fact

    J a cause

_____ **9.** To determine the meaning of _reputed,_ it would be _most_ helpful to consider the meaning of the more familiar word —

    A reply

    B put

    C punished

    D reputation

_____ **10.** Which of the following words or phrases signals that a writer is defining a term?

    F instead

    G then

    H most important

    J that is

Collection 4 Diagnostic Test

SELECTION TEST   *Student Edition page 356*

After Twenty Years O. Henry

COMPREHENSION (*40 points; 4 points each*)

On the line provided, write the letter of the *best* answer to each of the following items.

_____ 1. Which of the following statements *best* describes "Silky" Bob's reasons for returning to New York City?

   A He has come to see his dying mother.

   B He is trying to avoid being arrested.

   C He is meeting a girlfriend.

   D He is hoping to meet an old friend.

_____ 2. Why is the scene where Bob lights a match important?

   F It is when the police officer recognizes Bob as a criminal.

   G It lets readers know that he smokes.

   H It shows that the story takes place at night.

   J It increases the suspense and adds mystery.

_____ 3. What makes Bob stand out?

   A He has a limp.

   B He has a small white scar.

   C He has a large Roman nose.

   D He is very tall.

_____ 4. Bob's detailed explanation to the first police officer about his presence in the doorway suggests —

   F he feels guilty about not staying in touch with his old friend

   G the police officer immediately recognizes him as a wanted criminal

   H he is afraid of getting in trouble with the police

   J he likes to talk about his past

_____ 5. Bob feels that his old friend Jimmy Wells is a —

   A real genius

   B true friend

   C go-getter, always making clever deals

   D razor-sharp wit

_____ 6. Jimmy Wells is a —

   F police officer in uniform

   G criminal

   H plainclothes police officer

   J restaurant owner

Holt Assessment: Literature, Reading, and Vocabulary

_____ **7.** What does Bob notice about his old friend that is different?

    A He has grown taller.

    B He is bald.

    C He has a beard.

    D He now wears glasses.

_____ **8.** How can you predict that Jimmy will do the right thing?

    F Jimmy questions Bob for a long time.

    G Bob describes Jimmy as true, dependable, and good.

    H Jimmy is suspicious of Bob.

    J Jimmy envies Bob's diamond jewelry.

_____ **9.** Which of the following statements *best* describes what Jimmy and Bob have in common?

    A Both wish the old restaurant had not been torn down.

    B Both love New York City.

    C Both keep their promise to meet.

    D Both have made large fortunes.

_____ **10.** Why won't Jimmy arrest Bob?

    F Jimmy knows that Bob isn't really guilty of anything.

    G Jimmy isn't a real police officer.

    H Jimmy is going off duty.

    J Jimmy can't bring himself to turn in a friend.

LITERARY FOCUS *(20 points; 5 points each)*

On the line provided, write the letter of the *best* answer to each of the following items.

_____ **11.** Who is telling this story?

    A Jimmy Wells

    B "Silky" Bob

    C An unnamed narrator

    D The second police officer

_____ **12.** Which sentence reveals the story's point of view?

    F "The policeman on the beat moved up the avenue impressively."

    G "I dined here at 'Big Joe' Brady's with Jimmy Wells, my best chum…"

    H "I'll be on my way."

    J "I should say not!"

_____ **13.** You can tell this story is told from the omniscient point of view because —

    A readers know every character's thoughts

    B readers see events through Jimmy's eyes only

    C readers see events though Bob's eyes only

    D the writer uses the first-person pronoun "I"

_____ **14.** How would the story change if it were told from the first-person point of view?

    F Readers would get a more complete description of the characters.

    G Readers would see events through every character's eyes.

    H Readers would get an incomplete description of the characters.

    J Readers would see events through one character's eyes only.

VOCABULARY DEVELOPMENT *(20 points; 4 points each)*

Match the definition on the left with the Vocabulary word on the right. Write the letter of the Vocabulary word on the line provided.

_____ **15.** conceit; talking about oneself too much   **a.** habitual

_____ **16.** complicated; full of detail   **b.** intricate

_____ **17.** at the same time   **c.** dismally

_____ **18.** miserably; gloomily   **d.** egotism

_____ **19.** done or fixed by habit; customary   **e.** simultaneously

CONSTRUCTED RESPONSE *(20 points)*

20. "At the end of the story, Jimmy and Bob are both friends and enemies." Do you agree or disagree with this statement? Consider the story's point of view in your response. On a separate piece of paper, write a paragraph that explains your answer. Support your ideas with details from the story.

What's *Really* in a Name?   Joan Burditt

COMPREHENSION *(100 points; 10 points each)*

On the line provided, write the letter of the *best* answer to each of the following items.

_____ **1.** Who is Patsy in this selection?

    A The writer of the article

    B A well-known author

    C The friend of the writer's sister

    D A character in a book by Mark Twain

_____ **2.** Which phrase *best* describes Patsy?

    F A famous writer

    G A talented actress

    H A wrongly accused bank robber

    J A popular singer

_____ **3.** The writer called her sister to —

    A find out why Patsy's name had been left off the movie credits

    B invite her to see Elton John in concert

    C recommend a book by Stephen King that she had just read

    D discuss Patsy's career and life in Los Angeles

_____ **4.** Which writer took a pseudonym?

    F Ralph Lauren

    G Elton John

    H Norma Jean Baker

    J Samuel Clemens

_____ **5.** What was William Sydney Porter's pen name?

    A O. Henry

    B Mark Twain

    C Ralph Lauren

    D Richard Bachman

_____ **6.** People take pseudonyms for all of the following reasons *except* —

    F to hide their identity

    G to have a name that sounds better

    H to hold tight to their past

    J to make it easier to sell books

What's *Really* in a Name?

_____ **7.** Why does it bother the writer that Patsy took a pseudonym?

    A The writer was not asked her opinion.

    B The writer feels that Patsy was trying to get rid of her past.

    C The writer does not like the sound of the new name.

    D Patsy changes her name often.

_____ **8.** Which statement *best* describes the author's perspective?

    F Patsy needed a new name.

    G Always hold tight to your roots.

    H A name has no connection to the past.

    J The past has no roots.

_____ **9.** The writer conveys her perspective through —

    A speech and action

    B time and place

    C details and examples

    D pictures and symbols

_____ **10.** The author's purpose in this essay is to —

    F express her opinion about pseudonyms

    G explain how to change your name legally

    H tell a story about someone who made a mistake

    J argue that people should never change their name

_____ **7.** Who tells Yeh-Shen not to lose her magic shoes?

    A The spirit of the bones

    B Her stepmother

    C Her stepsisters

    D The king

_____ **8.** What happens when Yeh-Shen loses one of her magic shoes?

    F The fish bones become silent.

    G Her stepmother becomes kind.

    H The king returns the missing shoe.

    J The old man gives her a new pair.

_____ **9.** The story's theme is *best* expressed as —

    A hard work pays off in the end

    B everyone needs a fairy godmother

    C evil wins over good

    D good wins over evil

_____ **10.** This story has been popular throughout the ages because —

    F it has a sad ending that appeals to many people

    G people like to believe that good will be rewarded

    H it is part of the oral tradition

    J it has a clear point of view

LITERARY FOCUS *(20 points; 5 points each)*

On the line provided, write the letter of the *best* answer to each of the following items.

_____ **11.** Who is the story's narrator?

    A The author

    B The fish

    C Yeh-Shen

    D The stepmother

_____ **12.** What is the narrator's relationship to the story?

    F The narrator is a major character in the story.

    G The narrator is a minor character in the story.

    H The narrator is more than one character in the story.

    J The narrator is not in the story.

_____ **13.** "Yeh-Shen" is told from the —

    A first-person point of view

    B third-person-limited point of view

    C omniscient point of view

    D third-person-unlimited point of view

_____ **14.** The author likely selected this point of view to —

    F describe events more fully

    G include his opinion of events

    H show only Yeh-Shen's thoughts

    J experiment with point of view

CONSTRUCTED RESPONSE *(20 points)*

15. How would the story "Yeh-Shen" have changed if it had been told from a different point of view? Identify the point of view from which the story is told, and explain how changing point of view would affect the story. On a separate piece of paper, write a paragraph that explains your answer. Support your ideas with details from the story.

SELECTION TEST *Student Edition page 389*

Mirror, Mirror, on the Wall, Do I See Myself As Others Do? Joan Burditt

COMPREHENSION *(100 points; 10 points each)*

On the line provided, write the letter of the *best* answer to each of the following items.

_____ **1.** Who is the woman the narrator saw on television?

     A She is a neighbor.

     B She is a customer at the drugstore.

     C She works at the corner drugstore.

     D She is the narrator's sister.

_____ **2.** Why was the woman on television?

     F She was selling lottery tickets.

     G She had just won the lottery.

     H She was selling a new diet.

     J She was reporting on overweight teenagers.

_____ **3.** The woman on television was upset because —

     A she did not win the lottery

     B she wanted to be on television longer

     C she did not have designer clothing on

     D she thought she looked fat on television

_____ **4.** According to the writer, all of the following affect our perceptions of weight *except* —

     F television

     G test scores

     H magazines

     J peer pressure

_____ **5.** The writer believes that high-fashion models —

     A reinforce unrealistic body types

     B are beautiful

     C need more muscle

     D always wear name-brand clothing

_____ **6.** The writer would most likely —

    F buy her own child designer clothing

    G make her daughter stay slim

    H try to reinforce her daughter's self-confidence

    J read fashion magazines with her daughter

_____ **7.** What happens to students' self-esteem as they grow up?

    A It increases.

    B It decreases slightly.

    C It decreases sharply.

    D It stays the same.

_____ **8.** What may help girls gain self-esteem?

    F Humor

    G Sports

    H Magazines

    J Television

_____ **9.** The subject of this essay is —

    A accurate body image in the United States

    B distorted body image in the United States

    C the importance of staying in shape

    D how Americans are getting fatter

_____ **10.** What point is the author arguing in this essay?

    F If you believe in yourself, you will be thin.

    G The media are not a powerful force in the United States.

    H Weight gain is determined by society, not the individual.

    J Children need self-confidence, not unrealistic media images.

SELECTION TEST *Student Edition page 393*

Names/Nombres Julia Alvarez

COMPREHENSION *(40 points; 4 points each)*
On the line provided, write the letter of the *best* answer to each of the following items.

_____ **1.** Julia Alvarez's family is from —

    A Spain

    B Bermuda

    C the Middle East

    D the Dominican Republic

_____ **2.** How does Julia feel about the nicknames her friends give her?

    F She hates to hear her friends mispronounce her name.

    G She dislikes all nicknames.

    H She sees the nicknames as a sign of popularity.

    J She would prefer that her friends call her "Juliet."

_____ **3.** According to the passage, in the late 1960s, Americans began to treat "Third World names" —

    A rudely

    B indifferently

    C with more respect

    D as if they were silly

_____ **4.** Which of the following statements does *not* show the importance of names in Caribbean culture?

    F Julia's name reflects many generations of her family.

    G Julia allows her friends to call her "Judy."

    H Julia has the same name as her mother.

    J "Mauricia" combines the names of both grandmothers.

_____ **5.** Why was Alvarez's mother embarrassed in the hospital after giving birth to her first daughter?

    A She thought her baby's name was too noisy.

    B Her baby was named after a relative.

    C The other babies were more attractive.

    D Julia's family was poor.

_____ **6.** Which of the following statements *best* describes Julia?

    F She was born in the United States.

    G She is ashamed of her heritage.

    H She is proud of her name.

    J She graduated from high school.

_____ **7.** In the essay, which of the following is an example of ethnicity being "in"?

    A A stranger corrects Julia's pronunciation of her own sister's name.

    B Julia's classmate asks her to pronounce her name in Spanish.

    C The young mothers think the name "Mauricia" is odd.

    D Julia's large family comes to her graduation.

_____ **8.** What happens last in the essay?

    F Julia's parents become homesick.

    G Julia's family gives her a graduation party.

    H Julia has a difficult time introducing her family to her friends.

    J Julia becomes popular with her classmates.

_____ **9.** The essay's main idea is *best* stated as —

    A people had trouble pronouncing Julia's name

    B it is rude for people to mispronounce names

    C Julia's life is influenced by two cultures

    D many authors have unusual names

_____ **10.** The writer chose the title "Names/Nombres" to —

    F show that she speaks both Spanish and English

    G emphasize the importance of speaking two languages

    H show that she has a name in Spanish and a name in English

    J emphasize the importance of adapting to a new culture while keeping your heritage

LITERARY FOCUS (20 points; 5 points each)

On the line provided, write the letter of the *best* answer to each of the following items.

_____ **11.** Alvarez relates the events from her —

    A father's point of view

    B sister's point of view

    C mother's point of view

    D own point of view

_____ **12.** What is the narrator's relationship to the story?

   F She is a participant.

   G She is a bystander.

   H She is completely uninvolved.

   J She is involved to a small extent.

_____ **13.** "Names/Nombres" is told from the —

   A first-person point of view

   B third-person-limited point of view

   C omniscient point of view

   D third-person-unlimited point of view

_____ **14.** All of the following sentences help you identify the point of view *except* —

   F "By the time I was in high school, I was a popular kid, and it showed in my name."

   G "Sometimes, American tongues found even that mispronunciation tough to say and called her *Maria* or *Marsha* or *Maudy* from her nickname *Maury*."

   H "My little sister, Ana, had the easiest time of all."

   J "Our first few years in the States, though, ethnicity was not yet 'in.' "

VOCABULARY DEVELOPMENT *(20 points; 4 points each)*

Match the Vocabulary word on the left with its synonym or antonym on the right. In the space provided, write the letter of the synonym or antonym for each Vocabulary word.

_____ **15.** antonym for *convoluted*

_____ **16.** synonym for *ethnicity*

_____ **17.** antonym for *exotic*

_____ **18.** synonym for *heritage*

_____ **19.** synonym for *convoluted*

   a. common culture or nationality

   b. simple

   c. traditions

   d. complicated

   e. familiar or native

CONSTRUCTED RESPONSE *(20 points)*

20. How does the essay's **point of view** affect the **theme**? Be sure to identify both the point of view and the theme. On a separate sheet of paper, write a paragraph that explains your answer. Support your ideas with details from the story.

SELECTION TEST   *Student Edition page 402*

An Unforgettable Journey   Maijue Xiong

COMPREHENSION *(40 points; 4 points each)*

On the line provided, write the letter of the *best* answer to each of the following items.

_____ **1.** What purpose does the introduction serve?

    A It argues the author's main point.

    B It explains why the Hmong were uprooted.

    C It summarizes the story to follow.

    D It shows the author's point of view.

_____ **2.** The Hmong are —

    F people from only Vietnam and Laos

    G Communists from Southeast Asia

    H soldiers from Vietnam

    J people from Southeast Asia

_____ **3.** At the beginning of the story, the author's father was —

    A a soldier fighting with the Central Intelligence Agency against the Communists

    B a Communist soldier fighting with the Central Intelligence Agency

    C a simple farmer fighting with the Communists

    D a high-ranking Communist government official

_____ **4.** The author's family left the country as fast as possible because —

    F they had been planning to leave for ten years

    G they were thrown out

    H their lives were in danger

    J they hated their homeland

_____ **5.** Which of the following statements is a *fact*?

    A The journey felt very long.

    B Thailand is a beautiful country.

    C "For a month, my family walked through the dense tropical jungles…"

    D I was like a little ant placed in a field of tall grass.

_____ **6.** Which of the following statements is an *opinion*?

    F "We traveled in silence at night…"

    G "We…slept in the daytime."

    H "When it got dark, the fishermen came back with a small fishing boat…"

    J It was depressing and nerve-racking.

_____ **7.** The author compares her experience to —

   A a war

   B a fierce battle

   C a good dream because it brought her to the United States

   D a bad dream

_____ **8.** "We were then taken to a refugee camp in Nongkhai" is a *fact* because —

   F it is the author's own personal feeling

   G it cannot be proven true or false

   H it can be confirmed by outside sources

   J many people agree with it

_____ **9.** You can infer that the family survived their experience because they are —

   A rich and powerful

   B intelligent and determined

   C in good physical shape and well fed

   D clever and ruthless

_____ **10.** Why do you think the author told her story?

   F She wants others to understand what the refugees experienced.

   G She wants pity.

   H She wants admiration.

   J She does not think anyone would believe her otherwise.

LITERARY FOCUS *(20 points; 5 points each)*

On the line provided, write the letter of the *best* answer to each of the following items.

_____ **11.** Who is the narrator in the story?

   A The author's mother

   B The author's sister

   C The author

   D The author's father

_____ **12.** Which sentence reveals the story's point of view?

   F "Each person received a bowl of rice porridge…"

   G "Many families had been there for weeks…"

   H "The plane ride took a long time…"

   J "In the morning, I ran to get in line for breakfast."

An Unforgettable Journey

_____ **13.** How can you tell this story is told from the first-person point of view?

    A Readers see events through one character's eyes.

    B Readers know every character's thoughts.

    C The writer uses the pronouns *they* and *them*.

    D The narrator knows all.

_____ **14.** How would the story change if it were told from an omniscient point of view?

    F Readers would have an unreliable narrator.

    G The narrator would zoom in on one character.

    H Readers would know what other characters think and feel.

    J The writer would experiment with point of view more freely.

VOCABULARY DEVELOPMENT *(20 points; 4 points each)*

Match the definition on the right with the Vocabulary word on the left. Write
the letter of the Vocabulary word on the line provided.

_____ **15.** refuge

_____ **16.** transition

_____ **17.** persecution

_____ **18.** refugee

_____ **19.** deprivation

    a. act of willfully injuring others
    because of their beliefs

    b. loss; condition of having something
    taken away by force

    c. shelter; protection

    d. change; passing from one condition
    to another

    e. a person who flees his or her home or
    country to escape war or persecution

CONSTRUCTED RESPONSE *(20 points)*

20. Does the writer use a subjective or objective point of view? Provide
reasons why the writer chose that point of view. On a separate piece of
paper, write a paragraph that explains your answer. Support your ideas
with details from the story.

SELECTION TEST *Student Edition page 410*

Exile Eyes Agate Nesaule

COMPREHENSION *(100 points; 10 points each)*

On the line provided, write the letter of the *best* answer to each of the following items.

_____ **1.** Who is Agate Nesaule?

    A She is a hairdresser.

    B She is a newcomer to the United States.

    C She is a refugee from Latvia.

    D She is a refugee from Cambodia.

_____ **2.** The essay is set in —

    F Latvia

    G Laos

    H Vietnam

    J Wisconsin

_____ **3.** Each of the following details tells the narrator that the women are exiles *except* —

    A physical handicaps

    B details of their clothing

    C their extreme good manners

    D their look of pain and sorrow

_____ **4.** The purpose of "Exile Eyes" is to show the women's —

    F anger and hatred

    G harsh experiences

    H determination

    J severe poverty

_____ **5.** The narrator has seen eyes of exiles everywhere *but* in —

    A her mother

    B her teacher

    C women who survived Siberia

    D people who were tortured in Rwanda

_____ **6.** You can infer that the shop owner is kind to the women because he —

    F wants to make a profit

    G is trying to build a new business

    H shares their painful pasts

    J is a journalist too

_____ **7.** When she was twelve years old, the narrator —

    A visited Latvia

    B published her first story

    C came to the United States

    D had her braids cut off

_____ **8.** The last lines reveal that this essay is basically —

    F hopeful

    G despairing

    H frightening

    J cheerful

_____ **9.** The writer used the first-person point of view to —

    A be a reliable narrator

    B show everyone's thoughts and feelings

    C add her own experiences to those of the newcomers

    D persuade people to come to the United States

_____ **10.** The author's perspective is —

    F unbiased

    G neutral

    H negative

    J personal

SELECTION TEST *Student Edition page 414*

**LITERARY RESPONSE
AND ANALYSIS**

Elizabeth I Milton Meltzer

COMPREHENSION *(40 points; 4 points each)*
On the line provided, write the letter of the *best* answer to each of the following items.

_____ **1.** By the end of the reign of Elizabeth I, England —

    A experienced huge economic losses

    B was just starting to be respected around the world

    C had been brought to its lowest point in centuries

    D became a major world power

_____ **2.** As a child, Elizabeth I can *best* be described as —

    F lazy and foolish

    G intelligent and determined

    H sullen and depressed

    J unappealing but bright

_____ **3.** The order of succession was —

    A Edward, Mary, Elizabeth

    B Mary, Edward, Elizabeth

    C Elizabeth, Mary, Edward

    D Edward, Elizabeth, Mary

_____ **4.** In the time of Elizabeth I, the nobility and royalty married for all of the following reasons *except* —

    F to provide heirs

    G to strengthen a family's power

    H a create an alliance against common enemies

    J love

_____ **5.** Whom did Elizabeth I finally marry?

    A Philip II of Spain

    B No one

    C Henry VIII

    D Sir William Cecil

_____ **6.** Why was Elizabeth I an effective monarch?

    F She ruled alone without advisors.

    G She was ruthless and didn't care what the people thought.

    H She was skilled at state matters and comfortable wielding power.

    J She resisted great social change to create stability.

_____ **7.** Which of the following statements is an objective *fact*?

    A Sir William Cecil was both brilliant and cruel.

    B Sir Francis Drake was the most daring explorer of all.

    C William Shakespeare and Edmund Spenser wrote during the reign of Elizabeth I.

    D Christopher Marlowe was a better writer than John Donne.

_____ **8.** What can you infer about how Milton Meltzer feels about Queen Elizabeth I?

    F He admires her very much.

    G He feels she was not an effective ruler.

    H He believes that much of her success was due to her brilliant advisors.

    J He faults her for England's loss to the Spanish Armada.

_____ **9.** Which quality *best* describes the character of Elizabeth I?

    A Irritable

    B Lucky

    C Shrewd

    D Energetic

_____ **10.** "Elizabeth I" can be categorized as a story that is —

    F filled with the author's personal feelings

    G biased

    H highly subjective

    J basically objective

LITERARY FOCUS *(20 points; 5 points each)*

On the line provided, write the letter of the *best* answer to each of the following items.

_____ **11.** You can tell that "Elizabeth I" is a biography because —

    A the subject is writing about her own life

    B it is the story of another person's life

    C it is unbiased

    D it is well researched and full of facts

_____ **12.** Who is the story's narrator?

    F Sir William Cecil

    G William Shakespeare

    H Elizabeth I

    J an unnamed narrator

_____ **13.** What is the narrator's relationship to the story?

    A The narrator is not in the story.

    B The narrator is more than one character in the story.

    C The narrator is a major character in the story.

    D The narrator is a minor character in the story.

_____ **14.** "Elizabeth I" is told from the —

    F first-person point of view

    G third-person-limited point of view

    H omniscient point of view

    J third-person-unlimited point of view

VOCABULARY DEVELOPMENT *(20 points; 4 points each)*

Match the Vocabulary word on the left with its synonym or antonym on the right. In the space provided, write the letter of the synonym or antonym for each Vocabulary word.

_____ **15.** antonym for *arrogant*   **a.** regal; royal

_____ **16.** synonym for *monarch*   **b.** meek; shy

_____ **17.** synonym for *alliance*   **c.** bearable; tolerable

_____ **18.** antonym for *intolerable*   **d.** total market control

_____ **19.** synonym for *monopoly*   **e.** partnership between nations

CONSTRUCTED RESPONSE *(20 points)*

20. How would the biography "Elizabeth I" change if Elizabeth herself told the story? How would the biography's main idea change if the **point of view** shifted? On a separate sheet of paper, write a paragraph that explains your answer. Support your ideas with details from the story.

COLLECTION 4 SUMMATIVE TEST

Point of View: Can You See It My Way?

This test asks you to use the skills and strategies you have learned in this collection.
Read this short story excerpt, and then answer the questions that follow it.

from **Directions**
by Sara Baade

When there is a cat in the yard, we let the dog out to chase it away. He runs outside barking and snatching and usually the cat flits away in a second, up a tree or under a shrub. Sometimes, though, it doesn't move, being either too old or too lazy, or surprised. Occasionally, the cat is even mocking, confident that the dog will stop short, unsure of itself, still barking frantically. I can't help laughing at the dog, even when I see it hiding later, confused, or maybe ashamed of his cowardice.

The new girl made me think of this. She is standing in the doorway, stocky terrier stance <u>contradicted</u> by a hesitant, scared expression. I think maybe we will be friends, and I silently try to tell her not to look so frightened as she is introduced to the fourth grade, because this is the unguarded <u>demeanor</u> which commands mocking and taunts. Yet even as I sympathize I look over to Andrea, who meets my eye. Hers gleam, and while I nod knowingly back, as I too have <u>instinctively</u> been wondering how we can test this new girl, I commiserate with the stranger wavering in front of thirty similar sets of eyes. Maybe later she will be one of us, but for now she is an outsider, an outcast.

At recess, we pour out the side door and Andrea and I gather into a circle with the other girls, Janine, Flo, and Margaret. "Look," giggles Flo, pointing over to the paved area. We see the new girl, bouncing a ball against the wall, catching it, sometimes kicking it hard and having it leap high. We know she is watching us <u>furtively</u> without seeming to look— she can't and won't make the first move because she's the newcomer and it's up to us, and she knows this.

I stare, imagining how she must feel, but I can't call her over, not without approval. Suddenly she turns and fixes me with a daring, lofty expression. Instantly I cool. Everyone has seen; she has overstepped her boundary.

I call, "Come over here."

She is undecided, doesn't want to obey, but is <u>ravenous</u> for inclusion. She walks toward us, still tossing and catching the ball. Flo and Janine titter nervously. "What are you going to do?" they whisper. Suddenly, inexplicably, I wish I was playing kick-the-can with the boys instead.

The girls all wait expectantly, a jury awaiting the judge's condemnation of the criminal. Andrea nudges me with her elbow. I can't do it, ridicule this outsider. By now some of the boys are drifting over curiously; even the new girl is watching me almost interestedly, wondering what I will do, what torment I have planned. "Hello," I quaver, and the bell rings.

From "Directions" by **Sara Baade** from *B.C.E.T.A. Student Writing Journal*, 1989–1990. Copyright © 1990 by Sara Baade. Reproduced by permission of the author.

VOCABULARY SKILLS *(25 points; 5 points each)*

Each of the underlined words below has also been underlined in the selection. Re-read those passages in which the underlined words appear, and then use context clues and your prior knowledge to help you select an answer. On the line provided, write the letter of the word or words that *best* complete each sentence.

_____ **1.** If a theory is <u>contradicted</u>, it is _____.

    A historically proven

    B contrary to opinion

    C neutral

    D shown to be false

_____ **2.** Your best <u>demeanor</u> refers to _____.

    F attractive clothing

    G good behavior

    H excellent health

    J an impressive hairstyle

_____ **3.** When you do something <u>instinctively</u>, you do it _____.

    A with great skill

    B immediately

    C without thinking of it

    D with great creativity

_____ **4.** To act <u>furtively</u> is to act _____.

    F in a secret, hidden manner

    G in an open manner

    H in a bold manner

    J with other people at your side

_____ **5.** If you are <u>ravenous</u> for attention, you _____.

    A are eager to be noticed

    B do not want to be noticed

    C deserve to be noticed

    D do not care whether you are noticed

COMPREHENSION *(25 points; 5 points each)*

On the line provided, write the letter of the *best* answer to each of the following items.

_____ **6.** Why does Andrea have a gleam in her eye when the new girl enters?

    F She has been hoping to find a new friend.

    G She thinks it will be fun to test the new girl.

    H She is hungry and thinking about lunch.

    J The girls need a good ballplayer for their team.

_____ **7.** The new girl wears a "lofty expression" because she —

    A is acting as if she does not mind being alone

    B does not want to be friends with the other girls

    C does not think the other girls are as good as she is

    D is terrified of all the other girls

_____ **8.** According to the narrator, what sort of boundary does the new girl overstep?

    F A mark on the pavement

    G A language barrier

    H A line the girls draw on the ground

    J A social boundary

_____ **9.** Based on the details in the story, it is reasonable to assume that the author —

    A dislikes the new girl because she is a stranger

    B disapproves of the group's attitude toward the new girl

    C is disappointed that the new girl did not have a fight with the narrator

    D approves of the group's attitude toward the new girl

_____ **10.** All of the following details in the story support the prediction that the narrator will not harm the new girl *except* —

    F the narrator tries to imagine how the new girl feels

    G the narrator notices that the new girl wants to be included

    H the narrator gathers with her friends at recess

    J the narrator thinks that she and the new girl might become friends

READING SKILLS AND STRATEGIES: CONSTRUCTED RESPONSE *(30 points; 10 points each)*
Making Predictions

11. On the lines provided, write a brief paragraph in which you predict what
    you think happens between the narrator, the new girl, and the other girls at
    the end of the story. Support your ideas with details from the story.

    _____

    _____

    _____

    _____

    _____

    _____

Determining the Main Idea

12. Which of the following statements *best* describes the story's main idea? On the lines provided,
    write the letter of the answer you choose, and briefly defend your choice. There is more than
    one possible answer. Support your answer with details from the story.

    A Children can be cruel to newcomers.

    B Peer pressure often influences our decisions.

    C It is very difficult to make new friends.

    D People should try hard to welcome strangers to the group.

    _____

    _____

    _____

    _____

    _____

    _____

Collection 4 Summative Test

Distinguishing Facts from Opinions

13. Write *fact* by each statement that is a fact. Write *opinion* by each statement that is an opinion.

_____ **A.** The new girl was standing in the doorway.

_____ **B.** The new girl had a stocky terrier stance and looked scared.

_____ **C.** The new girl will become friends with the rest of the girls.

_____ **D.** The girls gathered in a circle and stared at the newcomer.

_____ **E.** The newcomer had overstepped her boundary.

LITERARY FOCUS: CONSTRUCTED RESPONSE *(20 points)*

14. On the lines provided, rewrite the following passage from the story, using the omniscient point of view. Be sure to look at the situation from different characters' viewpoints. Explain how the change in the point of view affects the story.

> At recess, we pour out the side door and Andrea and I gather into a circle with the other girls, Janine, Flo, and Margaret. "Look," giggles Flo, pointing over to the paved area. We see the new girl, bouncing a ball against the wall, catching it, sometimes kicking it hard and having it leap high. We know she is watching us furtively without seeming to look—she can't and won't make the first move because she's the newcomer and it's up to us, and she knows this.

_____

_____

_____

_____

_____

_____

_____

_____

Worlds of Words: Prose and Poetry

On the line provided, write the letter of the *best* answer to each of the following items.
(100 points; 10 points each)

_____ **1.** Which of the following elements is *most* often found in **nonfiction**?

   A Exaggeration

   B Unrealistic characters

   C Facts and true details

   D Unusual settings

_____ **2.** The main difference between a **novella** and a **short story** is seen in their —

   F subject matter

   G point of view

   H length

   J characters

_____ **3.** Which of the following sentences contains a **metaphor**?

   A In the fierce storm the ship was a tin can, bobbing up and down in the waves.

   B My face stung from the pelting rain, which felt like hard glass beads.

   C The wind howled like a wolf all night long and kept me awake.

   D Each post in the fence is as rough as sandpaper.

_____ **4.** Which of the following sentences contains an **image** that appeals to your sense of hearing?

   F Lightning flashed across the sky in the dark of night.

   G At dawn there was a gentle tapping at the window.

   H Downy feathers covered the tiny chicks.

   J Her old barn held the scent of summer straw.

_____ **5.** When poetry is written in **free verse,** it —

   A has a regular beat

   B sounds like ordinary speech

   C is divided into paragraphs

   D contains several themes

_____ **6.** Which of the following lines contains **internal rhyme**?

    F Lillie Lou lost the locket.

    G The oil hissed in the pan.

    H Corn spilled on the floor.

    J Daniel dove for the treasure trove.

_____ **7.** Which organizational pattern do writers often use when they **compare and contrast**?

    A Cause and effect

    B Point-by-point method

    C Chronological order

    D Problem and solution

_____ **8.** When the **main idea** of a paragraph is implied, you should —

    F re-read the previous paragraph to determine what the author is saying

    G question the author's knowledge of the subject

    H identify important details and think about what point they make

    J assume that the paragraph is not essential to the text

_____ **9.** The emotions associated with a word are called its —

    A connotations

    B derivations

    C context clues

    D denotations

_____ **10.** The pair of words *happy* and *glad* are —

    F antonyms

    G affixes

    H idioms

    J synonyms

Amigo Brothers Piri Thomas

COMPREHENSION *(40 points; 4 points each)*

On the line provided, write the letter of the *best* answer to each of the following items.

_____ **1.** When Antonio and Felix realize they must fight each other —

    A Antonio joins a gang

    B Felix trains longer and harder

    C they feel a barrier rising between them

    D Felix decides to quit boxing

_____ **2.** In order to fight each other, Felix and Antonio decide that each must —

    F think of his best friend as a stranger

    G force himself to hate the other

    H never see the other again

    J beat the other boy to a pulp

_____ **3.** When Felix tells Antonio that he wants to win the fight "fair and square," he means that he does not —

    A like the way that Antonio fights

    B want to go through with the fight

    C trust Antonio's trainer

    D want Antonio to let him win

_____ **4.** Which of the following statements about Felix and Antonio is *false*?

    F Felix is a stronger puncher.

    G The boys share a collection of *Fight* magazines.

    H Antonio is the better boxer.

    J Neither boy has ever represented his community in a match before.

_____ **5.** Felix and Antonio have all the following in common *except* —

    A gold-plated medals

    B scrapbooks of boxing match tickets

    C fancy boxing shoes

    D positive attitudes

_____ **6.** After Felix sees *The Champion*, he —

    F does not want to see Antonio beaten

    G sees himself as the champion and Antonio as the challenger

    H decides that winning the fight is not worth ending the friendship

    J knows that life never works out as neatly as movie plots

_____ **7.** Which of the following aspects of each boy is contrasted in the story?

    A Their appearance

    B Their memories of fight statistics

    C Their dedication to working out

    D Their commitment to their friendship

_____ **8.** The internal conflict that both Felix and Antonio face is how to —

    F end their friendship so they can fight each other

    G pursue their own goal without hurting their friend

    H avoid shame if they lose the fight

    J explain the fight to their friends

_____ **9.** The referee is stunned by —

    A the huge crowd

    B the boys' kindness to each other

    C Felix's bad fighting

    D the boys' savagery

_____ **10.** The external conflict is resolved when Antonio and Felix —

    F leave the ring together

    G decide not to fight each other

    H begin the fight

    J watch *The Champion* together

LITERARY FOCUS (20 points; 5 points each)

On the line provided, write the letter of the *best* answer to each of the following items.

_____ **11.** "Amigo Brothers" has all the following characteristics *except* —

    A a plot

    B characters

    C setting

    D rhyme

_____ **12.** This story is written in —

    F rhyme

    G poetry

    H prose

    J rhythm

_____ **13.** "Amigo Brothers" can be characterized as a(n) —

    A autobiography

    B biography

    C short story

    D novella

_____ **14.** The author likely selected this form of fiction because it allowed him to —

    F present a slice of life

    G discuss a limited topic and include many facts

    H write about a complex issue

    J tell the story of two real people

VOCABULARY DEVELOPMENT *(20 points; 4 points each)*

Think about the relationship between the first pair of words in each item. Then, choose the word for the second pair that *best* matches that relationship. Choose the word from the Vocabulary words listed below, and write it on the line provided.

dispelled   **pensively**   **barrage**

frenzied   **torrent**

15. *Accidentally* is to *carelessly* as *thoughtfully* is to _____.

16. *Shower* is to *burst* as *attack* is to _____.

17. *Dribble* is to *flood* as *trickle* is to _____.

18. *Enticed* is to *scattered* as *attracted* is to _____.

19. *Relaxed* is to *rested* as *crazed* is to _____.

CONSTRUCTED RESPONSE *(20 points)*

20. Identify the form of "Amigo Brothers," and explain how this form suits the author's purpose. On a separate piece of paper, write a paragraph that explains your answer. Support your ideas with details from the story.

Amigo Brothers   **123**

Right Hook—Left Hook: The Boxing Controversy Joan Burditt

COMPREHENSION *(100 points; 10 points each)*

On the line provided, write the letter of the *best* answer to each of the following items.

_____ **1.** The title "Right Hook—Left Hook" refers to —

 A getting "hooked" on a subject

 B injured boxers

 C the subject of boxing

 D why boxing is a great sport

_____ **2.** The writer opens with a story about a duck and pig cartoon to —

 F attract the reader's attention

 G suggest that boxing is only for children

 H imply that boxers are like pigs

 J make readers laugh

_____ **3.** How do many doctors feel about boxing?

 A They think that only professional boxers should be allowed to fight.

 B They support boxing as a healthy outlet for everyone.

 C They believe it is safe for adults, not children.

 D They believe it causes serious injuries.

_____ **4.** Who is Muhammad Ali?

 F A speaker for disabled people

 G A doctor who studied Parkinson's disease

 H A boxer who now has Parkinson's disease

 J A writer who interviewed people with Parkinson's disease

_____ **5.** Doctors have linked Muhammad Ali's diagnosis of Parkinson's disease to —

 A boxing success

 B boxing injuries

 C not enough vitamins

 D birth defects

_____ **6.** In 1984, the American Medical Association said that —

 F boxing is safe when done with protective gear

 G all boxing should be stopped

 H boxing outside the ring should be banned

 J boxing is a great way to make money

_____ **7.** What does the author mean by the phrase "verbally slugging it out"?

    A Boxers are cruel.

    B People are hitting each other.

    C People are arguing about boxing.

    D You can hurt people when you slug them.

_____ **8.** The author is comparing and contrasting —

    F famous boxers

    G doctors and boxers

    H different types of boxing moves

    J the disadvantages and advantages of boxing

_____ **9.** You can tell that the writer uses the block organizational pattern because —

    A one side is presented first, then the other side

    B the writer moves back and forth between the subjects

    C the writer knows a lot about the subject

    D the writer alternates sides

_____ **10.** The block pattern allows the writer to show —

    F point-by-point comparisons

    G similarities but not differences

    H all of one side at a time

    J differences but not similarities

Right Hook—Left Hook

SELECTION TEST *Student Edition page 499*

from Barrio Boy Ernesto Galarza

COMPREHENSION *(40 points; 4 points each)*

On the line provided, write the letter of the *best* answer to each of the following items.

_____ 1. Ernesto is nervous about starting school in America because —

    A he does not speak English

    B the school is in a bad neighborhood

    C he is not a good student

    D he wants to go back to Mexico

_____ 2. In what way is Ernesto like the other students in his class?

    F He is impressed with Miss Ryan's height.

    G He does not know English and needs private lessons.

    H He is afraid of the principal.

    J He is ashamed that he is a foreigner.

_____ 3. How is Ernesto's school in California different from his school in Mexico?

    A The teachers in California are tall and strict.

    B The school in California has a shingled roof and automatic doors.

    C The school in Mexico has a female principal.

    D The school in California does not have many foreign students.

_____ 4. How does Miss Ryan react when Ernesto tries to compare English and Spanish pronunciations?

    F She punishes Ernesto for speaking Spanish.

    G She listens and tries to pronounce the Spanish words.

    H She asks the class for the pronunciation of other words.

    J She does not let Ernesto change the subject from English.

_____ 5. One of the main reasons why students from all cultures feel safe being themselves at the school is that —

    A the teachers are very strict

    B the boys don't fight

    C the students learn that they can be Americans without giving up their traditions

    D criminals are punished harshly

Holt Assessment: Literature, Reading, and Vocabulary

_____ **6.** The insults that Galarza says the children learn from the elders probably refer to a person's —

    F income level

    G education

    H race or ethnic background

    J intelligence

_____ **7.** Which of the following statements is a *fact*?

    A "Then Miss Hopley did a formidable thing."

    B She had "thin lips that moved like steel springs."

    C "He was…faintly obnoxious."

    D One of "my pals…[was] Kazushi, whose parents spoke only Japanese."

_____ **8.** Miss Ryan had a "radiant, no-nonsense character." Why is this statement an *opinion*?

    F It is the author's personal belief.

    G It can be verified in a book or other reference text.

    H It can be proven true or false.

    J It is positive, not negative.

_____ **9.** Who is the "barrio boy" in the title?

    A Ernesto

    B All of Ernesto's friends

    C All Mexicans

    D All immigrants

_____ **10.** Miss Ryan can *best* be described as —

    F stern but effective

    G prejudiced and cunning

    H incompetent but determined

    J caring and competent

LITERARY FOCUS (20 points; 5 points each)

On the line provided, write the letter of the *best* answer to each of the following items.

_____ **11.** Which of the following is *not* true in this account from *Barrio Boy*?

    A The author made up a story that seems true.

    B The events in the story really did happen to the author.

    C Many people have experiences similar to the ones Ernesto describes.

    D By reading this story, Americans born here can learn how some immigrants feel.

Barrio Boy

_____ **12.** From the way the narrator tells this story, you can infer that Ernesto —

    F wishes that he and his family still lived in Mexico

    G had a difficult, unhappy childhood in America

    H learns to like school in America

    J learns to distrust people outside school

_____ **13.** This selection is told from the —

    A omniscient point of view

    B objective point of view

    C first-person point of view

    D third-person-limited point of view

_____ **14.** *Barrio Boy* is an autobiography because it is —

    F the story of a person's life written by someone else

    G a true story that uses many facts

    H objective rather than subjective

    J the story of a person's life written by that person

VOCABULARY DEVELOPMENT *(20 points; 4 points each)*

On the line provided, write the Vocabulary word that is *closest* in meaning to the word in italics. You will use one word twice.

        reassuring   **contraption**   **assured**   **formidable**

15. Ernesto's command of English was *impressive*. _____

16. Americans seem to have a *gadget* to help them with every chore. _____

17. Miss Ryan *guaranteed* Ernesto that he was an important member of the class. _____

18. A smiling face is *comforting* in a strange new situation. _____

19. We used a handy *device* to open the jar. _____

CONSTRUCTED RESPONSE *(20 points)*

20. Why do you think Ernesto Galarza chose to tell his life story as an autobiography rather than as a short story, novel, or essay? On a separate piece of paper, write a paragraph that explains your answer. Support your ideas with details from the story.

SELECTION TEST **Student Edition page 508**

Song of the Trees Mildred D. Taylor

COMPREHENSION *(40 points; 4 points each)*

On the line provided, write the letter of the *best* answer to each of the following items.

_____ **1.** "Song of the Trees" is set in the —

    A South during the 1830s

    B north woods around the turn of the century

    C South during the 1930s

    D north woods in the present

_____ **2.** Mr. Logan is away from the family because —

    F he has gone to take care of his parents

    G he is in prison

    H the only job he can find is away from home

    J a neighbor has threatened him, and he is in hiding

_____ **3.** Cassie loves the trees because —

    A she thinks she hears them sing their tales

    B they are worth money

    C they belong to her family

    D they are not important to her brothers

_____ **4.** Which of the following statements is the *best* generalization about Cassie's feelings toward the trees?

    F She wants them cut down.

    G She likes them because they produce gum.

    H She admires them because they are so tall.

    J She believes they are like human beings.

_____ **5.** Which of the following statements about the Logans is *not* true?

    A The children are willing to take risks when an important issue is at stake.

    B The children respect their parents.

    C The Logans are poor because they are not willing to work.

    D The land is important to the family's survival.

_____ **6.** What does Mr. Logan do *before* talking to Mr. Andersen?

    F He visits the sheriff.

    G He goes home to see his wife.

    H He sets sticks of dynamite throughout the forest.

    J He sells the trees to someone else at a higher price.

_____ **7.** Mr. Logan is *best* described as —

    A lucky

    B brave and honorable

    C wild and crazy

    D desperate

_____ **8.** Mr. Andersen and his men finally leave because they —

    F decide that Mr. Logan is right

    G think Mr. Logan might blow up the forest

    H are going to get the sheriff

    J do not really need Mr. Logan's trees

_____ **9.** What does Cassie learn about growing up after this incident?

    A Adults do not have to fight to settle their differences.

    B Adulthood is filled with easy decisions.

    C Money is more important than self-respect.

    D Self-respect is more important than money.

_____ **10.** One important theme in the story is —

    F money can help you get what you want

    G everyone has to deal with prejudice

    H children may be in danger if they do not obey their parents

    J personal honor is more important than wealth

LITERARY FOCUS *(20 points; 5 points each)*

On the line provided, write the letter of the *best* answer to each of the following items.

_____ **11.** How many main plotlines does "Song of the Trees" have?

    A One

    B Two

    C Three

    D Four

_____ **12.** "Song of the Trees" has —

    F one main conflict

    G two main conflicts

    H one main conflict and several minor conflicts

    J several main conflicts and several minor conflicts

_____ **13.** The main characters are —

   A Mama, David, Cassie

   B Mama, David

   C Big Ma, Stacey, Little Man, Christopher-John

   D Cassie and her father, David

_____ **14.** Because of its length and other characteristics, "Song of the Trees" can be classified as a(n) —

   F autobiography

   G novella

   H biography

   J short story

VOCABULARY DEVELOPMENT *(20 points; 4 points each)*

Match the Vocabulary word on the left with its definition on the right. Write the letter of the definition on the line provided.

_____ **15.** finicky

_____ **16.** dispute

_____ **17.** ambled

_____ **18.** delved

_____ **19.** curtly

a. walked slowly

b. rudely

c. fussy

d. searched

e. argument

CONSTRUCTED RESPONSE *(20 points)*

20. Explain the difference between a **novella** and a **short story**. Then, decide which type of prose *best* describes "Song of the Trees" and why. On a separate sheet of paper, write a paragraph that explains your answer. Support your ideas with details from the story.

SELECTION TEST *Student Edition page 527*

Fish Cheeks Amy Tan

COMPREHENSION *(40 points; 4 points each)*

On the line provided, write the letter of the *best* answer to each of the following items.

_____ 1. Why does Amy ignore Robert when he first comes to her house?

    A She is too shy to look at him.

    B She really doesn't like him.

    C She is ashamed of her family's poor home.

    D She has been taught to act that way.

_____ 2. For Christmas, Amy prays for Robert and —

    F a tweed miniskirt

    G a slim, American nose

    H an American-style turkey

    J a family like Robert's

_____ 3. The *best* example of the difference between Chinese and American culture is shown when —

    A Amy's family wrap their gifts in rumpled paper

    B Amy wears a miniskirt

    C the two families gather

    D Amy's father belches to show his appreciation of the food

_____ 4. Most descriptions of food in "Fish Cheeks" produce mental images that are —

    F delightful

    G ordinary

    H unusual

    J confusing

_____ 5. The phrase that does *not* describe the Chinese dinner in the essay is —

    A "white sponges" of tofu

    B "roasted turkey"

    C "slimy rock cod"

    D "soaking dried fungus"

_____ 6. The author's statement that her family arrives "in a clamor of doorbells and rumpled Christmas packages" appeals to the senses of —

    F sight and taste

    G taste and smell

    H sight and hearing

    J touch and smell

Holt Assessment: Literature, Reading, and Vocabulary

_____ **7.** Which of the following *best* describes a mental image of how Amy probably looked at the end of the dinner?

    A Pale, with downcast eyes

    B Flushed, with a big smile

    C Exhausted, with black circles under her eyes

    D Energetic, with a lively expression on her face

_____ **8.** Though the dinner seems painful to Amy at the time, how does she view it later?

    F She views it as even more unpleasant.

    G She has forgotten the incident.

    H She has blown it all out of proportion.

    J She is impressed that her mother prepared her favorite foods.

_____ **9.** The title "Fish Cheeks" indicates all of the following *except* —

    A the difference between Chinese and American customs

    B Amy's embarrassment over her family's customs

    C Amy's name for herself after the Christmas feast

    D Amy's favorite part of the fish

_____ **10.** Which of the following new titles *best* fits "Fish Cheeks"?

    F Culture Clash

    G My Favorite Memory

    H A Good Time

    J A Very Special Christmas

LITERARY FOCUS (20 points; 5 points each)

On the line provided, write the letter of the *best* answer to each of the following items.

_____ **11.** The author creates humor by —

    A making fun of Robert

    B making fun of herself and her parents

    C comparing and contrasting Chinese and American customs

    D explaining the true meaning of family holidays

_____ **12.** This selection is —

    F fiction

    G nonfiction

    H not true to life

    J a novella

Fish Cheeks

_____ **13.** All of the following characteristics fit "Fish Cheeks" *except* —

    A formal tone

    B brief

    C humorous

    D concerned with one subject

_____ **14.** "Fish Cheeks" is *best* classified as —

    F poetry

    G prose

    H a short story

    J an essay

VOCABULARY DEVELOPMENT *(20 points; 4 points each)*

On the line provided, write the Vocabulary word that is *closest* in meaning to the word or phrase in italics.

    appalling   **clamor**   **muster**

    wedges   **rumpled**

15. A *loud noise* fills the room as everyone greets one another. _____

16. She hopes that her outfit does not look *wrinkled*. _____

17. She tries to *call forth* the courage to face him at dinner. _____

18. She knows that it will taste good, but the food looks *horrifying*. _____

19. The *chunks* that are thick at one end and narrow at the other are cheese. _____

CONSTRUCTED RESPONSE *(20 points)*

20. "Fish Cheeks" is a humorous essay. First, describe the humorous elements you find in the essay. Then, tell how the author achieves her more serious purpose. On a separate sheet of paper, write a paragraph that explains your answer. Support your ideas with details from the story.

SELECTION TEST | *Student Edition page 533*

A Mason-Dixon Memory Clifton Davis

COMPREHENSION *(50 points; 10 points each)*
On the line provided, write the letter of the *best* answer to each of the following items.

_____ 1. In this selection, the difference between the North and the South is that —

    A in the North, there is no racial prejudice

    B in the North, African Americans are not allowed in some public places

    C in the South, whites and African Americans are never friends

    D in the South, African Americans are not allowed in some public places

_____ 2. When Clifton's chaperon tells Clifton that he cannot go to the park, she shows that she —

    F does not like Clifton

    G is upset with the park's discriminatory policy

    H is upset that she cannot go to visit the Lincoln Memorial

    J is nervous about the water balloons

_____ 3. Frank does not go to the amusement park because he —

    A thinks that standing by Clifton is more important than having fun

    B feels guilty about throwing water balloons

    C is afraid that he will lose Clifton's friendship

    D has also been excluded from the park

_____ 4. What evidence does the story offer that many people were outraged by what happened to Dondré?

    F He was asked to write an article about his experience.

    G He was given a scholarship to an expensive college.

    H Laws were passed to prevent the same thing from happening again.

    J He was invited to play golf at many other country clubs.

_____ 5. Clifton uses a flashback so the reader —

    A can be challenged with the two story lines

    B can predict the outcome of Dondré's speech

    C does not lose interest in the story

    D can understand that Clifton and Dondré are the same person

VOCABULARY DEVELOPMENT *(50 points; 10 points each)*

Match the definition on the right with the Vocabulary word on the left. Write the letter of the definition on the line provided.

_____ **6.** predominantly

_____ **7.** forfeit

_____ **8.** resolve

_____ **9.** ominous

_____ **10.** erupted

a. threatening

b. decide

c. burst forth

d. mainly

e. lose the right to compete

SELECTION TEST *Student Edition page 543*

INFORMATIONAL READING

Buddies Bare Their Affection for Ill Classmate *Austin American-Statesman*

COMPREHENSION *(100 points; 10 points each)*

On the line provided, write the letter of the *best* answer to each of the following items.

_____ **1.** The pun in the title refers to —

    A shaving your head

    B helping an ill classmate

    C supporting a classmate

    D having many close friends

_____ **2.** The boys are in the —

    F first grade

    G third grade

    H fifth grade

    J tenth grade

_____ **3.** Ian's health problem was located in his —

    A nose

    B head

    C skin

    D small intestine

_____ **4.** Mr. Alter was Ian's —

    F father

    G teacher

    H doctor

    J principal

_____ **5.** The boys shaved their heads to —

    A be different from boys in the other class

    B adopt the latest style

    C support Ian in his illness

    D meet a challenge from a rival group

_____ **6.** You can infer that the boys in Ian's class were —

    F sensitive and mature

    G callous and lacking judgment

    H easily led

    J very concerned about Ian's illness

_____ **7.** Why is Ian's father emotional?

    A He realizes that his son looks odd.

    B He very much appreciates the boys' decision to stand by Ian.

    C He is worried about paying all the medical bills.

    D He is concerned that his son's hair won't grow back.

_____ **8.** The essay's theme concerns —

    F the importance of being brave under pressure

    G a special teacher and school

    H a terrible illness that can afflict children

    J selfless acts of friendship

_____ **9.** Which is the *best* summary of this passage?

    A A class of fifth-grade boys shave their heads to support a classmate with cancer.

    B A class of tenth-grade boys shave their heads to protest school policy.

    C A boy with a serious illness asks his friends for support, and they agree to help him.

    D Undergoing chemotherapy is easier when your friends support you.

_____ **10.** You can infer that Ian feels —

    F resigned to death

    G hopeless

    H hopeful

    J numb

SELECTION TEST *Student Edition page 548*

**LITERARY RESPONSE
AND ANALYSIS**

I'm Nobody! Emily Dickinson

COMPREHENSION *(60 points; 6 points each)*
On the line provided, write the letter of the *best* answer to each of the following items.

_____ **1.** Who is the speaker in this poem?

    A Emily Dickinson

    B A frog

    C Somebody

    D Nobody

_____ **2.** From what point of view is the poem told?

    F Third-person-limited

    G First-person

    H Omniscient

    J Objective

_____ **3.** The speaker does *not* want to reveal —

    A her love of nature

    B where she goes

    C her love of frogs

    D her identity

_____ **4.** The speaker *most* values —

    F fame

    G money

    H privacy

    J frogs

_____ **5.** Why does the speaker think it would be "dreary to be Somebody"?

    A The public would never leave her alone.

    B She would be lonely.

    C She would be banished.

    D The public would not care about her.

_____ **6.** The figure of speech the poet uses to compare a famous person to a frog is —

    F simile

    G personification

    H metaphor

    J onomatopoeia

I'm Nobody!

139

_____ **7.** The figure of speech the author uses to compare the public to a bog is —

    A personification

    B onomatopoeia

    C metaphor

    D simile

_____ **8.** You can infer that the bog symbolizes —

    F her family

    G the public

    H dcath

    J a nearby lake filled with frogs

_____ **9.** The tone of this poem is *best* described as —

    A very serious

    B bitter

    C light

    D anxious

_____ **10.** If offered a spot on a talk show, the speaker of this poem would *most likely* —

    F appear on the show, but only with family close by

    G think about it for a while and then decline

    H accept immediately

    J decline quickly

LITERARY FOCUS *(20 points; 5 points each)*

On the line provided, write the letter of the *best* answer to each of the following items.

_____ **11.** You can classify "I'm Nobody!" as a poem because it —

    A has a regular rhyme scheme

    B is nonfiction

    C is short

    D uses compressed language

_____ **12.** This poem includes all of the following poetic elements *except* —

    F a strong rhythm and regular rhyme pattern

    G lines

    H similes

    J metaphors

_____ **13.** How many stanzas does "I'm Nobody!" have?

    A None

    B One

    C Two

    D Three

_____ **14.** How would this poem change if rewritten as a short story?

    F It would be nonfiction.

    G It would no longer have characters.

    H It would be longer.

    J It would be harder to read.

CONSTRUCTED RESPONSE *(20 points)*

15. The speaker of the poem feels fame is unimportant. Do you agree with the speaker? Write a paragraph that supports your opinion. In your argument, include both the advantages and disadvantages of being nobody. Then, tell how the short form of the poem fits the poet's purpose. On a separate piece of paper, write a paragraph that explains your answer. Support your ideas with details from the poem.

I'm Nobody!

SELECTION TEST *Student Edition page 551*

I Like to See It Lap the Miles Emily Dickinson

COMPREHENSION *(60 points; 6 points each)*

On the line provided, write the letter of the *best* answer to each of the following items.

_____ 1. When the speaker says, "I like to see it lap the Miles—" (line 1), she is referring to the train's —

    A size

    B noise

    C speed

    D steam

_____ 2. What action is the train performing in lines 4–5?

    F Picking up passengers on mountains

    G Helping to level mountains

    H Driving around mountains

    J Going through a tunnel in the mountains

_____ 3. The use of the word *supercilious* in line 6 makes the train seem like a —

    A powerful machine

    B modern car

    C disobedient horse

    D conceited person

_____ 4. Lines 8–10 appeal to the reader's sense of —

    F sight

    G hearing

    H taste

    J smell

_____ 5. Lines 11–12, "Complaining all the while / In horrid—hooting stanza—," describe the —

    A train's passengers

    B sounds the train makes

    C speaker in the poem

    D people watching the train

_____ **6.** In line 14, the train is compared to Boanerges in order to —

    F reveal that a storm has begun

    G describe how loud the train is

    H illustrate that the train is old

    J show that the train is a familiar sight

_____ **7.** What is the "stable door" (line 17) that the train stops at?

    A A barn door

    B A gate to a field

    C A train station

    D A bridge

_____ **8.** The train in the poem performs all of the following actions *except* —

    F going downhill

    G carrying coal

    H traveling through valleys

    J driving by shanties

_____ **9.** The train in the poem is *best* described as —

    A fast

    B cautious

    C tired

    D frightening

_____ **10.** You can infer that the speaker in the poem —

    F has never seen a real train

    G is an athletic person

    H lives in the city

    J is familiar with the behavior of horses

LITERARY FOCUS (20 points; 5 points each)

On the line provided, write the letter of the *best* answer to each of the following items.

_____ **11.** In line 3, "And stop to feed itself at Tanks—," the speaker uses a metaphor to describe —

    A a horse's appetite

    B a train conductor

    C how the train gets refueled

    D restaurants in nearby towns

I Like to See It Lap the Miles

_____ **12.** The poem uses an extended metaphor for all of the following purposes *except* to —

    F sustain a comparison throughout the whole poem

    G paint a vivid picture of the train and bring it to life

    H show similarities between trains and horses

    J reveal the speaker's fondness for her horses

_____ **13.** The rhythm of the poem can *best* be described as —

    A flowing

    B singsong

    C irregular

    D even

_____ **14.** What is the poet's tone in the poem?

    F Admiring

    G Critical

    H Regretful

    J Unconvinced

CONSTRUCTED RESPONSE *(20 points)*

15. Dickinson describes several features of the train in her poem, but she seems especially interested in developing the train's personality. How would you describe the train's personality in your own words? On a separate sheet of paper, write a paragraph that explains your answer. Support your ideas with details from the poem.

SELECTION TEST *Student Edition page 555*

I Am of the Earth Anna Lee Walters
Early Song Gogisgi/Carroll Arnett

COMPREHENSION *(60 points; 6 points each)*
On the line provided, write the letter of the *best* answer to each of the following items.

_____ 1. In "I Am of the Earth," the speaker describes the earth's —

  A relationship to other planets

  B history

  C human characteristics

  D physical characteristics

_____ 2. The speaker in "I Am of the Earth" is —

  F the earth

  G a human being

  H the sun

  J the moon

_____ 3. In "I Am of the Earth," line 10 refers to the —

  A earth's anger with the speaker

  B speaker's abuse of the earth

  C development of the earth

  D natural process of getting older

_____ 4. "I Am of the Earth" is *mainly* concerned with —

  F the speaker's relationship to the earth

  G how all living things relate to each other

  H how to keep the earth beautiful

  J how the earth was created

_____ 5. The image used in "Early Song" to describe the speaker's relationship to the earth is —

  A a circle

  B a time line

  C the four seasons

  D a mother and her child

_____ **6.** The prayers in "Early Song" are prayers of —

    F forgiveness

    G hope

    H thanks

    J despair

_____ **7.** How many prayers does the speaker of "Early Song" offer?

    A One

    B Two

    C Three

    D Four

_____ **8.** The speaker offers thanks for all of the following *except* —

    F her brothers and sisters

    G her great success as a poet

    H a clear fine day

    J good brown earth

_____ **9.** Why do you think these poems are paired?

    A They were written by the same author.

    B They both describe ways to help the earth.

    C They share similar themes and topics.

    D They have the same number of stanzas.

_____ **10.** Unlike "I Am of the Earth," "Early Song" describes —

    F the earth as female

    G the earth as male

    H only what the earth gives humans

    J what humans give back to the earth

LITERARY FOCUS *(20 points; 5 points each)*

On the line provided, write the letter of the *best* answer to each of the following items.

_____ **11.** These two poems use all of the following poetic techniques *except* —

    A rhyme

    B personification

    C figures of speech

    D rhythm

_____ **12.** Which of the following is an example of personification?

    F   The sun rises every day.

    G   The earth takes care of her children.

    H   The earth is made of deep, brown soil.

    J   All people share the benefits of the earth.

_____ **13.** In "I Am of the Earth," the poet personifies the earth by saying that —

    A   she longs to leave the earth

    B   the earth is her mother

    C   she comes from the brown earth

    D   she is one with the earth

_____ **14.** Why are these two works classified as poems?

    F   They both describe nature.

    G   They are both real-life stories.

    H   They use compressed language to describe an idea.

    J   They concern actual people.

CONSTRUCTED RESPONSE (20 points)

15. What feelings about life are described in these two poems? On a separate sheet of paper, write a paragraph that explains your answer. Support your ideas with details from the poems.

I Am of the Earth / Early Song

Madam and the Rent Man Langston Hughes

COMPREHENSION *(60 points; 6 points each)*

On the line provided, write the letter of the *best* answer to each of the following items.

_____ **1.** "Madam" is —

  A the woman who owns the apartment

  B the woman who lives in the apartment

  C a woman visiting the apartment

  D the speaker's grandmother

_____ **2.** All of the following things are wrong with the apartment *except* the —

  F front door won't lock

  G sink is broken

  H water doesn't work

  J back window is cracked

_____ **3.** Why won't the speaker pay her rent?

  A The rent man is rude to her.

  B She does not have the money.

  C She hates the landlord.

  D The landlord has not made the repairs he promised.

_____ **4.** The rent man reacts to the woman's speech by —

  F promising to help her

  G making some repairs right then

  H threatening her

  J telling her that there is nothing he can do

_____ **5.** At the end of the poem, what do the two characters finally agree on?

  A They are both displeased.

  B The woman is going to move.

  C The woman is going to pay part of her rent.

  D The landlord will reduce the rent.

_____ **6.** The poet uses the word *ain't* to show —

  F how angry the woman is at the end

  G how pleased the woman is at the end

  H how people really speak

  J his own anger at the rent collector's behavior

_____ **7.** You can infer that the woman is living —

    A in a middle-class apartment

    B in a slum

    C with her children

    D in a luxury building

_____ **8.** The woman in the poem shows a sense of humor by —

    F commenting on the rent man's looks

    G twisting the rent man's final comment

    H telling the rent man how well he does his job

    J talking about her children

_____ **9.** What contradiction does the poem contain?

    A The rent agent sounds friendly at first, but he is actually very angry.

    B The bathroom is broken but the attic leaks.

    C The woman was willing to talk to the rent man, but then she changed her mind.

    D The rent agent lives in the building himself.

_____ **10.** The dialogue imitates real conversation by —

    F having the woman speak in rhymes

    G using perfect grammar for both speakers

    H using everyday expressions such as "pass the buck"

    J having the woman twist the rent man's words

LITERARY FOCUS *(20 points; 5 points each)*

On the line provided, write the letter of the *best* answer to each of the following items.

_____ **11.** Which word *best* shows the poem's casual tone?

    A Squeaks

    B Madam

    C Howdy-do

    D Listen

_____ **12.** The poem's overall tone is *best* described as —

    F lighthearted

    G firm

    H sad

    J apologetic

Madam and the Rent Man

_____ **13.** The poem uses all of the following poetic techniques *except* —

    A rhythm

    B personification

    C rhyme

    D meter

_____ **14.** Hughes probably wrote this poem to —

    F entertain his readers

    G persuade his readers to learn to make home repairs

    H convince people to pay their rent on time

    J describe a common and upsetting situation

CONSTRUCTED RESPONSE *(20 points)*

15. Based on "Madam and the Rent Man," how is poetry different from prose? On a separate sheet of paper, write a paragraph that explains your answer. Support your ideas with details from the poem.

Holt Assessment: Literature, Reading, and Vocabulary

SELECTION TEST **Student Edition page 563**

Harlem Night Song *and* Winter Moon   Langston Hughes

COMPREHENSION *(60 points; 6 points each)*

On the line provided, write the letter of the *best* answer to each of the following items.

_____ **1.** In "Harlem Night Song" the speaker is *most likely* addressing —

    A an old friend

    B a person he or she is in love with

    C his or her neighbors

    D the moon

_____ **2.** Based on details in "Harlem Night Song," you can infer that the speaker lives —

    F near the ocean

    G in a city

    H on a farm

    J in the mountains

_____ **3.** In "Harlem Night Song" the speaker wants to —

    A climb over rooftops

    B dance in the street

    C sing and wander around

    D rest in a quiet place

_____ **4.** In lines 9–10 of "Harlem Night Song," the speaker compares stars to —

    F music

    G sunlight

    H lemon candy

    J dewdrops

_____ **5.** In describing the moon, the sky, and the stars in "Harlem Night Song," the speaker emphasizes their —

    A width

    B delicateness

    C color

    D permanence

_____ **6.** Which of the following statements *best* matches the description of the night in "Harlem Night Song"?

   F   On a clear night the moon and stars are visible in the sky.

   G   It is hot outside, and night has not completely fallen.

   H   The stars look like they are shooting through the night sky.

   J   The bright moon partially hides the stars in the sky.

_____ **7.** In "Harlem Night Song," where is the band playing?

   A   Nearby

   B   Inside the speaker's house

   C   A long walk away

   D   On a rooftop

_____ **8.** In "Winter Moon" the poet *most likely* describes the moon as "ghostly white" to show that it is —

   F   imaginary

   G   not alive

   H   pale and shadowy

   J   very thin

_____ **9.** Which of the following statements *best* describes the moon in "Winter Moon"?

   A   There is a full moon shining in the sky.

   B   The moon is covered by clouds.

   C   Tall buildings block part of the moon.

   D   The moon is out, but only a small crescent is visible.

_____ **10.** Viewing the moon, the speaker in "Winter Moon" can *best* be described as filled with —

   F   wonder

   G   confusion

   H   frustration

   J   regret

LITERARY FOCUS (20 points; 5 points each)

On the line provided, write the letter of the *best* answer to each of the following items.

_____ **11.** In "Harlem Night Song" the image of the band appeals to the reader's sense of —

   A   hearing

   B   sight

   C   touch

   D   smell

_____ **12.** Which element in "Harlem Night Song" makes the poem *most* similar to a song?

    F The use of short lines

    G The speaker's addressing an audience

    H The reference to a band playing

    J The use of repetition

_____ **13.** Which of the following statements about "Winter Moon" is *false*?

    A It contains only one stanza.

    B All of the lines rhyme.

    C The poet uses repetition in the poem.

    D A simile appears in the poem.

_____ **14.** The title of *each* poem provides information about its —

    F main character

    G setting

    H theme

    J purpose

CONSTRUCTED RESPONSE *(20 points)*

15. In "Harlem Night Song" and "Winter Moon," how does Langston Hughes help the reader see and hear what he is describing? On a separate sheet of paper, write a paragraph that explains your answer. Support your ideas with details from both poems.

SELECTION TEST *Student Edition page 568*

I Ask My Mother to Sing Li-Young Lee

COMPREHENSION *(60 points; 6 points each)*
On the line provided, write the letter of the *best* answer to each of the following items.

_____ **1.** In the first line of the poem, to whom does the word *she* refer?

    A The grandmother's mother

    B The speaker's mother

    C The speaker's sister

    D The speaker's daughter

_____ **2.** According to the speaker, what would his father do if he were still alive?

    F Sing with the women

    G Sail on a boat

    H Cry at the end of the song

    J Play his accordion

_____ **3.** The poem suggests that members of the speaker's family —

    A spent time at the Summer Palace

    B never visited the Summer Palace

    C disliked the Summer Palace

    D built the Summer Palace

_____ **4.** You can infer that the women sing about —

    F people crying

    G Peking

    H their children

    J their vacations

_____ **5.** Why are "the picnickers / running away in the grass" (lines 7–8)?

    A The Stone Boat is sinking.

    B It begins to rain.

    C They are going to hear the song.

    D They are not allowed to be at the lake.

_____ **6.** Lines 10–12 describe —

    F details from the women's song

    G a scene from the speaker's childhood

    H an event that the speaker is currently observing

    J an imaginary setting

_____ **7.** When the speaker describes the waterlilies as "spilling water into water" (line 11), he means that —

    A they pour rainwater into the lake

    B it is raining continuously

    C water drips from one flower to the next

    D the lake overflows

_____ **8.** What happens at the end of the poem?

    F Because they are crying, the women stop singing.

    G When both women start crying, one of them stops singing.

    H Both women continue to sing, even though they are crying.

    J The women stop crying and continue their song.

_____ **9.** The title of the poem helps to explain —

    A the character of the mother

    B where the speaker is

    C the subject of the song

    D the action described in line 1

_____ **10.** "I Ask My Mother to Sing" is *mostly* about —

    F the history of China

    G memories of the past

    H the loss of the speaker's father

    J the speaker's view of nature

LITERARY FOCUS *(20 points; 5 points each)*

On the line provided, write the letter of the *best* answer to each of the following items.

_____ **11.** Line 2, "Mother and daughter sing like young girls," contains —

    A a metaphor

    B personification

    C a simile

    D a symbol

_____ **12.** The images in lines 3–4 appeal to the senses of —

    F sight and smell

    G touch and sight

    H hearing and sight

    J hearing and taste

I Ask My Mother to Sing

_____ **13.** This poem is an example of a lyric poem because it —

    A discusses music

    B is short

    C tells a story

    D focuses on expressing emotions

_____ **14.** What makes this poem a sonnet?

    F It contains fourteen lines, divided into three quatrains and a couplet.

    G The sentence structure and word choice are old-fashioned.

    H The speaker discusses various aspects of one subject.

    J The poet writes about complex thoughts and ideas.

CONSTRUCTED RESPONSE *(20 points)*

15. Think about how the speaker and the women feel about the song. Do they respond differently to it? Why do you think they have these reactions? On a separate sheet of paper, write a paragraph that explains your answer. Support your ideas with details from the poem.

Holt Assessment: Literature, Reading, and Vocabulary

SELECTION TEST *Student Edition page 572*

Ode to Family Photographs Gary Soto

COMPREHENSION *(60 points; 6 points each)*

On the line provided, write the letter of the *best* answer to each of the following items.

_____ 1. The speaker describes photographs of all of the following subjects *except* —

    A a trash can

    B a bird

    C the front bumper of a car

    D his mother

_____ 2. What do all of the photographs have in common?

    F The speaker is visible in each picture.

    G The family members seem shy in the pictures.

    H The pictures are action shots.

    J The pictures contain images from everyday life.

_____ 3. You can conclude that the mother is an unskilled photographer based on all of the following photographs *except* —

    A snapshots of the speaker's feet

    B a picture of Pedro standing on one leg

    C a picture in which the speaker's head is cut off

    D a snapshot of the speaker's father with his eyes half-closed

_____ 4. Some of the photographs are out of focus because —

    F they were taken a long time ago

    G the mother has poor vision

    H the mother sneezed while taking the pictures

    J the mother used an inexpensive camera

_____ 5. What can you infer about the photographs described in lines 1–2?

    A Some of the photographs were shot in a rural setting.

    B Most of the photographs were taken at night.

    C All of the photographs were taken on the same day.

    D A few of the photographs were taken recently.

_____ **6.** The poet *most likely* paired the pictures of the bird and Pedro in one stanza (lines 11–13) because both the bird and Pedro are —

    F standing on one leg

    G shown with food

    H next to the car

    J resting on a rock

_____ **7.** Why does the speaker know that his family had fun when his mother took pictures?

    A His parents told him that everyone enjoyed those times.

    B His mother was known for her great sense of humor.

    C Looking at the pictures makes him smile now.

    D His family is laughing in the photographs.

_____ **8.** In the last stanza, the poet *most likely* uses the image of the speaker with candy in his mouth to show that the —

    F speaker's mother loves him

    G speaker is hungry

    H speaker is a young boy

    J speaker is happy

_____ **9.** The poem is *mostly* in the form of a(n) —

    A story

    B list

    C argument

    D comparison

_____ **10.** You can infer that the speaker in the poem is talking to —

    F a person to whom he is showing each photograph

    G himself

    H his brother

    J his sister

LITERARY FOCUS *(20 points; 5 points each)*

On the line provided, write the letter of the *best* answer to each of the following items.

_____ **11.** This poem is an ode because it —

    A is written in praise of family photographs and what they stand for

    B pays tribute to famous people and their actions

    C describes personal experiences and feelings

    D tells the life story of the speaker

_____ **12.** The style of the poem is —

    F conversational

    G elegant

    H wordy

    J technical

_____ **13.** The tone of the poem is *best* described as —

    A respectful

    B impatient

    C affectionate

    D mocking

_____ **14.** Line 16, *"The angles dizzy as a spin on a merry-go-round,"* contains an example of —

    F a metaphor

    G repetition

    H a simile

    J rhyme

CONSTRUCTED RESPONSE *(20 points)*

15. What generalizations can you make about Gary Soto's family, based on the poet's descriptions and on what you "see" in the photographs he describes? What comment do you think Soto is making about the significance of his family photographs? On a separate sheet of paper, write a paragraph that explains your answer. Support your ideas with details from the poem.

SELECTION TEST *Student Edition page 578, 582*

**LITERARY RESPONSE
AND ANALYSIS**

Father William Lewis Carroll
Sarah Cynthia Sylvia Stout Would Not Take
the Garbage Out Shel Silverstein

COMPREHENSION *(60 points; 6 points each)*

On the line provided, write the letter of the *best* answer to each of the following items.

_____ **1.** In Carroll's poem, why is Father William unconcerned about standing on his head all the time?

    A He can balance well, so he will not fall over.

    B Since the top of his head is flat, he won't dent it.

    C He can't hurt his brain, since he doesn't think he has one.

    D Because he has a strong back, he won't injure himself.

_____ **2.** Father William explains that he can do a back somersault because he —

    F learned how to do somersaults when he was a young boy

    G makes money by teaching people how to do somersaults

    H has applied a special ointment to his limbs to keep them flexible

    J takes medicine to prevent him from getting dizzy

_____ **3.** Father William tells his son that he strengthened his jaw muscles by —

    A chewing goose bones and beaks

    B balancing an eel on his chin

    C eating the fatty part of meat

    D arguing law cases with his wife

_____ **4.** The son is shocked by Father William's behavior because the youth —

    F is embarrassed by his father's actions

    G thinks his father is too old to perform such actions

    H is incapable of performing these actions himself

    J had assumed that such actions were impossible for any person to perform

_____ **5.** Father William *most likely* refuses to answer more questions at the end of the poem because he —

    A thinks the questions are insulting

    B believes his son is invading his privacy

    C is bored by the questions

    D is late for an appointment

Holt Assessment: Literature, Reading, and Vocabulary

_____ **6.** In the beginning of Silverstein's poem, although Sarah wouldn't take the garbage out, she would —

    F help her father in the yard

    G wash dishes and prepare food

    H clean her room and make her bed

    J go to the grocery store

_____ **7.** Toward the end of the poem, Sarah *most likely* agreed to take out the garbage because —

    A she had to sleep on top of it

    B the garbage drove her friends away

    C the garbage began to smell

    D piles of garbage blocked the door of the house

_____ **8.** Why was it too late for Sarah to take out the garbage?

    F No one cared about the garbage anymore.

    G Sarah's father did not allow her to clean up the garbage.

    H The garbage had spread across the United States.

    J Other people had already thrown out the garbage.

_____ **9.** When the speaker says that Sarah met "an awful fate" (line 43), you can infer that she *most likely* —

    A was forced out of the house by her father

    B went to jail for not taking out the garbage

    C was kidnapped by her neighbors

    D died in the piles of garbage

_____ **10.** The speaker is telling Sarah's story to —

    F children

    G Sarah's mother

    H the public

    J the authorities

LITERARY FOCUS *(20 points; 5 points each)*

On the line provided, write the letter of the *best* answer to each of the following items.

_____ **11.** Carroll's poem is in the form of a —

    A dialogue

    B story

    C summary

    D speech

_____ **12.** Carroll's poem contains all of the following literary elements *except* —

    F rhyme

    G repetition

    H rhythm

    J personification

_____ **13.** You can tell that Silverstein uses meter when he writes, "The garbage rolled on down the hall, / It raised the roof, it broke the wall . . ." (lines 21–22), because —

    A the two lines contain almost the same number of words

    B the stressed and unstressed syllables are arranged in a regular pattern

    C he uses mostly short words in the lines

    D the lines are easy to read aloud

_____ **14.** In Silverstein's poem, "Prune pits, peach pits, orange peel" (line 15) contains —

    F onomatopoeia

    G alliteration

    H idioms

    J figurative language

CONSTRUCTED RESPONSE *(20 points)*

15. Both Lewis Carroll and Shel Silverstein rely on exaggeration in their poems. How does each poet use exaggeration to make a point? On a separate sheet of paper, write a paragraph that explains your answer. Support your ideas with details from the poems.

Holt Assessment: Literature, Reading, and Vocabulary

The Runaway Robert Frost

COMPREHENSION *(60 points; 6 points each)*

On the line provided, write the letter of the *best* answer to each of the following items.

_____ **1.** What feelings does the colt arouse in the speaker?

    A Protective and nourishing

    B Angry and bitter

    C Fearful and intimidating

    D Joyful and pleasant

_____ **2.** All of the following words describe the colt *except* —

    F little

    G frightened

    H winter-broken

    J quick-footed

_____ **3.** Why does the speaker describe the sound of the colt's fleeing as "miniature thunder"?

    A It is raining out.

    B The colt is afraid of lightning.

    C The colt's hooves sound like thunder.

    D The snow muffles the noise of the colt's fleeing.

_____ **4.** When the speaker says that the colt isn't "winter-broken," he means that —

    F no one has put a saddle on the colt this winter

    G the colt can still run quickly

    H the colt has not gotten used to winter yet

    J the colt was born in the spring

_____ **5.** Why does the colt look like "a shadow against the curtain of falling flakes"?

    A The colt is moving so quickly you can barely see him.

    B The snow makes it impossible to see the colt.

    C The colt is playing a game with the speaker.

    D The colt looks dim and gray against a white background.

_____ **6.** Why does the colt need to bolt?

    F He wants to find other horses.

    G He is afraid of the men.

    H He wants to play.

    J He is afraid of the snow.

_____ **7.** How does the speaker seem to feel about the colt's owners?

    A Disapproving

    B Disappointed

    C Friendly and neighborly

    D Angry

_____ **8.** What words sum up the lesson the colt's mother might have taught him?

    F Keep out of the field in this kind of weather.

    G The snow won't hurt you; you'll get used to it.

    H The thunder makes a loud noise, but it is nothing to be frightened of.

    J The men are there to protect you; trust them.

_____ **9.** How does the poet feel the colt would respond to his mother's words?

    A He would calm down suddenly.

    B He would think she was angry at him for not knowing better.

    C He wouldn't believe her.

    D He would run away from her.

_____ **10.** If you think of the colt as representing all runaways, what might the poet be telling us through this poem?

    F Young people need to learn about life for themselves.

    G People are like horses.

    H Adults always know better.

    J Don't be scared of the weather.

LITERARY FOCUS _(20 points; 5 points each)_

_____ **11.** You can tell that "The Runaway" is a poem, not prose, because it —

    A contains figurative language

    B is short

    C is written in lines, not sentences

    D is written by Robert Frost

_____ **12.** All of the following items contain words that rhyme _except_ —

    F fall/wall

    G eyes/flies

    H straight/late

    J flakes/play

Holt Assessment: Literature, Reading, and Vocabulary

_____ **13.** The rhyme scheme of a poem —

    A   is its pattern of rhyme

    B   is the way words rhyme within a line

    C   is always *abab*

    D   changes from line to line

_____ **14.** Which statement is *true* about the rhyme scheme of "The Runaway"?

    F   It does not follow a regular pattern.

    G   Only the first four lines end in rhymes.

    H   It is *abacbc*.

    J   It is too complicated to describe with letters.

CONSTRUCTED RESPONSE *(20 points)*

15. Like prose, "The Runaway" makes use of a first-person narrator. Describe the role of the first-person narrator in this poem. Explain what you learn from him. On a separate piece of paper, write a paragraph that explains your answer. Support your ideas with details from the poem.

SELECTION TEST   *Student Edition page 589*

The Pasture *and* A Minor Bird   Robert Frost

COMPREHENSION   (60 points; 6 points each)

On the line provided, write the letter of the *best* answer to each of the following items.

_____ **1.** In the first stanza of "The Pasture," the speaker says he is going out to —

    A plant seeds

    B clean out the leaves from the spring

    C fetch a calf

    D take a long swim

_____ **2.** In the last line of the first stanza in "The Pasture," the speaker offers a(n) —

    F lesson

    G apology

    H compliment

    J invitation

_____ **3.** The little calf in "The Pasture" *most likely* totters, or is unsteady, because —

    A the speaker frightens it

    B it is cold

    C it wants to stand near its mother

    D its legs are weak

_____ **4.** You can infer that events in "The Pasture" take place in —

    F the city

    G the country

    H an earlier century

    J the speaker's youth

_____ **5.** Which of the following statements expresses a possible theme of "The Pasture"?

    A A helping hand makes work easier.

    B Farm life is sometimes lonely.

    C Many small, everyday aspects of life are worth sharing.

    D Few people fully appreciate their friends.

Holt Assessment: Literature, Reading, and Vocabulary

_____ **6.** In "A Minor Bird," what is the main reason that the speaker wishes the bird would fly away?

    F The bird is asking to be fed.

    G The bird built a nest near the speaker's house.

    H The speaker does not like the sound of the bird's song.

    J The bird disrupts the speaker's sleep.

_____ **7.** What does the speaker in "A Minor Bird" do in an attempt to make the bird leave?

    A Claps his hands

    B Shouts

    C Waves the bird away

    D Closes the door

_____ **8.** What does the speaker admit in "A Minor Bird"?

    F His negative reaction to the bird is his own fault.

    G He does not know how to make the bird leave.

    H He does not appreciate music.

    J He often criticizes others.

_____ **9.** By the end of the poem, the speaker in "A Minor Bird" realizes that —

    A he is not a patient person

    B all creatures should be allowed to sing their songs

    C the bird has become good company

    D the quiet is peaceful

_____ **10.** Which of the following words *best* characterizes the speaker?

    F stubborn

    G cruel

    H thoughtful

    J lonely

LITERARY FOCUS *(20 points; 5 points each)*

On the line provided, write the letter of the *best* answer to each of the following items.

_____ **11.** All of the following statements about stanzas are true *except* —

    A they are made up of a group of lines in a poem

    B they express a unit of thought

    C to form a stanza, the lines of a poem must rhyme

    D they can be any length

The Pasture / A Minor Bird

_____ **12.** In "The Pasture," Frost expresses his point through the use of —

    F similes and rhythm

    G visual imagery and repetition

    H personification and rhyme

    J tone and figures of speech

_____ **13.** What is the *most* significant aspect of the title "A Minor Bird"?

    A The title tells you that the poem is about a bird.

    B The title refers to something from nature.

    C Frost plays with two meanings of the word *minor* in the title.

    D Like the poem, the title is short and uses simple language.

_____ **14.** Frost uses each couplet in "A Minor Bird" to —

    F express a complete thought

    G list a series of related things

    H show how the speaker has changed

    J praise the bird

CONSTRUCTED RESPONSE *(20 points)*

15. Both "The Pasture" and "A Minor Bird" describe interactions between people and nature. What similarities and differences do you see in the subject matter of the two poems and in the speakers' views of nature? On a separate sheet of paper, write a paragraph that explains your answer. Support your ideas with details from the poems.

Holt Assessment: Literature, Reading, and Vocabulary

SELECTION TEST *Student Edition page 593*

**LITERARY RESPONSE
AND ANALYSIS**

Names of Horses Donald Hall

COMPREHENSION *(60 points; 6 points each)*
On the line provided, write the letter of the *best* answer to each of the following items.

_____ **1.** At the start of the poem, the speaker addresses his or her thoughts to —

 A a farmer

 B a horse

 C himself

 D an unknown audience

_____ **2.** What type of labor did the horse perform during the winter?

 F Plowing the fields

 G Bringing equipment to the house

 H Carrying wood

 J Transporting grain into town

_____ **3.** On summer afternoons the horse would —

 A move loads of hay

 B fertilize the fields

 C travel to church

 D graze in the meadow

_____ **4.** All of the following adjectives describe the horse as it is portrayed in the first four stanzas *except* —

 F strong

 G hardworking

 H reliable

 J excitable

_____ **5.** The horse was *most likely* "shuddering in" its "skin" (line 20) because it —

 A sensed that its owner was digging a grave

 B was restless and needed exercise

 C had reached old age

 D felt nervous near the water

_____ **6.** Which of the following actions *best* indicates that the man cared deeply about the horse?

    F He had the horse carry a small load on Sundays.

    G He placed padding on the horse's collar.

    H He fed the horse and harnessed him every morning.

    J He placed a goldenrod plant on the horse's grave.

_____ **7.** By the end of the poem, it is clear that the speaker's focus is on —

    A farmwork

    B a group of horses

    C the farmer

    D lost youth

_____ **8.** The poem is set in a time —

    F when farmers did not understand the benefits of technology

    G before modern machinery and cars were available to farmers

    H when a farmer's life was hard because the land did not produce many crops

    J before farmers were knowledgeable about horses

_____ **9.** The speaker conveys the passage of time by referring to all of the following items *except* —

    A a number of years

    B the names of months

    C the time of day

    D dates

_____ **10.** The speaker shows that —

    F horses made essential contributions to life on a farm

    G the loss of an animal does not compare with the loss of a person

    H all things are forgotten with time

    J people have always struggled against nature

LITERARY FOCUS *(20 points; 5 points each)*

On the line provided, write the letter of the *best* answer to each of the following items.

_____ **11.** "Names of Horses" is an example of free verse because it —

    A tells a story

    B uses figurative language

    C does not rely on a regular rhyme scheme or meter

    D is written in couplets

_____ **12.** Which of the following phrases contains an example of alliteration?

    F "you mowed the grass"

    G "uphill to the chaffy barn"

    H "hanging wide from the hayrack"

    J "the same acres"

_____ **13.** The image of the horse "smoothing the wood as the sea smooths glass" (line 16) suggests an action that is —

    A repeated

    B rebellious

    C unusual

    D brief

_____ **14.** In line 8, "the sun walked high in the morning" is an example of —

    F personification

    G exaggeration

    H a simile

    J onomatopoeia

CONSTRUCTED RESPONSE *(20 points)*

15. Explain why "Names of Horses" is considered an elegy. What is the speaker's attitude toward the horses he or she describes? On a separate sheet of paper, write a paragraph that explains your answer. Support your ideas with details from the poem.

**LITERARY RESPONSE
AND ANALYSIS**

maggie and milly and molly and may E. E. Cummings

COMPREHENSION *(60 points; 6 points each)*

On the line provided, write the letter of the *best* answer to each of the following items.

_____ 1. The setting of "maggie and milly and molly and may" is a —

    A swamp

    B forest

    C beach

    D lake

_____ 2. Cummings probably selected the words *maggie, milly, molly,* and *may* —

    F to honor close friends

    G for their sound

    H for their meaning

    J because they represent the sea

_____ 3. Which statement *best* describes the four girls in relation to one another?

    A They do not like each other.

    B They are exactly alike.

    C They are completely different.

    D They have similar experiences.

_____ 4. What do maggie, milly, molly, and may find at the sea?

    F Each girl finds something she has always wanted.

    G Each girl discovers something that scares her.

    H Each girl finds something to share with the others.

    J Each girl learns something about herself.

_____ 5. Maggie discovers a —

    A sea creature that roars

    B shell that sings

    C discarded plastic slipper

    D pretty pile of pebbles

Holt Assessment: Literature, Reading, and Vocabulary

_____ **6.** Milly finds a —

    F rubber inner tube

    G smelly crab

    H stranded star

    J delicious lobster

_____ **7.** Which of the following is an example of exact rhymes?

    A May/day

    B Milly/molly

    C Thing/bubbles

    D Stranded/languid

_____ **8.** Which of the following is an example of slant rhymes?

    F May/day

    G Sang/and

    H Thing/bubbles

    J Stone/alone

_____ **9.** Which of the following words *best* describes a reaction the poem might evoke?

    A Sadness

    B Fear

    C Curiosity

    D Despair

_____ **10.** In this poem, Cummings suggests that going to the sea —

    F may teach us something

    G is always fun

    H is usually scary

    J gives us time to be alone

LITERARY FOCUS *(20 points; 5 points each)*

On the line provided, write the letter of the *best* answer to each of the following items.

_____ **11.** This poem is unusual for its —

    A subject matter

    B characters

    C lack of capitalization

    D figures of speech

_____ **12.** This poem shows that Cummings also experimented with —

    F the spacing of words

    G themes

    H topics

    J setting

_____ **13.** Which of the following statements is *not* true about Cummings's poetry?

    A He does not follow the standard rules of punctuation.

    B He never uses punctuation.

    C He does not follow the standard rules of capitalization.

    D His poems are thoughtful.

_____ **14.** This poem does *not* contain —

    F rhyme

    G rhythm

    H humor

    J figures of speech

CONSTRUCTED RESPONSE *(20 points)*

15. Describe how Cummings's poetry, based on "maggie and milly and molly and may," is similar to and different from other poetry you have read in this collection. On a separate piece of paper, write a paragraph that explains your answer. Support your ideas with details from the poem.

SELECTION TEST *Student Edition page 601*

All in green went my love riding E. E. Cummings

COMPREHENSION *(60 points; 6 points each)*

On the line provided, write the letter of the *best* answer to each of the following items.

_____ **1.** In line 1, "my love" refers to the —

    A hunter

    B speaker

    C great horse

    D stags, or male deer

_____ **2.** The deer *most likely* represent —

    F the inexperience of youth

    G women

    H the cruelty of nature

    J early death

_____ **3.** The deer can *best* be described as —

    A sneaky and dangerous

    B calm and patient

    C fearful and cautious

    D lively and good-natured

_____ **4.** The role of the hounds in the poem is to —

    F help capture the deer

    G warn the deer of danger

    H find food

    J control the horse

_____ **5.** During what time of day does the action in the poem take place?

    A Late afternoon

    B Midday

    C Night

    D Daybreak

_____ **6.** The poem's setting includes all of the following elements *except* —

    F a valley

    G meadows

    H mountains

    J gardens

_____ **7.** The poet *most likely* uses the word *flown* in line 18 to show that the deer —

    A are far from their usual territory

    B have disappeared from view

    C are running away at great speed

    D are on a hill above the hunter

_____ **8.** Which of the following statements is the *best* explanation of "Paler be they than daunting death" (line 26)?

    F Those who try to avoid death will not succeed.

    G They are paler than death itself.

    H Experiences with death have frightened them.

    J People are very pale when they die.

_____ **9.** The hunter is *most likely* described as being "lucky" (line 30) because —

    A the deer are within his range

    B he has wealth and fine clothes

    C he is a good rider

    D the area is filled with animals to hunt

_____ **10.** The *most* logical conclusion to draw at the end of the poem is that the —

    F hunter rides away empty-handed

    G deer attack the hunter

    H speaker has fallen in love

    J hunter kills the hounds

LITERARY FOCUS *(20 points; 5 points each)*

On the line provided, write the letter of the *best* answer to each of the following items.

_____ **11.** In this poem, the poet imitates the style and subject matter of —

    A modern fairy tales and fables

    B songs and poems written centuries ago

    C songs that were sung in his day

    D descriptions of daily life found in old history books

_____ **12.** All of the following lines are repeated in the poem *except* —

    F "four lean hounds crouched low and smiling"

    G "All in green went my love riding"

    H "on a great horse of gold"

    J "the merry deer ran before"

_____ **13.** The poem includes imagery that appeals to all of the following senses *except* —

    A hearing

    B smell

    C sight

    D touch

_____ **14.** In which of the following phrases does the poet use personification?

    F "the famished arrow"

    G "four lean hounds"

    H "the red rare deer"

    J "on a great horse of gold"

CONSTRUCTED RESPONSE *(20 points)*

15. "All in green went my love riding" is a musical poem. What does the poet's use of alliteration, repetition, and rhyme contribute to the overall feeling or effect of the poem? On a separate sheet of paper, write a paragraph that explains your answer. Support your ideas with details from the poem.

SELECTION TEST Student Edition page 606

Arithmetic Carl Sandburg

COMPREHENSION (60 points; 6 points each)

On the line provided, write the letter of the *best* answer to each of the following items.

_____ 1. The description of numbers flying in and out of a person's head (stanza 1) suggests all of the following actions *except* —

    A thinking

    B subtracting

    C running

    D adding

_____ 2. The speaker points out in stanza 2 that arithmetic can tell you —

    F whether you will win or lose something

    G the quantity of something that will be added or taken away

    H how much of something you originally had

    J why you should keep or get rid of something

_____ 3. The image of squeezing numbers (stanza 4) suggests that solving an arithmetic problem can be —

    A hard work

    B confusing

    C quick

    D simple

_____ 4. Which of the following situations does the speaker contrast in stanza 5?

    F Appreciating a beautiful day with watching the sky become cloudy

    G Using arithmetic with avoiding arithmetic

    H Finding the right answer with getting the wrong answer

    J Looking out the window with doing your work

_____ 5. The purpose of arithmetic in stanza 6 is to —

    A make a number smaller

    B prevent a number from getting too large

    C list one number after another

    D calculate a number

_____ **6.** Carrying the multiplication table "in your head" (stanza 7) means —

    F remembering it

    G reading it

    H writing it down

    J reciting it

_____ **7.** The speaker's purpose in stanza 8 is to —

    A explain how to solve an arithmetic problem

    B link arithmetic to nature

    C make fun of a certain type of arithmetic problem

    D use arithmetic to determine how much someone has eaten

_____ **8.** The mother in the last stanza *most likely* gives her child two fried eggs because she —

    F enjoys cooking a lot of food

    G thinks that one egg is not enough

    H wants the child to share the eggs

    J misunderstood what her child had said

_____ **9.** To present his observations about arithmetic, the speaker uses all of the following elements *except* —

    A questions

    B exclamations

    C definitions

    D comparisons

_____ **10.** Arithmetic is portrayed in the poem as being —

    F dull and useless

    G knowledge that you are born with

    H a modern invention

    J connected to everyday life

LITERARY FOCUS (20 points; 5 points each)

On the line provided, write the letter of the *best* answer to each of the following items.

_____ **11.** Which of the following statements about free verse is *true*?

    A It comments on many different subjects.

    B Its subject matter is personal.

    C It lacks a regular rhyme scheme and meter.

    D Its stanzas are a standard length.

_____ **12.** What is the *main* characteristic of a catalog poem?

     F It contains a list of things or ideas.

     G It is short and simple.

     H It is addressed to a person.

     J It does not contain a theme.

_____ **13.** Which of the following words *best* describes the style of this poem?

     A graceful

     B old-fashioned

     C rigid

     D informal

_____ **14.** The poem's tone is *best* described as —

     F humorous

     G judgmental

     H neutral

     J flattering

CONSTRUCTED RESPONSE *(20 points)*

15. Although "Arithmetic" may seem similar to prose in some ways, the poem contains a number of traditional poetic elements. What poetic devices does Carl Sandburg use in the poem to express his thoughts about arithmetic? On a separate sheet of paper, write a paragraph that explains your answer. Support your ideas with details from the poem.

SELECTION TEST *Student Edition page 609*

LITERARY RESPONSE AND ANALYSIS

For Poets Al Young

COMPREHENSION *(48 points; 8 points each)*

On the line provided, write the letter of the *best* answer to each of the following items.

_____ **1.** When the speaker tells poets not to become moles (line 3), he *most likely* means that poets should —

    A be flexible

    B be true to themselves

    C not isolate themselves

    D respect others

_____ **2.** What do a worm, a root, and a stone have in common?

    F They can be found under the earth.

    G They need water.

    H They are hard to move.

    J They cannot be seen during the day.

_____ **3.** When the speaker says, "Breathe in trees" (line 8), he *most likely* means that poets should —

    A appreciate nature

    B plant trees

    C rest and relax

    D write about the woods

_____ **4.** When the speaker tells poets, "Poke your head up / & blink" (lines 12–13), he is talking to them as if they were —

    F flowers

    G the sun

    H birds

    J moles

_____ **5.** The speaker reminds poets to perform all of the following actions *except* —

    A walk

    B run

    C swim

    D think

_____ **6.** What does the speaker *most likely* mean by stating, "Dont forget to fly" (line 17)?

    F Work hard and practice.

    G Forget the past.

    H Challenge yourself.

    J Fulfill your responsibilities.

LITERARY FOCUS *(32 points; 8 points each)*

On the line provided, write the letter of the *best* answer to each of the following items.

_____ **7.** An ars poetica is a poem about —

    A nature

    B dreams

    C poetry

    D youth

_____ **8.** An unusual feature of this poem is its —

    F short lines

    G everyday language

    H use of repetition

    J lack of punctuation

_____ **9.** In line 7, "sunlight" is *most likely* a figure of speech meaning —

    A world

    B summer

    C warmth

    D morning

_____ **10.** Lines 12–16 contain —

    F meter

    G rhyme

    H a simile

    J onomatopoeia

CONSTRUCTED RESPONSE *(20 points)*

11. What do you think the theme of "For Poets" is? How does the poet use figurative language to convey that message? On a separate sheet of paper, write a paragraph that explains your answer. Support your ideas with details from the poem.

Worlds of Words: Prose and Poetry

This test asks you to use the skills and strategies you have learned in this collection. Read this poem, and then answer the questions that follow it.

grandmother
by Ray A. Young Bear

if i were to see
her shape from a mile away
i'd know so quickly
that it would be her.
the purple scarf
and the plastic
shopping bag.
if i felt
hands on my head
i'd know that those
were her hands
warm and damp
with the smell
of roots.
if i heard
a voice
coming from
a rock
i'd know
and her words
would flow inside me
like the light
of someone
stirring ashes
from a sleeping fire
at night.

"grandmother" from *Winter of the Salamander* by **Ray A. Young Bear**. Copyright ©
1980 by Ray A. Young Bear. Reproduced by permission of the author.

VOCABULARY SKILLS *(25 points; 5 points each)*

The underlined words below are included in the selection. Re-read the passages
in which the underlined words appear, and then use context clues and your
prior knowledge to help you select an answer. On the line provided, write the
letter of the word or words that best complete each sentence.

_____ **1.** The phrase her shape from a mile away is *not* an analogy because —

    A the language can be taken at face value

    B the poet does not use the word *like* or *as*

    C a comparison is being made

    D a comparison is not being made

_____ **2.** If the poet wanted to create a simile with the purple scarf/and the plastic/shopping
bag, what word would have to be added?

    F is

    G like *or* as

    H appears

    J had

_____ **3.** If the poet said his grandmother's hands were the smell of roots, he would be
creating a(n) —

    A simile

    B metaphor

    C idiom

    D setting

_____ **4.** The last seven lines are a(n) —

    F analogy

    G idiom

    H metaphor

    J simile

_____ **5.** What is being compared in the last seven lines?

    A The grandmother's words and sleep

    B The grandmother's words and getting burned with fire

    C The grandmother's words and light

    D Fire and love

Holt Assessment: Literature, Reading, and Vocabulary

COMPREHENSION *(25 points; 5 points each)*

On the line provided, write the letter of the *best* answer to each of the following items.

_____ **6.** In the poem "grandmother," the speaker is —

    F the grandmother

    G a voice from the rock

    H an outside observer

    J the grandchild

_____ **7.** In which of the following ways is Ray Young Bear's poem unconventional?

    A He does not use periods.

    B He does not use apostrophes.

    C He uses quotation marks to emphasize certain words.

    D He does not use capital letters or commas.

_____ **8.** The image that appeals to the sense of touch is —

    F "a voice / coming from / a rock"

    G "her hands / warm and damp"

    H "the purple scarf"

    J "a sleeping fire"

_____ **9.** The image of "stirring ashes / from a sleeping fire" suggests that the speaker's —

    A grandmother is a good cook

    B grandmother makes him angry

    C grandmother's words fill him with love

    D grandmother's house is warm and cozy

_____ **10.** How many stanzas does this poem have?

    F One

    G Two

    H Three

    J Four

READING SKILLS AND STRATEGIES: CONSTRUCTED RESPONSE *(30 points; 10 points each)*

Identifying Personification

11. When writers give human qualities to nonhuman things, writers are using *personification.* Write a paragraph in which you identify the personification in this poem and explain its effect.

_____

_____

_____

_____

_____

Making Generalizations

12. A generalization is a broad statement that tells about something in general. Based on "grandmother," what generalization can you make about poetry? Explain your generalization in a paragraph.

_____

_____

_____

_____

_____

Describing Mental Images: Appealing to the Senses

13. Which images from the poem appeal to the senses most strongly? From the following options, choose the one you think is the *best* response to this question. On the lines provided, write the letter of the answer you chose, and briefly defend your choice.

A "the purple scarf / and the plastic / shopping bag"

B "if i felt / hands on my head / i'd know that those / were her hands / warm and damp"

C "with the smell / of roots"

D "if i heard / a voice / coming from / a rock"

_____

_____

_____

_____

_____

LITERARY FOCUS: CONSTRUCTED RESPONSE *(20 points)*

14. Complete the following chart to distinguish among kinds of prose and poetry. Under each category, write the specific characteristics of each type of writing.

Prose			Poetry
novels	*novellas*	*short stories*	*poems*

COLLECTION 6 DIAGNOSTIC TEST ███████

Our Literary Heritage: Greek Myths and World Folk Tales

On the line provided, write the letter of the *best* answer to each of the following items.
(100 points; 10 points each)

_____ **1.** Which of the following statements about the ancient Greek and Roman **myths** is *false*?

 A Some of the myths explain the creation of the world.

 B These myths are historically accurate records of the ancient world.

 C A number of myths explain mysterious or frightening forces in the universe.

 D These myths have influenced art and literature over the course of centuries.

_____ **2.** Which of the following statements about the gods and goddesses in *most* Greek and Roman **myths** is *false*?

 F They have the power to reward or punish humans.

 G They may be identified with aspects of nature.

 H They display human emotions.

 J They stay removed from the human world.

_____ **3.** Which statement about **folk tales** is *true*?

 A They are passed down by word of mouth from generation to generation.

 B Each one is unique and has little in common with stories from other cultures.

 C They present realistic descriptions of everyday life in the past.

 D They are widely read because their authors are famous.

_____ **4.** Many stories contain a **moral,** or a(n) —

 F lesson about the right way to behave

 G conflict between the forces of good and evil

 H test that the hero must pass

 J ending based on magical or fantastic events

_____ **5.** When characters undergo a **metamorphosis,** they —

 A go on a journey

 B die a heroic death

 C marry their true love

 D change shape or form

Holt Assessment: Literature, Reading, and Vocabulary

_____ **6.** Which of the following sentences contains an **opinion**?

    F Zeus, whose Roman name is Jupiter, is king of the Greek gods.

    G When the Romans conquered the Greeks, they adopted the Greek myths.

    H Fables are more interesting than the ancient Greek and Roman myths.

    J Storytelling festivals take place in many parts of the United States.

_____ **7.** A very brief story told to make a point is called a(n) —

    A inference

    B anecdote

    C generalization

    D conclusion

_____ **8.** When you **summarize** an informational text, you should leave out —

    F the author's name

    G minor details

    H the topic of the work

    J the title

_____ **9.** When you add a **prefix** to a word, you —

    A restate the word

    B make the word plural

    C change the word's meaning

    D add an accent to the word

_____ **10.** **Context clues,** which provide clues to a word's meaning, appear in —

    F the word itself

    G a footnote

    H a dictionary

    J surrounding sentences

The Origin of the Seasons

retold by Olivia Coolidge

COMPREHENSION *(60 points; 6 points each)*
On the line provided, write the letter of the *best* answer to each of the following items.

_____ **1.** Farmers call Demeter "the great mother" because she —

    A has many children

    B has raised Persephone well

    C is generous to them

    D likes to be admired

_____ **2.** Hades kidnaps Persephone because he —

    F is an enemy of her mother

    G wants to marry her

    H longs to be immortal

    J seeks revenge against Zeus

_____ **3.** Demeter asks Apollo for information about her daughter because Apollo —

    A is related to her

    B can predict the future

    C may have helped kidnap Persephone

    D sees everything from his chariot in the heavens

_____ **4.** Which response *best* explains why Demeter neglects her duties as goddess of the harvest?

    F She is grief-stricken over the loss of her daughter.

    G She wants to teach Hades a lesson.

    H She needs Persephone's help to make crops grow.

    J She doesn't think the gods and other goddesses respect her.

_____ **5.** Demeter places Demophoon in the fire in order to —

    A make him immortal

    B keep him warm

    C hide him from Hades

    D frighten his mother

_____ **6.** As a result of Metaneira's interference, Demeter —

    F kills Demophoon

    G loses hope of ever caring for a child again

    H reveals her identity as a goddess

    J wants Zeus to punish Metaneira

_____ **7.** Zeus decides that Persephone must be returned to Demeter to —

    A stop the fighting among the gods and goddesses

    B make Persephone happy again

    C prevent humankind from dying of hunger

    D show Demeter that he loves her

_____ **8.** Persephone agrees to eat something before she leaves Hades because she —

    F is trying to be kind to him

    G is weak from a lack of food

    H wants to prove to him that she is happy to be leaving

    J wishes to avoid arguing with him and delaying her departure

_____ **9.** As a result of eating the pomegranate seeds, Persephone —

    A forgets her previous life on Earth

    B must return to the Underworld for seven months of each year

    C is transformed into a beautiful tree

    D will never age and die

_____ **10.** In this myth, who is the *most* powerful of the immortals?

    F Zeus

    G Hades

    H Iris

    J the Fates

LITERARY FOCUS (20 points; 5 points each)

On the line provided, write the letter of the *best* answer to each of the following items.

_____ **11.** The story of Demeter and Persephone is an origin myth because it —

    A was first told long ago in ancient Greece

    B explains the reason for the changing seasons

    C examines the problems that can be caused by love

    D describes a power struggle between gods and goddesses

The Origin of the Seasons

_____ **12.** Persephone is characterized as being —

    F beautiful and innocent

    G strong and stubborn

    H thoughtful and cautious

    J calm and patient

_____ **13.** When the author refers to Hades' "heart of stone," she is using figurative language to convey that the god is —

    A huge

    B immortal

    C brave

    D unfeeling

_____ **14.** When the author states in the last line of the story, "Everywhere the heavens . . . weep sudden showers of gladness upon the springing earth," she is using figurative language to explain that —

    F Zeus is crying about Demeter and Persephone's situation

    G it rains when Persephone returns from the Underworld in the spring

    H Hades and Persephone find happiness together part of the year

    J Persephone feels sorry for herself and suffers great sorrow

CONSTRUCTED RESPONSE *(20 points)*

15. As she takes care of Demophoon, Demeter behaves like both a human and a goddess. How does she reveal both sides of her character? On a separate sheet of paper, write a paragraph that explains your answer. Support your ideas with details from the myth.

SELECTION TEST | *Student Edition page 664*

Orpheus, the Great Musician

retold by Olivia Coolidge

COMPREHENSION *(40 points; 4 points each)*

On the line provided, write the letter of the *best* answer to each of the following items.

_____ **1.** In the beginning of the myth, what inspires Orpheus to sing so beautifully?

    A His love of nature

    B His passion for Eurydice

    C His desire to be admired

    D His sense of loneliness

_____ **2.** Eurydice dies because she —

    F is chosen to be Hades' bride

    G does not want to marry Orpheus

    H is bitten by a snake on her wedding day

    J falls into the river Styx

_____ **3.** As Orpheus travels to the Underworld, all of the creatures he encounters —

    A attempt to stop him at the gate

    B lead him toward the hissing flame

    C express their sorrow for his loss

    D become hushed and still

_____ **4.** When Hades hears Orpheus's music, he —

    F weeps at its beauty

    G asks Orpheus to describe his troubles

    H is angry that Orpheus has entered the Underworld

    J fears Orpheus's power

_____ **5.** As Orpheus leaves the Underworld, he —

    A thanks the gods and goddesses

    B takes the flock of ghosts with him

    C listens for any sound from Eurydice

    D vows never to play music again

_____ **6.** Which of the following words *best* characterizes Orpheus's attitude toward Hades?

    F admiring

    G loyal

    H distrustful

    J snobbish

_____ **7.** Orpheus loses Eurydice a second time when he —

    A looks back to see if she is following him

    B takes a wrong path out of the Underworld

    C angers the creatures in the Underworld

    D climbs too slowly to the upper world

_____ **8.** What happens when Orpheus tries to return to the Underworld?

    F He is unable to persuade the ferryman to take him there.

    G Hades refuses to talk to him.

    H He is frightened away by the monsters.

    J He is unable to see in the grayness and the smoke.

_____ **9.** How does losing Eurydice a second time affect Orpheus?

    A He vows to take revenge.

    B He never returns to the light of day.

    C He asks the god Dionysus to help him.

    D He cannot sing for seven days.

_____ **10.** Orpheus is finally reunited with Eurydice after —

    F Hades takes Eurydice back to the upper world

    G Eurydice brings him to the Underworld

    H he dies at the hands of an angry mob

    J he kills himself

LITERARY FOCUS *(24 points; 6 points each)*

On the line provided, write the letter of the *best* answer to each of the following items.

_____ **11.** Orpheus's journey to the Underworld is unusual because —

    A his stirring music brings the dead back to life

    B only the souls of the dead typically go there

    C he takes Hades' place as ruler of the Underworld

    D he finds the Underworld to be filled with strange creatures

_____ **12.** For the ancient Greeks, one purpose of this myth was *most likely* to —

    F portray a man who is transformed into a different creature

    G examine death and the afterlife

    H show that music brings hope to people

    J advise people never to give up their dreams

_____ **13.** The monster that guards the gates of the Underworld is —

    A Cerberus

    B Charon

    C Tantalus

    D Sisyphus

_____ **14.** The queen of the Underworld is described as being —

    F young and lively

    G quiet and shy

    H mature and refined

    J pale and unhappy

VOCABULARY DEVELOPMENT *(16 points; 4 points each)*

On the line before each sentence, write the Vocabulary word that has a similar meaning to the italicized word or phrase in the sentence.

inconsolable	**ghastly**	**reluctance**	**ascended**

_____ **15.** The *horrible* flocks of ghosts made Orpheus shiver.

_____ **16.** Orpheus showed some *unwillingness* to leave the Underworld.

_____ **17.** Orpheus slowly *moved up* until he reached the sunny earth.

_____ **18.** Orpheus was *brokenhearted* when Eurydice disappeared.

CONSTRUCTED RESPONSE *(20 points)*

19. In this myth the god Hades does not behave the way he ordinarily does. In what ways is his behavior surprising? On a separate sheet of paper, write a paragraph that explains your answer. Support your ideas with details from the myth.

Orpheus, the Great Musician

SELECTION TEST | *Student Edition page 672*

The Power of Music Nadja Salerno-Sonnenberg

COMPREHENSION *(100 points; 10 points each)*

On the line provided, write the letter of the *best* answer to each of the following items.

_____ **1.** What does the author claim to "know for a fact"?

    A She is a brilliant musician because she fought hard to perfect her art.

    B Although you may struggle to achieve your dream, you may not fully attain it.

    C Everyone should strive to love and understand music.

    D Achieving your most important goals requires the greatest effort.

_____ **2.** The author says that when you love music, you face the challenge every day of —

    F memorizing new pieces of music

    G improving your playing

    H performing in front of an audience

    J displaying patience when mastering a new instrument

_____ **3.** Which of the following sentences is the *best* paraphrase of the statement "But whenever you fall in love with music, you'll never sit still again"?

    A An appreciation for music will motivate you to play an instrument better each day.

    B If you love music, your schedule will be filled with concerts and tours.

    C Liking music means that you will always have a song running through your head.

    D An enjoyment of music can distract you from doing other things.

_____ **4.** The author believes that music has the "power" to —

    F make people more intelligent

    G unite different types of people

    H lead to the enjoyment of other art forms

    J cause strong emotional reactions in people

_____ **5.** The author feels that the struggle to be a musician is "noble" and "heroic" because musicians —

    A run the risk of severely injuring themselves

    B face overwhelming obstacles in their careers

    C are greatly admired in society

    D can help other people feel fulfilled and uplifted

Holt Assessment: Literature, Reading, and Vocabulary

6. As a musician, the author has experienced all of the following emotions *except* —

    F pride

    G frustration

    H hatred

    J happiness

7. Which of the following statements expresses a fact?

    A Music is the most important art form.

    B Some people reveal a talent for music at a very young age.

    C Only people who enjoy music have good taste.

    D Musicians are more admirable than politicians.

8. When the author describes a period of time when she felt discouraged, she is presenting —

    F an anecdote

    G a stereotype

    H foreshadowing

    J a prediction

9. Which of the following questions is *not* answered in the selection?

    A What is the author's favorite type of music?

    B Why does the author value music?

    C What is the author's view of the role of musicians in society?

    D What has the author's life as a musician been like?

10. The author's tone can *best* be described as —

    F enthusiastic

    G matter-of-fact

    H argumentative

    J uncertain

SELECTION TEST *Student Edition page 675*

The Flight of Icarus *retold by* Sally Benson

COMPREHENSION *(60 points; 6 points each)*

On the line provided, write the letter of the *best* answer to each of the following items.

_____ **1.** Which of the following events occurs *first* in the myth?

    A Daedalus designs wings for himself and Icarus.

    B Theseus escapes from King Minos's labyrinth.

    C Daedalus and Icarus watch how birds fly.

    D Daedalus names the land Icaria.

_____ **2.** Daedalus decides to escape from Crete by air because —

    F other prisoners have escaped by flying

    G his son, Icarus, is a poor swimmer

    H he is unfamiliar with the roads in Crete

    J King Minos will not have the power to stop him

_____ **3.** From his behavior in the beginning of the myth, you can infer that Icarus —

    A is still a young boy

    B is worried about his father

    C feels lonely

    D is a gifted athlete

_____ **4.** Daedalus warns his son that if he flies too low, —

    F he will crash into the ground

    G the spray from the sea will clog his wings

    H their enemies will see him

    J he will be attacked by gulls

_____ **5.** Icarus flies higher and higher because he —

    A is angry at his father

    B cannot see where he is going

    C enjoys the sense of freedom

    D is frightened by the wild sea

_____ **6.** What warning sign indicates that Icarus is in danger?

    F Small feathers fall off his wings.

    G His father flies toward earth.

    H A cool wind blows on his face.

    J He begins to feel faint.

Holt Assessment: Literature, Reading, and Vocabulary

_____ **7.** Icarus's wings finally fall apart because —

    A he flutters them too much

    B the heat of the sun melts the wax

    C the gods and goddesses want to punish him

    D they are too small for him

_____ **8.** Daedalus does not hear his son's cries because —

    F Icarus is shouting in the wrong direction

    G he is flying too far ahead of Icarus

    H he is focused on trying to save himself

    J Icarus's voice is muffled by the sea

_____ **9.** What happens to Daedalus at the end of the myth?

    A He dies of grief.

    B Apollo rewards him.

    C King Minos forgives him.

    D He finds safety in Sicily.

_____ **10.** At the end of the myth, Daedalus views flying with —

    F appreciation

    G curiosity

    H wonder

    J bitterness

LITERARY FOCUS *(20 points; 5 points each)*

On the line provided, write the letter of the *best* answer to each of the following items.

_____ **11.** Which of the following statements *best* expresses a moral of the myth?

    A If at first you don't succeed, try again.

    B It is better to be true to yourself than to follow others.

    C Know your limits before you leap into action.

    D Freedom is a goal worth sacrificing for.

_____ **12.** In the myth, Icarus is compared to —

    F the sun

    G a butterfly

    H a bird

    J the wind

_____ **13.** Which of the following generalizations can be made about Icarus's personality?

   A He is fearful and careful.

   B He is innocent and foolish.

   C He is respectful and patient.

   D He is intelligent and experienced.

_____ **14.** Which words *best* describe Daedalus's attitude toward Icarus?

   F loving and concerned

   G critical and controlling

   H unfeeling and neglectful

   J boastful and encouraging

CONSTRUCTED RESPONSE *(20 points)*

15. One critic has noted that the situation of Icarus and Daedalus is similar to the situation of a teenager asking for the keys to the family car. Do you agree or disagree with this comparison? On a separate sheet of paper, write a paragraph that explains your answer. Support your ideas with details from the myth.

SELECTION TEST *Student Edition page 682*

**LITERARY RESPONSE
AND ANALYSIS**

King Midas and the Golden Touch

retold by Pamela Oldfield

COMPREHENSION *(60 points; 6 points each)*

On the line provided, write the letter of the *best* answer to each of the following items.

_____ **1.** In the opening of the myth, Midas is described as feeling —

    A dissatisfied

    B insulted

    C deceived

    D aimless

_____ **2.** Silenus is resting in Midas's garden because he —

    F is hiding from Dionysus

    G was being chased by other satyrs

    H became lost and drank too much

    J and Midas are old friends

_____ **3.** Silenus's appearance is remarkable because he —

    A has wings

    B is very old

    C grins foolishly

    D has hoofs

_____ **4.** Dionysus offers to give Midas a gift as a —

    F reward for taking care of Silenus

    G prize for his beautiful garden

    H repayment for money that he is owed

    J token of appreciation for honoring the god

_____ **5.** Why does Midas want everything he touches to turn to gold?

    A He is trying to learn the secrets of the universe.

    B He wants to become the most powerful king in the world.

    C He would like to give his wife and daughter everything they want.

    D He hopes to become immortal, like a god.

_____ **6.** After Midas turns the plants in his garden into gold, he is —

    F filled with joy to have been given such a gift

    G disturbed by how lifeless the garden has become

    H depressed because he has no more plants to turn into gold

    J overcome by the desire for even more gold

_____ **7.** Which event *first* persuades Midas to beg Dionysus to take back the gift?

    A He accidentally turns his daughter into gold.

    B He discovers that his power makes it impossible for him to eat or drink.

    C His fingers tremble, and he feels ill.

    D He has to walk by himself for many miles.

_____ **8.** To save his daughter, Midas must —

    F wash himself in the river Pactolus

    G return to his palace

    H ask his daughter to forgive him

    J agree never to ask a god for anything again

_____ **9.** Midas is able to smell the flowers at the end of the myth because —

    A they are new flowers that have just been planted

    B his daughter is alive

    C the plants are no longer made of gold

    D he is no longer rich

_____ **10.** At the end of the myth, Midas feels —

    F happy but somewhat regretful

    G resentful but relieved

    H joyful and satisfied

    J tired and slightly foolish

LITERARY FOCUS *(20 points; 5 points each)*

On the line provided, write the letter of the *best* answer to each of the following items.

_____ **11.** "King Midas and the Golden Touch" addresses all of the following topics typically covered in myths *except* —

    A the creation of the world

    B people's fears and hopes

    C the way people should live

    D the relationship between humans and gods

_____ **12.** This myth helps explain why —

    F visitors should be treated well

    G roses are beautiful

    H statues can be found in palaces

    J gold can be found in rivers

_____ **13.** What is the irony in the myth?

    A Midas's daughter increasingly annoys her father.

    B Greed saves Midas from starving to death.

    C Midas's new power turns out to be a terrible curse.

    D Nature can affect humans in a positive manner.

_____ **14.** Which of the following words *best* describes Dionysus in this myth?

    F jealous

    G ambitious

    H self-centered

    J forgiving

CONSTRUCTED RESPONSE *(20 points)*

15. What lesson about life does King Midas learn in this myth? How does the reader know that King Midas's views have changed? On a separate sheet of paper, write a paragraph that explains your answer. Support your ideas with details from the myth.

SELECTION TEST **Student Edition page 688**   INFORMATIONAL
                                                              READING

The Funeral Banquet of King Midas

John Fleischman

COMPREHENSION *(60 points; 6 points each)*

On the line provided, write the letter of the *best* answer to each of the following items.

_____ **1.** King Midas lived in an area that is now known as —

   A   Greece

   B   Turkey

   C   Assyria

   D   Egypt

_____ **2.** Midas was buried with all of the following items *except* —

   F   bronze vessels

   G   textiles

   H   gold

   J   wooden furniture

_____ **3.** Scientists were able to determine the age of the burial mound by —

   A   performing chemical tests on the sludge found in vessels

   B   analyzing the level of oxygen in the tomb

   C   translating symbols that were carved into the coffin

   D   studying the pattern of tree rings in the tomb's inner wall

_____ **4.** The funeral banquet was part of a —

   F   celebration that lasted for sixty days

   G   service honoring past rulers of the kingdom

   H   festival for gods and goddesses

   J   religious ceremony for the dead king

_____ **5.** Because the burial mound was built with such precision, Dr. Simpson compares it to —

   A   an Egyptian pyramid

   B   Apollo's shrine at Delphi

   C   the Great Wall of China

   D   modern skyscrapers

_____ **6.** Which sentence *best* summarizes the main idea of the last paragraph?

    F King Midas never achieved King Tut's level of fame throughout the world.

    G Although most pharaohs have been forgotten, people still remember King Midas because of the story of his golden touch.

    H People cannot recall how many emperors Persia had over the centuries.

    J Most rulers are remembered only for their monuments, not for their contributions to society.

VOCABULARY DEVELOPMENT *(40 points; 10 points each)*

On the line provided, write the Vocabulary word that *best* completes each sentence.

    archaeologists   **excavating**   **avalanche**   **interior**

7. The miners dug a tunnel to explore the _____ of the burial mound.

8. After the _____ the miners had to clear away the fallen rocks.

9. Rodney Young's _____ of the burial mound led to important discoveries.

10. Chemists and _____ worked together to learn what people ate at King Midas's funeral banquet.

The Funeral Banquet of King Midas

SELECTION TEST *Student Edition page 698*

Oni and the Great Bird *retold by* Abayomi Fuja

COMPREHENSION *(40 points; 4 points each)*

On the line provided, write the letter of the *best* answer to each of the following items.

_____ **1.** During the war between his people and another village, Oni discovers that he —

    A cannot be killed

    B is destined to become a famous warrior

    C was born wearing boots

    D has never been well liked

_____ **2.** Oni is banished from his village because —

    F he sets fire to a house

    G the king of Ajo summons him

    H he loses his magic boots

    J everyone is afraid of him

_____ **3.** Why do the bells in Ajo ring as dusk approaches?

    A To scare off evil spirits and bring good luck

    B To show that the people in the town are united

    C To signal that it is time to hide from the giant eagle

    D To acknowledge Oni's arrival in the town

_____ **4.** Why does the king discourage Oni from trying to kill the eagle?

    F He wants to prove his courage by killing the bird himself.

    G He does not want to give Oni the reward and divide his kingdom.

    H He feels that enough hunters have already been killed.

    J He wants to protect the bird from harm.

_____ **5.** Oni sings to Anodo about the coming battle because Oni —

    A is hoping to avoid a struggle

    B is demonstrating his bravery

    C wants the people of Ajo to join him in the fight

    D needs more time to prepare his weapons

_____ **6.** How is the conflict between Oni and the hunter resolved?

    F A witness who saw the fight between Oni and Anodo speaks up.

    G Oni and the hunter agree to share the reward for killing Anodo.

    H The king arranges a duel between Oni and the hunter to test their bravery.

    J Oni proves that he killed the eagle by revealing the location of his missing boot, which fits only him.

_____ **7.** At the end of the tale, the people of Ajo are free to —

    A dance and rejoice in the streets at night

    B honor their king

    C earn a living again

    D welcome visitors into their homes

_____ **8.** In his village and in Ajo, Oni is a(n) —

    F hero

    G outsider

    H prince

    J beggar

_____ **9.** Which of the following statements about Oni is *false*?

    A He is knocked unconscious during his fight with the eagle.

    B Oni takes a canoe that does not belong to him.

    C He has killed dangerous creatures in the past.

    D He asks an old man for help when he arrives in Ajo.

_____ **10.** Which of the following statements *best* summarizes the message of the tale?

    F Everyone should help others.

    G It is unfair to pass judgment on someone.

    H The truth is always discovered, even though it may be temporarily hidden.

    J Love is brief, but hatred lasts forever.

LITERARY FOCUS (20 points; 5 points each)

On the line provided, write the letter of the *best* answer to each of the following items.

_____ **11.** Like a typical superhero, Oni performs all of the following actions *except* —

    A resisting the force of bows and arrows

    B slaying the enemy

    C rescuing a village from harm

    D winning the love of a fair maiden

_____ **12.** What makes Oni similar to an ordinary person?

    F His guilt

    G His boots

    H His determination

    J His fear of death

_____ **13.** Which event marks the climax of the tale?

    A The conversation in which Oni tells the king he will try to kill Anodo that night

    B The fight between Oni and the eagle

    C The banishment of Oni from his village

    D The old man's attempt to persuade Oni not to challenge the eagle

_____ **14.** To emphasize the eagle's power, the author repeatedly refers to its —

    F great wings

    G song

    H sharp beak

    J talons

VOCABULARY DEVELOPMENT *(20 points; 4 points each)*

On the line before each sentence, write the Vocabulary word that has a similar meaning to the italicized word or phrase in the sentence.

implored   commenced   invincible   hovered   imposter

_____ **15.** Oni accused the hunter of being a *person who pretends to be someone he is not.*

_____ **16.** The eagle *began* its nightly raid on the village.

_____ **17.** The old man *begged* Oni to stay inside.

_____ **18.** The giant eagle *hung in the air* above the village.

_____ **19.** Oni proved that the eagle was not *unbeatable*.

CONSTRUCTED RESPONSE *(20 points)*

20. "Oni and the Great Bird" contains many popular motifs that have appeared in other stories throughout time. What motifs from the folk tale seem familiar to you? Did any aspects of the tale surprise you? On a separate sheet of paper, write a paragraph that explains your answer. Support your ideas with details from the folk tale.

SELECTION TEST *Student Edition page 707*

Master Frog *retold by* Lynette Dyer Vuong

COMPREHENSION *(40 points; 4 points each)*
On the line provided, write the letter of the *best* answer to each of the following items.

_____ **1.** Which of the following events happens *first* in the tale?

    A The king orders his guards to kill Master Frog.

    B Giang Dung comes to live in the palace.

    C Master Frog turns into a prince.

    D Kien Tien's sisters throw her into the sea.

_____ **2.** Giang Dung decides to raise the frog because —

    F her husband would have wanted her to

    G she realizes that she may be rewarded in some way

    H she knows the frog's true identity

    J she is afraid that no one else will ever love her

_____ **3.** When Giang Dung tries to discourage Master Frog from seeking the princess as his bride, Master Frog displays —

    A anger

    B alarm

    C determination

    D shame

_____ **4.** When Master Frog says that he would like to marry the king's daughter, the king is *first* —

    F enraged

    G amused

    H embarrassed

    J sympathetic

_____ **5.** Who are Master Frog's vassals?

    A Master Frog's classmates

    B Silkworms

    C Wild beasts

    D Foreign soldiers

_____ **6.** Kien Tien offers to marry the frog because she —

    F wants to protect the kingdom

    G finds the frog handsome

    H wants to make her father happy

    J knows her marriage will make her sisters jealous

_____ **7.** Master Frog, a son of Jade Emperor, could only regain his true shape once —

    A he had fallen in love

    B he had succeeded in the world

    C his father had forgiven him

    D he had lived among other frogs for twenty years

_____ **8.** Bich Ngoc burns Master Frog's skin because she —

    F is trying to kill Jade Emperor

    G hopes that a prince will arise from the smoke

    H is angry over her failure to find a prince for herself

    J does not want Kien Tien to know that she touched it

_____ **9.** Master Frog reclaims his bride by —

    A threatening Kien Tien's father

    B asking the Dragon King of the Waters for help

    C turning back into a frog

    D offering up his own life as a sacrifice

_____ **10.** Which of the following statements is *not* a lesson taught in the story?

    F Don't trust first impressions.

    G Good things come in small packages.

    H Children should be seen and not heard.

    J Good marriages are based on companionship.

LITERARY FOCUS *(20 points; 5 points each)*

On the line provided, write the letter of the *best* answer to each of the following items.

_____ **11.** A metamorphosis occurs in "Master Frog" when —

    A the king realizes that the frog is powerful

    B Kien Tien learns to love her husband

    C Giang Dung gives birth to a frog

    D Master Frog takes a human form

_____ **12.** When Kien Tien's sisters learn that Master Frog is a prince, they become —

      F thoughtful and forgiving

      G kind and gentle

      H bold and adventurous

      J bitter and envious

_____ **13.** Which motif, typically found in folk tales, does "Master Frog" contain?

      A A handsome prince who saves a young woman

      B An evil witch

      C A fairy godmother

      D A quest to slay a monster

_____ **14.** Compared with her sisters, Kien Tien is —

      F more open-minded

      G trickier

      H less trusting

      J greedier

VOCABULARY DEVELOPMENT *(20 points; 4 points each)*

On the line before each sentence, write the Vocabulary word that has a similar meaning to the italicized word or phrase in the sentence.

    admonished   **entreaties**   **charade**   **presumptuous**   **cowered**

_____ **15.** Until the king heard the frog croak, he thought that Master Frog's request to marry a princess was a *pretense*.

_____ **16.** The king accused Master Frog of being *arrogant* when Master Frog asked for Kien Tien's hand in marriage.

_____ **17.** Kien Tien's sisters *urged* her to drink the tea, which contained sleeping powder.

_____ **18.** Kien Tien's older sisters *trembled in fear* when they saw that she was alive.

_____ **19.** Giang Dung gave in to Master Frog's *earnest requests* to go to the palace.

CONSTRUCTED RESPONSE *(20 points)*

20. Choose any character other than Master Frog whose actions in the tale demonstrate the old saying that "beauty is only skin-deep." How does this character's reaction to Master Frog help express this idea? On a separate sheet of paper, write a paragraph that explains your answer. Support your ideas with details from the folk tale.

SELECTION TEST *Student Edition page 718*

The Crane Wife *told by* Sumiko Yagawa

COMPREHENSION *(60 points; 6 points each)*
On the line provided, write the letter of the *best* answer to each of the following items.

_____ **1.** What is the setting of this folk tale?

    A A snowy mountain village

    B A bustling, modern city

    C A cozy farmhouse

    D A wealthy capital city

_____ **2.** Yohei rescues a crane by —

    F releasing it from the jaws of an animal

    G freeing it from a trap

    H removing an arrow from its wing

    J giving it shelter during a storm

_____ **3.** The wife's character can *best* be described as —

    A kind and faithful

    B angry and resentful

    C sad and irritable

    D reckless and foolish

_____ **4.** What problem results from Yohei's marriage?

    F Yohei's wife becomes bored.

    G Yohei's friends will no longer associate with him.

    H Yohei's house is too small for the couple.

    J Yohei becomes poorer than before.

_____ **5.** Yohei's wife warns Yohei —

    A not to look at her while she is weaving

    B to try to earn money himself

    C not to tell anyone they are married

    D to be honest with her

_____ **6.** After she has finished weaving, Yohei's wife seems —

    F cheerful and relieved

    G self-confident and proud

    H thin and weak

    J insecure and nervous

Holt Assessment: Literature, Reading, and Vocabulary

_____ **7.** Yohei's neighbor offers to —

    A have his own wife weave cloth for Yohei

    B lend Yohei's wife a loom

    C provide Yohei's wife with better thread

    D help Yohei sell his wife's fabric

_____ **8.** What is Yohei's wife's view of money?

    F She thinks money is useless.

    G She wants only enough money to live on.

    H She desires great wealth.

    J She thinks money is more important than love.

_____ **9.** Why does Yohei's wife agree to weave one last time?

    A She knows her last creation will be her most beautiful.

    B She thinks weaving will restore her husband's health.

    C She hates to see her husband worry about money.

    D She needs to weave three times in order to break her curse.

_____ **10.** What happens to Yohei's wife at the end of the tale?

    F She flies off as a crane.

    G She cuts herself while weaving.

    H She becomes lost in the snow.

    J She dies.

LITERARY FOCUS (20 points; 5 points each)

On the line provided, write the letter of the *best* answer to each of the following items.

_____ **11.** Which of the following statements *best* summarizes a moral of the folk tale?

    A Kind deeds are rare in the world.

    B Warnings should be obeyed.

    C True love does not last.

    D One can never be too rich.

_____ **12.** A metamorphosis occurs in the folk tale when —

    F the crane's wounded wing heals

    G Yohei lives more grandly than he did before his marriage

    H the crane turns into a woman

    J Yohei's wife is revealed to be an excellent weaver

_____ **13.** Onomatopoeia refers to words —

    A   that rhyme

    B   with multiple meanings

    C   that evoke specific feelings

    D   whose sounds echo their sense

_____ **14.** The crimson thread in the white fabric mentioned at the end of the tale *most likely* represents —

    F   the crane's blood

    G   the royal background of Yohei's wife

    H   the riches that can be gained by selling the fabric

    J   Yohei and his wife's marriage

CONSTRUCTED RESPONSE *(20 points)*

15. At the end of the story, Yohei's wife says that she fell in love with Yohei because of his gentle heart and simplicity. In what way does Yohei's personality change during the folk tale? How do the changes in his character contribute to his breaking of the taboo? On a separate sheet of paper, write a paragraph that explains your answer. Support your ideas with details from the folk tale.

SELECTION TEST | *Student Edition page 726*

Aunty Misery Judith Ortiz Cofer

COMPREHENSION *(60 points; 6 points each)*

On the line provided, write the letter of the *best* answer to each of the following items.

_____ **1.** Aunty Misery spends *most* of her time —

    A hosting guests

    B cleaning her hut

    C looking after her pear tree

    D taking care of her children

_____ **2.** How do the neighborhood children treat Aunty Misery?

    F They insult her.

    G They lie to her.

    H They throw fruit at her.

    J They threaten her.

_____ **3.** The first stranger who spends the night at Aunty Misery's hut is a(n) —

    A sorcerer

    B prince

    C man who is lost

    D explorer

_____ **4.** Aunty Misery wishes for —

    F good health

    G a companion in her old age

    H harm to come to the neighborhood children

    J protection for her pear tree

_____ **5.** Aunty Misery does not release children from her tree until they —

    A pay her for the fruit they have eaten

    B promise never to steal fruit again

    C agree to help her care for the tree

    D give back the fruit they have taken

_____ **6.** In the course of the tale, the tree is described as —

    F bearing less and less fruit

    G becoming more lovely

    H aging along with Aunty Misery

    J losing its leaves

_____ **7.** When a second traveler shows up at her door, Aunty Misery —

    A views him with suspicion

    B believes he is the same stranger who visited her before

    C welcomes him into her home

    D asks him to grant her a wish

_____ **8.** In order to trick Death into getting stuck in her tree, Aunty Misery —

    F tells Death that the pears taste delicious

    G claims that she is too old to climb to the top of the tree

    H convinces Death that he can make money by selling the pears

    J reveals that there are children stuck in the tree

_____ **9.** Aunty Misery agrees to free Death if he will —

    A allow her to live for another twenty years

    B grant immortality to everyone in her town

    C promise never to come for her again

    D protect her pear tree forever

_____ **10.** Which of the following sentences *best* restates the main idea of the last paragraph?

    F Everyone encounters misery and death at some point.

    G Promises are worth keeping.

    H Be careful whom you blame for your problems.

    J Life can be unfair.

LITERARY FOCUS *(20 points; 5 points each)*

On the line provided, write the letter of the *best* answer to each of the following items.

_____ **11.** In folk tales, wishes are often granted because —

    A someone tells a lie

    B someone does a good deed

    C one character loves another

    D a character is greedy

_____ **12.** Which of the following motifs is an element of "Aunty Misery"?

    F A superhero

    G A wicked stepmother

    H A test that a character must pass

    J A character who disguises his or her true identity

_____ **13.** Which of the following adjectives *best* characterizes Aunty Misery?

    A jealous

    B patient

    C clever

    D fearful

_____ **14.** The author uses personification to portray —

    F Aunty Misery's hearth

    G Aunty Misery's hut

    H death

    J time

CONSTRUCTED RESPONSE *(20 points)*

15. In many folk tales the granting of a wish leads to great unhappiness or regret. What are the consequences of Aunty Misery's wish? Are the consequences positive or negative? On a separate sheet of paper, write a paragraph that explains your answer. Support your ideas with details from the folk tale.

SELECTION TEST   **Student Edition page 732**

The Hummingbird King

retold by **Argentina Palacios**

COMPREHENSION *(60 points; 6 points each)*

On the line provided, write the letter of the *best* answer to each of the following items.

_____ 1. The thirteenth day of the month is considered lucky in Mayan culture because it —

    A is the day that a great chief was born

    B marks the time of the harvest

    C represents the thirteen Mayan heavens

    D is a day on which prayers are answered

_____ 2. The messenger of the gods sends Kukul's parents a sign that their son —

    F will be an admired ruler

    G will be extraordinary

    H may bring them bad luck

    J may be defeated by his enemies

_____ 3. What gift does the high priest give to the chief and his wife?

    A The granting of eternal life

    B A feather for their son's protection

    C The promise that they will have another son

    D A beautiful bird

_____ 4. Why does the birth of Kukul make Chirumá unhappy?

    F Chirumá has no son of his own.

    G Chirumá's brother no longer spends time with him.

    H Chirumá fears that Kukul's life will be filled with suffering.

    J Chirumá knows that Kukul will become the next chief.

_____ 5. During the battle with the nomadic tribe, Kukul —

    A kills all the enemy soldiers

    B stays with the wounded to avoid getting injured himself

    C destroys the nomads' weapons

    D saves his uncle's life

_____ **6.** After his brother's death, Chirumá tries to convince the youngest priest that Kukul is —

    F cowardly

    G compassionate

    H experienced

    J untruthful

_____ **7.** What kind of ruler does Kukul become?

    A One who brings peace and prosperity to the land

    B One who conquers many enemies

    C One who establishes schools for the study of the stars

    D One who devotes himself to amusements, such as hunting

_____ **8.** The hummingbird warns Kukul that —

    F his uncle dislikes him

    G his father will return from the dead

    H the priests have put a curse on him

    J a man will try to kill him

_____ **9.** Why is Kukul able to be killed at the end of the tale?

    A Chirumá had killed the hummingbird, which was Kukul's guardian.

    B Chirumá had stolen the charm that had protected Kukul.

    C Chirumá's magical powers are greater than Kukul's.

    D Chirumá kills Kukul with a charmed arrow taken from the gods.

_____ **10.** In Mayan culture, the beautiful bird with the scarlet chest is a symbol of —

    F youth

    G heroism

    H freedom

    J tragedy

LITERARY FOCUS (20 points; 5 points each)

On the line provided, write the letter of the *best* answer to each of the following items.

_____ **11.** "The Hummingbird King" is an origin story because it —

    A explains the political system of an ancient culture

    B describes how the quetzal bird came to be

    C tells about the birth of a future king

    D shows the reason for a character's jealousy

_____ **12.** What metamorphosis does the main character undergo in this tale?

    F He loses his magical powers.

    G He begins as an underdog and ends up a hero.

    H He turns into a bird.

    J He is appointed chief of a great city.

_____ **13.** The main conflict in this tale takes place between —

    A Chirumá and the priests

    B Kukul and Chirumá

    C Kukul's people and a nomadic tribe

    D Chirumá and the people he rules

_____ **14.** The character of Chirumá can *best* be described as —

    F ambitious and scheming

    G lucky and stubborn

    H weak and thoughtless

    J unconquerable and courageous

Constructed Response *(20 points)*

15. In the folk tale, Kukul is first presented as a superhero. Think of another story besides "The Hummingbird King" that features a character who is a superhero. What similarities and differences do you see between that story and "The Hummingbird King"? On a separate sheet of paper, write a paragraph that explains your answer. Support your ideas with details from the folk tale.

Holt Assessment: Literature, Reading, and Vocabulary

SELECTION TEST **Student Edition page 739**

INFORMATIONAL
READING

The Search Goes On

Carolyn Meyer *and* Charles Gallenkamp

COMPREHENSION *(50 points; 10 points each)*

On the line provided, write the letter of the *best* answer to each of the following items.

_____ **1.** Thieves used all of the following methods to loot the Mayan pyramids *except* —

    A digging trenches around the pyramids

    B tunneling into the pyramids

    C splitting the pyramids open

    D setting fire to the pyramids

_____ **2.** Looting results in tragic consequences because —

    F thieves often get killed when trying to retrieve treasures

    G objects are often destroyed or damaged before they can be sold

    H archaeologists cannot gain information by studying objects if they have been stolen

    J it damages the environment

_____ **3.** What motivates thieves to loot new sites?

    A They want to be seen as heroes.

    B They know people will pay high prices for ancient objects.

    C They believe beautiful objects should not be hidden from sight.

    D They want to decorate their homes with valuable objects.

_____ **4.** At E. W. Adams's urging, Congress passed a law —

    F preventing people from bringing national treasures looted from other countries into the United States

    G allowing the United States to keep certain lost or stolen ancient objects

    H pardoning those who have looted ancient sites in the past

    J preventing archaeologists from further disturbing Mayan pyramids

_____ **5.** Which of the following sentences *best* summarizes the last paragraph?

    A The tomb, which dates from the Classic period, most likely contains the body of a ruler's relative.

    B E. W. Adams was astonished to find that the tomb still existed.

    C The Mayan people often buried relatives near one another.

    D Pyramids are far more likely to be looted than small tombs.

VOCABULARY DEVELOPMENT *(50 points; 10 points each)*

On the line before each sentence, write the Vocabulary word that has a similar meaning to the italicized word or phrase in the sentence.

decipher	ransacked	artifacts	connoisseurs	unscrupulous

_____ **6.** The *dishonest* thieves stole valuable pottery from the tombs.

_____ **7.** When thieves *thoroughly searched* the tombs, there were no guards to prevent the looting.

_____ **8.** In the tomb the skeleton of the nobleman was surrounded by *man-made objects*.

_____ **9.** The collections of *experts* sometimes contain objects stolen from ancient sites.

_____ **10.** It can be difficult for archaeologists to *interpret* the writing of ancient cultures.

Holt Assessment: Literature, Reading, and Vocabulary

Our Literary Heritage: Greek Myths and World Folk Tales

This test asks you to use the skills and strategies you have learned in this collection. Read "The Frogs Who Wished for a King," and then answer the questions that follow it.

The Frogs Who Wished for a King
by Aesop

The Frogs were tired of governing themselves. They had so much freedom that it had spoiled them, and they did nothing but sit around croaking in a bored manner and wishing for a government that could entertain them with the <u>pomp</u> and display of royalty and rule them in a way to make them know they were being ruled. No milk-and-water government for them, they declared. So they sent a <u>petition</u> to Jupiter asking for a king.

Jupiter saw what simple and foolish creatures they were, but to keep them quiet and make them think they had a king, he threw down a huge log, which fell into the water with a great splash. The Frogs hid themselves among the reeds and grasses, thinking the new king to be some fearful giant. But they soon discovered how tame and peaceable King Log was. In a short time the younger Frogs were using him for a diving platform, while the older Frogs made him a meeting place, where they complained loudly to Jupiter about the government.

To teach the Frogs a lesson, the ruler of the gods now sent a Crane to be king of Frogland. The Crane proved to be a very different sort of king from old King Log. He gobbled up the poor Frogs right and left and they soon saw what fools they had been. In <u>mournful</u> croaks they begged Jupiter to take away the cruel <u>tyrant</u> before they should all be destroyed.

"How now!" cried Jupiter. "Are you not yet content? You have what you asked for, and so you have only yourselves to blame for your <u>misfortunes</u>."

Be sure you can better your condition before you seek to change.

VOCABULARY DEVELOPMENT *(25 points; 5 points each)*

Each of the underlined words below has also been underlined in the selection. Re-read those passages in which the underlined words appear, and then use context clues and your prior knowledge to help you select an answer. On the line provided, write the letter of the word or words that *best* complete each sentence.

_____ **1.** If an occasion calls for <u>pomp</u>, then it is a(n) _____ event.

    A dull

    B formal

    C unimportant

    D comical

_____ **2.** If a number of people sign a petition, they are _____.

    F signing a contract

    G paying someone money

    H sending greetings to someone

    J making a written request

_____ **3.** When he sang the mournful song, the audience felt _____.

    A sad

    B cheerful

    C soothed

    D encouraged

_____ **4.** Because he was a tyrant, his treatment of the people in his kingdom was always _____.

    F thoughtful

    G good-natured

    H brutal

    J fair

_____ **5.** My friend's misfortunes in life included _____.

    A a happy family life

    B wise financial investments

    C good health

    D an inability to hold a job

COMPREHENSION *(25 points; 5 points each)*

On the line provided, write the letter of the *best* answer to each of the following items.

_____ **6.** The Frogs want a government that provides —

    F opportunities for becoming wealthy

    G fewer restrictions on their activities

    H a ruler who will keep them in line

    J an equal balance of power between Jupiter and themselves

_____ **7.** How does Jupiter first respond to the Frogs' request for a king?

    A He ignores the Frogs' demand.

    B He throws a log down to Frogland.

    C He decides to govern the Frogs himself.

    D He tells the Frogs that they should rule themselves.

_____ **8.** Jupiter views the Frogs as —

    F unwise

    G dangerous

    H tricky

    J indecisive

_____ **9.** The Frogs are dissatisfied with King Log because he —

    A is not a frog

    B scares them

    C socializes with the younger Frogs

    D does not take action

_____ **10.** Why doesn't Jupiter honor the Frogs' request to remove the Crane as king of Frogland?

    F He does not believe the Frogs' lives are at risk.

    G The king has become more powerful than Jupiter.

    H He wants the Frogs to understand the consequences of their actions.

    J Being a god, he refuses to listen to the Frogs.

READING SKILLS AND STRATEGIES: CONSTRUCTED RESPONSE *(30 points; 15 points each)*
Summarizing

11. In your own words, summarize what happens after the Frogs ask Jupiter to appoint a king.

_____

_____

_____

_____

_____

_____

_____

Understanding Cause and Effect

12. What causes Jupiter to send the Crane to the Frogs? What are two effects of Jupiter's action?

_____

_____

_____

_____

_____

LITERARY FOCUS: CONSTRUCTED RESPONSE (20 points)

13. Explain the moral of "The Frogs Who Wished for a King." What lesson do you think Aesop is trying to teach by describing the Frogs' experiences? Do you think this moral can be applied to life today? Write a paragraph that explains your answer. Support your ideas with details from the fable.

_____

_____

_____

_____

_____

_____

_____

_____

COLLECTION 7 DIAGNOSTIC TEST ███████

Literary Criticism: Where I Stand

On the line provided, write the letter of the *best* answer to each of the following items.
(100 points; 10 points each)

_____ **1.** You should consider a story's **theme** to decide if —

    A the story says something meaningful to you

    B you like the author's writing style

    C the characters seem true to life

    D the plot is clear and logical

_____ **2.** When you analyze a **poem**, it is *most* helpful to consider all of the following items *except* —

    F tone

    G imagery

    H the author's popularity

    J rhythm and rhyme

_____ **3.** All of the following elements help make a work of **nonfiction** successful *except* —

    A a logical pattern of organization

    B a clear purpose

    C minimal evidence

    D accurate information

_____ **4.** In a response to a **story**, it is *most* important to include —

    F details from the text to support each main idea

    G a retelling of the plot

    H a variety of topics

    J a description of all the characters

_____ **5.** What is a **legend**?

    A A tale in which the main characters are usually animals

    B A very old story that combines historical facts and fictional events

    C An explanation, particular to a culture, of how the universe was created

    D The true life story of a famous person

_____ **6.** In ancient stories, when a hero goes on a **quest**, he —

  F faces a life-or-death struggle to overcome a powerful enemy

  G is lost and must find a way to return home

  H undertakes a long journey in search of something of great value

  J must pass a test to prove that he should be king

_____ **7.** What is a **stereotype**?

  A A broad statement based on facts

  B An unfair, fixed idea about a group of people

  C An educated guess based on prior knowledge

  D An opinion that is generally accepted as valid

_____ **8.** If an author reveals a **bias** in an article, he or she is presenting a(n) —

  F little-known truth

  G reason for a conclusion

  H opposing view

  J one-sided treatment of an issue

_____ **9.** Which of the following items is a common **suffix**?

  A _sub–_

  B _–spec–_

  C _mis–_

  D _–tion_

_____ **10.** To find out the **origin** of a word, you should —

  F check the footnotes in a dictionary

  G read the information in brackets in a dictionary entry

  H look in the glossary at the back of a thesaurus

  J look up the word _derivation_ in an encyclopedia

Holt Assessment: Literature, Reading, and Vocabulary

SELECTION TEST *Student Edition page 792*

King Arthur: The Sword in the Stone Hudson Talbott

COMPREHENSION *(40 points; 4 points each)*

On the line provided, write the letter of the *best* answer to each of the following items.

_____ **1.** Arthur's birth is marked by the appearance of —

    A a traitor

    B a great dragon formed by the stars

    C beautiful music

    D a small crown formed by the stars

_____ **2.** You can infer that Uther was —

    F a weak but well-meaning ruler

    G controlled by Merlin and his magic

    H a powerful and effective king

    J friends with everyone

_____ **3.** Merlin created the magical sword and stone to —

    A prove that Arthur is the rightful King of England

    B trick the archbishop

    C create a special Christmas celebration

    D create support for himself and the archbishop as co-rulers

_____ **4.** Sir Kay wishes to become —

    F Arthur's prime minister and chief advisor

    G archbishop of England

    H King of England

    J a famous magician

_____ **5.** You can infer from story clues that Sir Ector is —

    A young and hot-blooded

    B determined to be king himself

    C willing to stop at nothing to help his son achieve his ambitions

    D an honest, honorable man

_____ **6.** Why is it ironic that Arthur says to the sword, "Thank you, sword, for saving me"?

    F Ironically, the sword has not saved him.

    G Ironically, Sir Kay wants the sword.

    H Ironically, the sword kills Arthur.

    J Ironically, the sword saves Arthur in more than one way.

_____ **7.** When he gets the sword, Sir Kay attempts to —

    A put the sword back

    B pretend that he took it from the stone and is thus the rightful King of England

    C hide the sword until later

    D save his brother Arthur from getting in trouble

_____ **8.** According to Merlin, Arthur's glorious destiny is —

    F weakened by tragedy

    G determined by others

    H unclear

    J in his own hands

_____ **9.** Arthur's speech at his coronation demonstrates that he is —

    A unfit to be king

    B too young to assume the throne

    C depending on the public to lead

    D a true leader

_____ **10.** This story is classified as a legend because of all of the following _except_ —

    F it is based on historical truth

    G it does not include true heroes

    H it contains fantastic events

    J it has been passed down through the ages

LITERARY FOCUS _(20 points; 5 points each)_

On the line provided, write the letter of the _best_ answer to each of the following items.

_____ **11.** Arthur can be described by all of the following character traits _except_ —

    A sneaky

    B intelligent

    C modest

    D loyal

_____ **12.** You can predict that Arthur's life will one day become a legend because of his —

    F bravery at the tournament

    G happiness at becoming king

    H success at pulling the sword from the stone

    J speech at the coronation

_____ **13.** What motivates Merlin to help Arthur assume the throne?

    A Merlin secretly wants the throne for himself.

    B Merlin plans to rule with Arthur.

    C Arthur and Merlin are related to each other.

    D Merlin wants a true and strong ruler—Arthur—to unite England.

_____ **14.** What plot event made this legend especially interesting?

    F The bloody tournament created drama.

    G The contest with the sword and stone created suspense.

    H Sir Kay's character created conflict.

    J Arthur's birth created happiness.

VOCABULARY DEVELOPMENT *(20 points; 4 points each)*

On the line provided, write a synonym or antonym for each Vocabulary word, as directed.

15. *turbulent*   synonym   _____

16. *integrity*   antonym   _____

17. *congregation*   synonym   _____

18. *tournament*   synonym   _____

19. *turbulent*   antonym   _____

CONSTRUCTED RESPONSE *(20 points)*

20. What is the theme of this legend? How did the theme help you appreciate the legend? On a separate sheet of paper, write a paragraph that explains your answer. Support your ideas with details from the story.

Three Responses to Literature

COMPREHENSION *(60 points; 6 points each)*

On the line provided, write the letter of the *best* answer to each of the following items.

_____ **1.** The introduction to Essay 1 contains —

    A an example

    B a question

    C the name of the author who wrote the work

    D the title of the work being discussed

_____ **2.** According to Essay 1, Sir Kay is —

    F persistent

    G a moody character

    H a typical boy

    J wise beyond his years

_____ **3.** Which of the following qualities is *not* attributed to Arthur in Essay 1?

    A Courage

    B Consideration of others

    C Disloyalty

    D Insight

_____ **4.** According to Essay 2, Arthur would rather not be a king, but instead would prefer to —

    F get an education

    G spend time with his family and animals

    H act as an advisor to the king

    J travel around the world

_____ **5.** Which sentence from Essay 2 cannot be proved?

    A "First, Arthur is kind."

    B "Second, Arthur is honest."

    C "A great person cannot ever give up."

    D "Fourth, Arthur is courageous."

Holt Assessment: Literature, Reading, and Vocabulary

_____ **6.** The writer of Essay 2 uses the transitions "first," "second," "third," and "fourth" to —

    F draw conclusions

    G organize ideas

    H prove points

    J introduce specific examples

_____ **7.** Essay 3 mainly describes —

    A Arthur's character

    B Arthur's role in the legend of the sword and the stone

    C Sir Kay's relationship with Arthur

    D Arthur's family history

_____ **8.** Essay 3 can *best* be described as a(n) —

    F argument

    G paraphrase

    H retelling

    J outline

_____ **9.** How are all three essays similar?

    A They all contain quotations.

    B They all discuss Merlin's role in the story.

    C They all criticize Arthur.

    D They all explore the same topic.

_____ **10.** How do all three essays differ?

    F Unlike the other two essays, Essay 1 uses comparison and contrast to answer the question.

    G Each essay does not refer to Arthur's destiny.

    H Each essay does not discuss the taking of the sword.

    J Each writer does not show a real familiarity with the story.

LITERARY FOCUS (20 points; 5 points each)

On the line provided, write the letter of the *best* answer to each of the following items.

_____ **11.** An effective literary response fulfills all of the following requirements *except* —

    A answering the question

    B using specific details from the text to support points

    C always focusing on a character

    D always sticking to the topic

Three Responses to Literature

_____ **12.** Essay 1 is well written because it —

    F answers the question indirectly

    G clearly states the main ideas

    H is loosely organized

    J contains long sentences

_____ **13.** Which of the following criticisms of Essay 2 is valid?

    A It has many errors in grammar, usage, and spelling.

    B It is not well organized.

    C It does not contain enough textual support.

    D It is not focused.

_____ **14.** Why is the third essay the least successful of all?

    F It provides plot summary rather than literary analysis.

    G It contains details that are concrete.

    H It is too brief.

    J It offers too many examples.

CONSTRUCTED RESPONSE *(20 points)*

15. Choose two criteria for a good essay, and explain why you think they make an essay successful. On a separate sheet of paper, write a paragraph that explains your answer. Support your ideas with details from Essay 1, Essay 2, or Essay 3.

He's No King

COMPREHENSION *(100 points; 10 points each)*

On the line provided, write the letter of the *best* answer to each of the following items.

_____ **1.** This speech is told from the —

   A third-person point of view

   B first-person point of view

   C omniscient point of view

   D third-person-limited point of view

_____ **2.** Whom are the speakers addressing?

   F Themselves

   G People in the kingdom

   H Arthur only

   J Merlin only

_____ **3.** In the second paragraph, the speakers express a bias against —

   A outsiders

   B horses

   C people who fight with their hands

   D people who refuse to wear helmets

_____ **4.** In the third paragraph, the speakers express a bias against people who are —

   F comfortable in big cities

   G physically strong

   H hot-tempered

   J little known

_____ **5.** In the fourth paragraph, the speakers —

   A portray Arthur as shrewd and conniving

   B set up Merlin as the villain

   C claim that Arthur is selfish

   D call Merlin "a puppet on a string"

_____ **6.** In paragraph 5, the speakers refer to the stereotype that —

   F physically strong people are not intelligent

   G only physically strong people can be rulers

   H all children are weak

   J appointed rulers are corrupt and untrustworthy

_____ **7.** The tone of this speech can *best* be described as —

    A calm

    B neutral

    C fiery

    D reasoned and rational

_____ **8.** This speech is *best* described as —

    F supporting Arthur

    G objective in tone

    H supporting fair play

    J highly subjective in tone

_____ **9.** The speakers' purpose is to —

    A entertain their audience

    B persuade their audience

    C educate their audience

    D tell their audience a story

_____ **10.** In their conclusion, the speakers call for another contest to —

    F try to discredit Arthur

    G try to support Arthur

    H show that Merlin has used his enchantment

    J prove that the speakers would not be good kings

SELECTION TEST *Student Edition page 820*   **LITERARY RESPONSE**
AND ANALYSIS

Merlin and the Dragons Jane Yolen

COMPREHENSION *(40 points; 4 points each)*
On the line provided, write the letter of the *best* answer to each of the following items.

_____ **1.** Arthur feels that the crown is too heavy. This feeling symbolizes —

    A the weight of old-fashioned crowns

    B his very small size

    C his uneasiness with being king

    D why kings should always keep their crowns on

_____ **2.** What can you infer about Arthur's joy at being told a story?

    F He gets bored easily.

    G He wants to be a writer.

    H He is still very much a boy.

    J He likes stories more than poems.

_____ **3.** The story Merlin tells Arthur takes place in the —

    A present, in England

    B past, in Wales

    C future, in Wales

    D past, in a make-believe land

_____ **4.** Emrys's dreams and abilities suggest that —

    F all people from Wales have special powers

    G he is a powerful magician

    H he comes from a family of magicians

    J heroes always have magical powers

_____ **5.** Vortigern functions as the story's —

    A narrator

    B storyteller

    C hero

    D villain

_____ **6.** The High King's tower keeps falling down because of —

    F poor workmanship

    G deliberate sabotage

    H shoddy materials

    J dragons hatching underground

_____ **7.** As the men dig under the tower, they discover that —

    A Emrys is telling the truth

    B Emrys is lying

    C the dragons are dead

    D Vortigern is really a dragon

_____ **8.** You can infer that the dragon battle symbolizes —

    F the battle between good and evil

    G the future of King Arthur

    H the end of the British Empire

    J nature's distrust of human-made structures

_____ **9.** Merlin would most likely agree with the slogan —

    A "trust yourself"

    B "might makes right"

    C "revenge is sweet"

    D "only the good die young"

_____ **10.** The dragon tooth proves that —

    F dragons have fierce yellow teeth

    G Vortigern was defeated

    H dragons still exist

    J Merlin was Emrys

LITERARY FOCUS (20 points; 5 points each)

On the line provided, write the letter of the *best* answer to each of the following items.

_____ **11.** Emrys is heroic because he —

    A has special powers

    B is lucky

    C withstands peer pressure

    D stands up to Vortigern

_____ **12.** Both Arthur and Emrys are —

    F of royal blood

    G young, alone, and powerful

    H from Wales

    J fierce warriors

Holt Assessment: Literature, Reading, and Vocabulary

_____ **13.** The plot is *best* described as —

    A exciting

    B dull

    C plodding

    D predictable

_____ **14.** The storyteller keeps your interest by providing all of the following *except* —

    F a surprise plot twist at the end

    G rhythm and rhyme

    H interesting characters

    J fast-paced action

VOCABULARY DEVELOPMENT *(20 points; 4 points each)*

Match the definition on the right with the Vocabulary word on the left. Write the letter of the definition on the line provided. You will use one Vocabulary word twice.

_____ **15.** ruthless   **a.** knowing again

_____ **16.** bedraggled   **b.** without pity

_____ **17.** insolence   **c.** dirty

_____ **18.** recognition   **d.** hanging limp and wet

_____ **19.** bedraggled   **e.** disrespect

CONSTRUCTED RESPONSE *(20 points)*

20. What function does the frame story serve in "Merlin and the Dragons"?
On a separate sheet of paper, write a paragraph that explains your answer.
Support your ideas with details from the story.

SELECTION TEST *Student Edition page 833*

LITERARY RESPONSE
AND ANALYSIS

Sir Gawain and the Loathly Lady *retold by* Betsy Hearne

COMPREHENSION *(40 points; 4 points each)*

On the line provided, write the letter of the *best* answer to each of the following items.

_____ **1.** While hunting, Arthur is astonished when —

   A Sir Gromer tries to kill him

   B he is attacked in the forest

   C his shot misses the deer

   D he kills a deer and a strange knight appears

_____ **2.** Arthur's belief that it is shameful to kill an unarmed man shows —

   F why he is not strong enough to be King of England

   G his trickery

   H his cowardice

   J his values and strict code of behavior

_____ **3.** The characters speak in a formal style with old-fashioned words to —

   A make the legend more complex

   B make the characters sound intelligent

   C capture the flavor of the times

   D show what knights were really like

_____ **4.** What quest does Sir Gawain undertake?

   F To find the answer to the riddle

   G To find the mysterious knight

   H To find the loathly lady

   J To get married within the year

_____ **5.** Dame Ragnell is called the "loathly lady" because —

   A she is related to a horrible knight

   B she is terribly ugly

   C that is her family's name

   D all women were called that in medieval times

_____ **6.** Dame Ragnell promises to answer the riddle if —

   F Sir Gawain will kiss her

   G King Arthur will marry her

   H Sir Gawain will marry her

   J she is made Queen of England

_____ **7.** What is the answer to the riddle?

    A Every woman wants a knight in shining armor.

    B Every woman wants to be beautiful.

    C Every woman wants to get married.

    D Every woman desires to rule over men.

_____ **8.** Near the end of the story, readers learn that Sir Gromer is really —

    F Dame Ragnell's father

    G Dame Ragnell's brother

    H an evil sorcerer

    J a knight of the Round Table

_____ **9.** What choice does Dame Ragnell give Sir Gawain?

    A She will reveal the truth about her family if he will leave King Arthur.

    B She will be beautiful or charming, but not both.

    C She will be beautiful by day and ugly by night, or vice versa.

    D She will be young or old.

_____ **10.** What is Sir Gawain's response?

    F He leaves the decision up to her.

    G He asks King Arthur for advice.

    H He throws up his hands and leaves her in a fury.

    J He tells her he wants everything or nothing.

LITERARY FOCUS *(20 points; 5 points each)*

On the line provided, write the letter of the *best* answer to each of the following items.

_____ **11.** The author creates suspense in the plot through —

    A the riddle

    B dialogue

    C the setting

    D figurative language

_____ **12.** Sir Gawain emerges as —

    F dense but handsome

    G heroic but cruel

    H loyal and brave

    J brave but foolish

Sir Gawain and the Loathly Lady

_____ **13.** What moral does Dame Ragnell illustrate?

    A People are all beautiful inside.

    B Women want power and control.

    C Each person is beautiful in his or her own way.

    D We can't always get what we want.

_____ **14.** Dame Ragnell's character is revealed in all of the following ways *except* —

    F through her actions

    G through her dialogue

    H through the speech and reactions of others

    J by the setting

VOCABULARY DEVELOPMENT *(20 points; 4 points each)*

On the line provided, write a synonym or antonym for each Vocabulary word, as directed.

15. *chivalry*   synonym   _____

16. *loathsome*   antonym   _____

17. *loathsome*   synonym   _____

18. *countenance*   synonym   _____

19. *sovereignty*   antonym   _____

CONSTRUCTED RESPONSE *(20 points)*

20. Select one of the following characters from "Sir Gawain and the Loathly Lady," and explain how the author makes him or her appealing: King Arthur, Sir Gawain, Dame Ragnell. On a separate piece of paper, write a paragraph that explains your answer. Support your ideas with details from the story.

COLLECTION 7 SUMMATIVE TEST

Literary Criticism: Where I Stand

This test asks you to use the skills and strategies you have learned in this collection. Read this passage from *River Notes,* and then answer the questions that follow it.

from River Notes
by Barry Holstun Lopez

A storm came this year, against which all other storms were to be measured, on a Saturday in October, a balmy afternoon. Men in the woods cutting firewood for winter, and children outside with melancholy thoughts lodged somewhere in the memory of summer. It built as it came up the valley as did every fall storm, but the steel-gray thunderheads, the first sign of it anyone saw, were higher, much higher, too high. In the stillness before it hit, men looked at each other as though a fast and wiry man had pulled a knife in a bar. They felt the trees falling before they heard the wind, and they dropped tools and scrambled to get out. The wind came up suddenly and like a scythe, like piranha after them, like seawater through a breach in a dike. The first blow bent trees half to the ground, the second caught them and snapped them like kindling, sending limbs raining down and twenty-foot splinters hurtling through the air like mortar shells to stick quivering in the ground. Bawling cattle running the fences, a loose lawnmower bumping across a lawn, a stray dog lunging for a child racing by. The big trees went down screaming, ripping open holes in the wind that were filled with the broken-china explosion of a house and the yawing screech of a pickup rubbed across asphalt, the rivet popping and twang of phone and electric wires.

It was over in three or four minutes. The eerie, sucking silence it left behind seemed palpably evil, something that would get into the standing timber, like insects, a memory.

No one was killed. Roads were cut off, a bridge buckled. No power. A few had to walk in from places far off in the steep wooded country, arriving home later than they'd ever been up. Some said it pulled the community together, others how they hated living in the trees with no light. No warning. The next day it rained and the woods smelled like ashes. It was four or five days before they got the roads opened and the phones working, electricity back. Three sent down to the hospital in Holterville. Among the dead, Cawley Besson's dog. And two deer, butchered and passed quietly in parts among neighbors.

Of the trees that fell into the river, a number came up like beached whales among willows at the tip of an island.

From "The Log Jam" from *River Notes: The Dance of the Herons* by Barry Holstun Lopez. Copyright © 1976 by Barry Holstun Lopez. All rights reserved. Reproduced by permission of **Sterling Lord Literistic, Inc.**

VOCABULARY SKILLS *(30 points; 6 points each)*

Each of the underlined words below has also been underlined in the selection. Re-read those passages in which the underlined words appear, and then use context clues and your prior knowledge to help you select an answer. On the line provided, write the letter of the word or words that *best* complete each sentence.

_____ **1.** When people are <u>melancholy</u>, they are _____.

    A sad

    B furious

    C cruel

    D proud

_____ **2.** A <u>breach</u> in a dam is a _____.

    F bridge

    G stone

    H window

    J gap

_____ **3.** If trees snap like <u>kindling</u>, they are breaking _____.

    A slowly

    B with difficulty

    C easily

    D into parts of equal size

_____ **4.** When an animal is <u>lunging</u>, it is _____.

    F panting

    G rushing forward

    H swimming upstream

    J howling

_____ **5.** When something seems <u>palpably</u> evil, it can almost be _____.

    A tasted

    B felt

    C smelled

    D erased

COMPREHENSION *(30 points; 6 points each)*
On the line provided, write the letter of the *best* answer to each of the following items.

_____ **6.** Before the storm, people are —

    F going into town to attend a festival

    G going about their everyday activities

    H buying supplies in preparation for the storm

    J preparing breakfast and going to work

_____ **7.** The part of the storm that causes the most damage is the —

    A wind

    B rain

    C lightning

    D hail

_____ **8.** The adjective that *best* describes the trees during the storm is —

    F sheltering

    G indestructible

    H strong

    J helpless

_____ **9.** The storm was unusually frightening because —

    A many people died

    B it lasted for hours

    C it was unexpected

    D people had no electricity

_____ **10.** After the storm, people on the mountain —

    F make their houses stronger by adding shutters

    G move out of the woods into the city

    H see both good and bad aspects of the storm

    J write books and movies about the storm

LITERARY FOCUS: CONSTRUCTED RESPONSE *(40 points)*

11. When you read nonfiction, you evaluate the work by examining the writer's objectivity. You also talk about the writer's use of primary sources to see if the sources are historically accurate. Evaluate *River Notes* by completing the following chart.

Criteria	Method of Evaluating	Proof
Objectivity	_____ _____	_____ _____ _____ _____
Primary sources	_____ _____	_____ _____ _____ _____

Holt Assessment: Literature, Reading, and Vocabulary

Reading for Life

On the line provided, write the letter of the *best* answer to each of the following items.
(100 points; 10 points each)

_____ **1.** A **consumer** is a person who —

    A uses a great quantity of something

    B sells products for a living

    C does not grow his or her own food

    D buys what someone else sells

_____ **2.** People read **advertisements** to —

    F learn where to buy a product and how much it costs

    G expand their knowledge of a subject

    H find out how to complete a task

    J understand their rights and responsibilities

_____ **3.** If you want to know what a product is made of, you should read —

    A a work permit

    B the label

    C the contract

    D a guidebook

_____ **4.** Once you have purchased a new mechanical device, you should —

    F skim the product information for the main idea

    G read the instruction manual carefully

    H use your prior knowledge to operate the item

    J compare and contrast the item with similar ones

_____ **5.** What is a **warranty**?

    A An outdated or inferior item

    B A document explaining a company's policy for repairing an item

    C The person or company that makes an item

    D The location where an item is produced

_____ **6.** A **business letter** would *most likely* contain —

    F news from your former neighbor who is employed by a company in France

    G information from a bank about your new checking account

    H a description from a classmate of his baby-sitting job

    J an update from your older sister about her career plans

_____ **7.** When you are looking for a job, you may have to complete a(n) —

    A application

    B employee manual

    C public document

    D memo

_____ **8.** **Technical directions** would be *most* useful if you were —

    F traveling by train to visit a friend

    G reading a difficult book

    H setting up a new computer

    J taking a dance class

_____ **9.** If you wanted to use the Internet to find out where to bike in your new hometown of Austin, Texas, which **key words** would be the *most* useful?

    A biking new Austin

    B biking and street safety

    C biking sports Texas

    D bike paths Austin Texas

_____ **10.** If you were searching an airline's Web site to find out how many bags you can bring on a plane, which **link** would be the *most* useful?

    F Arrivals and Departures

    G Travel Insurance

    H Special Offers

    J Travel Information

Holt Assessment: Literature, Reading, and Vocabulary

SELECTION TEST *Student Edition page 888*

Analyzing Information in Public Documents

COMPREHENSION *(100 points; 10 points each)*

On the line provided, write the letter of the *best* answer to each of the following items.

_____ **1.** A "Casting Call" is an announcement for —

    A actors

    B dog trainers

    C senior citizens

    D bike manufacturers

_____ **2.** People who want this job must be all of the following *except* —

    F skilled at riding a BMX-type bike

    G owners of a BMX-type bike

    H professional stunt riders

    J between the ages of twelve and fifteen

_____ **3.** Why did Sam want more information about the casting call?

    A She knew the casting call was fake.

    B She wanted to share the information with her friends.

    C She wanted to make an informed decision.

    D She thought that some facts were missing.

_____ **4.** Sam found more information by —

    F conducting an Internet search

    G interviewing friends

    H watching television

    J going to the movies

_____ **5.** *Hollywood Beat* is a(n) —

    A interview

    B novel

    C private document

    D newsmagazine

_____ **6.** Sam learns that the StreetWheelie Productions movie —

    F will be filmed in London, England

    G is a new version of Tolkien's novel about hobbits

    H is a Batman movie

    J stars Mr. Rogers

Analyzing Information in Public Documents

_____ **7.** To get a work permit, Sam must first complete and file a(n) —

    A letter

    B application

    C novel

    D Internet search

_____ **8.** As she completes the work permit, Sam must supply all of the following information _except_ —

    F her name, address, and date of birth

    G her height and weight

    H health information

    J a photograph

_____ **9.** All of the following are public documents _except_ —

    A work permits

    B announcements

    C casting calls

    D short stories

_____ **10.** These are public documents because they —

    F describe a process

    G argue a point

    H provide information

    J tell a story

Analyzing Information in Workplace Documents

COMPREHENSION *(100 points; 10 points each)*

On the line provided, write the letter of the *best* answer to each of the following items.

_____ **1.** Workplace documents include all of the following *except* —

    A business letters

    B poems

    C memos

    D instructions

_____ **2.** StreetWheelie Productions sends Sam a business letter to —

    F get to know her a little better

    G describe her duties and responsibilities

    H discover what she likes to do in her spare time

    J persuade her to take the job with them

_____ **3.** A business letter is —

    A the same format as a friendly letter

    B less formal than a personal letter

    C more formal than a personal letter

    D usually handwritten

_____ **4.** According to the letter, Sam —

    F will be driven to the movie set by a driver from StreetWheelie Productions

    G must dye her hair bright lime green

    H must take care of her own makeup, costumes, and hair styling

    J cannot change her hair color

_____ **5.** To make sure that she fulfills her responsibilities, Sam is given —

    A a manager who goes everywhere with her

    B a stern lecture by the producer

    C her own e-mail account

    D workplace instructions

_____ **6.** Sam is *not* allowed to —

    F have a horse on the set

    G play electronic games with the sound on

    H read books while on the movie set

    J play electronic games with the sound off

_____ **7.** Sam learns that e-mail is important on the set because it —

    A helps her keep up with each day's schedule

    B helps her pass the time when she is not filming

    C lets her tell her parents when she is going to be late

    D gives her information about other casting calls

_____ **8.** You can infer that the movie producers communicate with e-mail for all of the following reasons *except* its —

    F speed

    G efficiency

    H low cost

    J possibility for misunderstanding

_____ **9.** How often does Sam receive e-mail from the production company?

    A Every few days

    B Once a day

    C At least twice a day

    D At least six to ten times a day

_____ **10.** Workplace documents help —

    F people pass stories down through the ages

    G workers express their feelings

    H businesses function well

    J bosses communicate with their families

SELECTION TEST   *Student Edition page 899*

Analyzing Information in Consumer Documents

COMPREHENSION *(100 points; 10 points each)*

On the line provided, write the letter of the *best* answer to each of the following items.

_____ **1.** Consumer documents help —

    A entertain people

    B workplaces function more efficiently

    C manufacturers sell goods and services

    D people purchase goods and services

_____ **2.** All consumer documents —

    F persuade or convince

    G explain or inform

    H tell a story

    J argue a point

_____ **3.** BART provides information about all of the following *except* —

    A rules for bringing bicycles aboard

    B hours of service

    C the company's founders

    D cost

_____ **4.** Before consumers read all the documents on a Web page, they should —

    F check the information against a print source

    G call the toll-free telephone help line

    H read the FAQs (frequently asked questions)

    J speak with people who have used the product

_____ **5.** How do the BART's bike restrictions affect Sam?

    A They do not affect her at all.

    B She must ride the BART before all the regular commuters ride.

    C She cannot bring her bike on the train.

    D She must pay 25% more for carrying her bike.

_____ **6.** From the ticket guide, Sam discovers that —

    F she can get a discount because she is under age twelve, but her grandfather must pay full fare

    G she and her grandfather can get discount fares

    H her grandfather can get a senior citizen discount, but she pays full fare

    J all the fares are the same, regardless of passenger age

Analyzing Information in Consumer Documents

253

_____ **7.** On the BART, children age four and under —

    A travel for free

    B travel for four dollars

    C travel for half price

    D pay the same as adults

_____ **8.** All of the following information is contained in the ticket guide *except* —

    F how tickets are sold

    G what tickets cost

    H what the tickets look like

    J how to buy weekly and monthly passes

_____ **9.** What consumer document does Sam need to figure out what time the trains run?

    A She needs a schedule.

    B She needs a system map.

    C She needs a ticket guide.

    D She needs an instruction manual.

_____ **10.** Consumer documents can be in all the following forms *except* —

    F maps

    G schedules

    H novels

    J guides

Following Technical Directions

COMPREHENSION *(100 points; 10 points each)*

On the line provided, write the letter of the *best* answer to each of the following items.

_____ **1.** Technical directions can be all of the following *except* —

    A workplace documents

    B fiction

    C public documents

    D consumer documents

_____ **2.** Technical directions provide information about a(n) —

    F place

    G person

    H event

    J process

_____ **3.** Why is it important to change a flat tire immediately?

    A Driving on a flat tire feels strange.

    B Driving on a flat tire looks funny.

    C Driving on a flat tire can damage the tire and your car.

    D Your car won't work at all if the tire is flat.

_____ **4.** The lug nuts —

    F are decorative but have no real function

    G hold the tailpipe on

    H hold the tire in place

    J help prevent a tire from getting a flat

_____ **5.** You can tell from the illustration that lug nuts —

    A are very large, about the size of apples

    B come in pairs

    C are very small, about the size of peas

    D are on top of the wheel cover

_____ **6.** What must you do *before* you loosen the lug nuts?

    F Always take off the flat tire

    G Remove the spare tire from the trunk

    H Replace the flat tire with the good tire

    J Lift the car with the jack

_____ **7.** What must you do *after* you remove the flat tire?

    A Jack up the car

    B Remove the wheel cover

    C Loosen the lug nuts

    D Replace it with the spare tire

_____ **8.** The last step in changing a flat tire is —

    F parking the car as far off the road as possible

    G removing the spare tire from the trunk

    H replacing all the tools in your trunk

    J loosening the lug nuts

_____ **9.** The illustrations are provided to —

    A make it easier for people to follow the directions

    B make the directions look nicer

    C take up space

    D make the directions look like a picture book

_____ **10.** You can infer from the way these directions are written that —

    F the order is somewhat flexible

    G you must follow the directions in the exact order

    H the order is very flexible

    J the order doesn't matter at all

COLLECTION 8 SUMMATIVE TEST

Reading for Life

This test asks you to use the skills and strategies you have learned in this collection. Read "Yosemite Safety," and then answer the questions that follow it.

Yosemite Safety

Backcountry hazards

The risks of wilderness travel or danger from accidents, wildlife, and natural phenomena must be accepted as part of the wilderness experience. Common sense and some knowledge of safe travel and camping techniques are required to protect yourself and others from harm. Be alert to the following situations:

Weather

Sudden changes in weather catch many unaware. Drenching thunderstorms can form in a matter of hours, and snow can fall at any time during the year. Be prepared for all weather conditions. Afternoon thunderstorms are a frequent and spectacular occurrence in the Yosemite wilderness. These summer storms often bring intense rain, hail, and lightning strikes, particularly in mid- to late afternoon. Plan to be over passes and away from high open areas by noon. During a storm, stay away from peaks (particularly Half Dome), ridges, caves, water, and open areas. Seek shelter in low forested areas, but avoid tall, <u>solitary</u> trees. By setting up camp in a safe location before lightning begins, you can enjoy the power and spectacle of a mountain thunderstorm without <u>apprehension</u>.

High water

During early spring and summer, run-off from melting snow can cause high water levels and swift currents in rivers and streams. Please remember that any unbridged stream crossing may be <u>hazardous</u>. Cross in a wide, shallow spot that is not above rapids or falls. Unbuckle waist straps, use a long stick for stability, and face upstream while crossing. **Don't** tie yourself in to "safety ropes"—they can drown you. Water will be extremely cold. Caution should be used to prevent conditions that may lead to hypothermia.[1]

---

1. hypothermia n.: body temperature that is below normal.

Tick-borne diseases

There are two known diseases carried by ticks in this area: Lyme disease and relapsing fever (borelliosis). Not all ticks carry these diseases. If you are bitten by a tick and later experience flu-like symptoms, contact your doctor and mention you had a tick bite. If you are diagnosed as having Lyme disease or relapsing fever, and you believe you got it in Yosemite, have your doctor contact the park sanitarian.

Giardia lamblia

Giardiasis is an intestinal disease caused by *Giardia lamblia*, a water-borne protozoan.[2] Giardia is carried by humans and some domestic and wild animals. Giardia may contaminate lakes and streams. All water or melted snow must be treated by boiling for at least five minutes, using an iodine-based purifier or using a Giardia-rated water filter. Associated symptoms include chronic diarrhea, abdominal cramps, bloating, fatigue, and loss of weight. Treatment by a physician is necessary to kill the organisms.

Safety Hints

- It is your responsibility to be aware of potential dangers and to take steps necessary to minimize the chance that you will become lost or injured.

- Let someone know your itinerary and instruct them to contact Park Service emergency personnel if you are overdue.

- Stay on the trail!!! In addition to causing severe erosion and damage to fragile habitat, hiking off–trail increases the potential for injury or becoming lost.

- When hiking with a group, keep track of each other, and wait at all trail junctions.

- Always carry extra food and water, rain gear, and warm clothing in case you have to spend the night out unexpectedly.

- If you become ill or injured on the trail and are unable to hike, send someone in your party or a passing hiker for help. Write down and give the messenger your exact location, age, gender, height, weight, and a description of your illness/injury in order to ensure the appropriate emergency response.

- If you become disoriented or lost, attempt to fix your location using a map, compass, and visible landmarks. If you are unable to locate the trail, stay put! Use a mirror or reflective object to signal for help. Any signal done three times in a series is a universal distress call.

---

2. protozoan n.: a single-celled, microscopic organism.

VOCABULARY SKILLS (25 points; 5 points each)
Each of the boldface words below has been underlined in the selection.
Re-read those passages in which the words appear, and then use context clues
and your own knowledge to help you select an answer. On the line provided,
write the word that *best* completes each sentence.

solitary	hazardous	disoriented
apprehension	itinerary	

1. After walking in circles for two hours, the hikers felt confused and _____.
They no longer knew where they were.

2. A sense of _____ overwhelmed them as they began to fear that they would
never find their way out of the woods.

3. If only they had let their friends know their _____, or plan for the path
they would take!

4. Up ahead of them was a bridge, but it was creaky and old and too _____
to cross.

5. What relief they felt when they saw a _____ sign standing in the woods.
"Home base—1/2 mile," it read.

COMPREHENSION (50 points; 5 points each)
On the line provided, write the letter of the *best* answer to each of the following items.

_____ **6.** The risks of wilderness travel include all of the following *except* —

    F danger from slipping in your bathtub

    G problems with wildlife attacks

    H danger from accidents

    J being hit by lightning

_____ **7.** You can help protect yourself from injury during a thunderstorm in Yosemite by —

    A traveling through high open areas in the late afternoon

    B setting up camp after the storm

    C seeking shelter under tall, solitary trees

    D being over passes and away from high open areas by lunchtime

Collection 8 Summative Test

_____ **8.** While you are crossing a stream, do all of the following *except* —

    F select a wide, shallow spot

    G tie yourself in to "safety ropes"

    H unbuckle your waist straps

    J use a long stick to help you keep your balance

_____ **9.** If you are bitten by a tick, you should —

    A call the park health official at once

    B immediately call your doctor

    C wait to see if you have flu-like symptoms before taking action

    D get hypothermia treatment

_____ **10.** Ticks —

    F all carry diseases

    G all carry Lyme disease

    H may or may not carry Lyme disease or relapsing fever

    J are not found at Yosemite

_____ **11.** Giardiasis is —

    A a mountain in Yosemite

    B a disease that causes problems in your stomach

    C found in food sources

    D something you can cure yourself

_____ **12.** *Giardia lamblia* is —

    F a serious illness

    G a rare animal found in Yosemite

    H an insect that stings

    J a protozoan found in water

_____ **13.** This document was written for —

    A visitors to Yosemite

    B weather forecasters

    C park rangers in Yosemite

    D people who want to buy land in the public park

_____ **14.** This document would be classified as a —

    F literary essay

    G short story

    H public document

    J workplace document

_____ **15.** This document is designed mainly to —

    A   help protect the creatures in Yosemite National Park

    B   help keep you safe when you travel through Yosemite National Park

    C   persuade people to visit Yosemite National Park

    D   describe the beauty of Yosemite National Park

INFORMATIONAL FOCUS: CONSTRUCTED RESPONSE *(25 points)*

16. Consumer, workplace, and public documents improve our lives by giving us the information we need. Complete the following chart to explain what type of information people get from "Yosemite Safety." Write the warning in the center column and the specific examples in the right-hand column.

Category	Warning	Safety Measures
Weather		
High water		
Tick-borne diseases		
Giardia lamblia		
Safety hints		

End-of-Year Test

Reading and Literary Analysis

DIRECTIONS: Read each selection. Then, read each question about the selection. Decide which is the best answer to the question. Mark the space for the answer you have chosen.

SAMPLE

American painter George Luks was born in 1867. He studied art in Philadelphia, Germany, London, and Paris. On returning to the United States in 1894, Luks took a job as an illustrator for the *Philadelphia Press.*

Later, Luks began to paint images of people—especially New Yorkers. He became a member of a group of painters called the Ashcan School. The unusual name of the group is based on their realistic paintings depicting city life.

A **George Luks painted portraits of —**

    A New Yorkers
    B Parisians
    C Germans
    D Englishmen

B **A painting by a member of the Ashcan School might show a —**

    F tall mountain
    G grazing cow
    H night sky
    J busy street

Reading and Literary Analysis

Something of Value

Mark Twain, one of the world's most famous humorists and writers, was born in Missouri in 1835 and named Samuel L. Clemens. Many of his books, such as The Adventures of Tom Sawyer *and* Life on the Mississippi, *are based on Clemens's own adventures. The following story describes one such experience.*

In 1864, Samuel Clemens traveled with his friend Jim Gillis to Angel's Camp, a California mining town, to pan for gold. While they were there, the weather was often rainy, so they spent much of their time at their hotel. They entertained themselves by sitting around a stove with a group of men, swapping tales. One slow-talking storyteller in the group was a former riverboat pilot named Ben Coon. One of Coon's stories involved a trained frog that competed in jumping contests. The tale amused Clemens, and he wrote some notes about it.

Later, the weather cleared, and Clemens and Gillis decided to look for gold on a hillside outside of town. They divided the task—Gillis scooped soil into a round pan and washed it, and Clemens brought him buckets of water.

After a while, Gillis began to spot flecks of gold in the pan. Filled with "gold rush fever," he became more and more excited as they climbed higher and higher up the hill. Then, gray clouds formed overhead, and a chill rain started to fall. Although the change of weather didn't disturb Gillis, Clemens grew colder and more uncomfortable with each passing moment. Finally, just as Gillis filled the pan with a promising scoop of soil, Clemens insisted that they leave the disagreeable task and return to the hotel. Gillis pleaded for one more bucket of water. Clemens refused. Gillis pleaded some more.

"Jim, I won't do it!," Clemens replied. "No, sir, not a drop, not if I knew there were a million dollars in that pan!"

Sighing, Gillis ripped a piece of paper out of his notebook and hastily wrote a note claiming the pan of dirt for himself should anyone find it. He placed the note by the pan, and the men left. As the day wore on, rain washed the soil out of the pan, revealing several glistening nuggets of gold.

Later, two Austrian gold hunters spotted the pan, the nuggets, and Gillis's claim. They sat down next to the pan and began to wait for the claim to run out. Thirty days later, when Gillis's claim ran out, the men became the rightful owners of the gold nuggets. They found even more gold in a nearby *vein*. The Austrians had struck it rich! They went home with about ten or twenty thousand dollars for their efforts.

Although Clemens and Gillis went home without a single nugget of gold, Clemens left with something even more valuable—his notes about the jumping frog. In November 1865, he published a story using his pen name, Mark Twain. The story, called "The Celebrated Jumping Frog of Calaveras County," was published in a New York periodical *The Saturday Press*. A huge hit, it was reprinted in newspapers around the country, and it brought Twain his first national fame.

---

1. **Gillis and Clemens went to Angel's Camp to —**

   A pan for gold
   B swap tales
   C see Ben Coon
   D write a book

2. **Clemens refused to bring Gillis any more water because —**

   F he didn't think that Gillis needed it
   G it was time to meet Ben Coon
   H it was time for dinner at the hotel
   J he was cold and wet

3. **The Austrians sat by the pan because they wanted to —**

   A rest during the storm
   B claim the gold nuggets
   C read Clemens's story
   D swap tales

4. **Clemens's point of view, as compared with that of Gillis, was that he —**

   F did not think the gold was worth much money
   G would rather haul water than pan for gold
   H valued money more than comfort
   J valued comfort more than money

GO ON

Reading and Literary Analysis

5. **As Clemens listened to stories being told at the hotel, he probably felt —**

   A entertained and inspired
   B anxious to search for gold
   C bored and restless
   D mildly interested

6. **What theme is present in this story?**

   F It pays to hold on to friendships.
   G Ideas can be more important than money.
   H Some amusing stories are untrue.
   J Efforts are always rewarded.

7. **Which statement is an *opinion*?**

   A Samuel Clemens used the pen name Mark Twain.
   B Mark Twain was born in Florida in 1835 as Samuel L. Clemens.
   C Clemens left Angel's Camp with something more valuable than gold.
   D Mark Twain's story was published in *The Saturday Press*.

8. **How did Gillis probably feel as he walked away from the pan of dirt on the hill?**

   F Relieved
   G Frustrated
   H Contented
   J Bored

9. **This story *best* reveals —**

   A Clemens's character traits
   B life as a miner
   C the history of Angel's Camp
   D the value of work

10. **In this story the word *vein* means a —**

    F blood vessel in the body
    G line of thought
    H part of the framework of a leaf
    J rich source or supply

GO ON

Reading and Literary Analysis

How Gold Rush Miners Found Gold

After the discovery of gold at Sutter's Mill in 1848, people swarmed to California to strike it rich. Within two years, more than 40,000 prospectors, called "forty-niners," had arrived there. Forty-niners used a variety of methods to comb rivers and riverbeds for nuggets of gold. In the following article you will learn about some of these methods.

Panning   Prospectors used a large tin or iron pan with slanted sides to wash gravel in water. They panned in streams, near sandbars, and along low-lying gravel banks. They stooped or squatted in freezing water, swirling and shaking the pan so that sand washed over the rim and gold flecks sank to the bottom.

Dry washing   Miners threw soil from dry streambeds onto a sheet and tossed the contents into the air. The lighter particles of *debris* blew away and gold flakes remained on the sheet.

Rocking   A rocker, or cradle, was an improvement over the pan. The rocker was a wooden box, open at one end, that was mounted on rockers. It resembled a baby's cradle. Miners shoveled gold-bearing gravel onto a metal sieve atop the box and poured in water while vigorously rocking the cradle. The tiny gold particles collected behind grooves (or riffles) at the bottom of the box.

Using toms   A tom was a long wooden box, from eight to twenty feet long, with riffles on the bottom and a metal screen on top. Miners would dump large amounts of dirt and gravel into the tom. Then they would pour water over the dirt and gravel, washing most of it away and leaving behind the gold. A tom used a huge amount of water, and two or three people were needed to manage one.

"Tricks of the Trade" by Leslie Anderson Morales from *Footsteps*, vol. 2, issue 1, January 2000, page 19. Copyright © 2000 by **Cobblestone Publishing Company,** 30 Grove Street, Suite C, Peterborough, NH 03458. All rights reserved. Reproduced by permission of the publisher.

Reading and Literary Analysis

Hydraulic mining In hydraulic mining, hillsides were blasted with thousands of gallons of water forced through large hoses. The water pressure blasted away tons of earth, which was then washed into sluices—troughs with ridges along the bottom to catch gold flakes.

River damming Miners diverted whole rivers with heavy timbers and boulders on the chance that gold could be found in the exposed riverbed.

11. **Prospectors used water as they panned for gold because —**

   A the water cleaned the gold
   B the water washed the sand out of the pan
   C gold is more easily spotted when it is damp
   D the gold would float

12. **After miners blocked whole rivers with dams, the miners —**

   F blasted the hillsides with water pressure
   G threw soil from the banks of the river onto sheets
   H used expensive equipment to find gold in the water
   J looked for gold in the exposed riverbed

13. Which of these techniques would a miner working alone *most* likely use?

A Rocking

B Using a tom

C River damming

D Hydraulic mining

14. In a rocker, the gold collects —

F on a sheet held in the air

G at the front of the box

H on heavy timbers or boulders

J behind grooves at the bottom of the box

15. The purpose of this article is to —

A persuade readers to look for gold

B explain techniques once used by miners

C entertain readers with a story about the gold rush

D describe how miners used a rocker

16. If you wanted to find out more information about rockers, which keyword would be *most* helpful?

F Rivers

G Mining

H Timbers

J Dams

17. The title of this article helps readers by —

A introducing a new vocabulary word

B providing details about the first paragraph

C telling what the article is mainly about

D using words from the article

18. In this article, the word *debris* means small pieces of —

F dirt

G gold

H wood

J boulders

GO ON

Reading and Literary Analysis

The Wooden Chest

Jacob took a deep breath and slowed his horse to a trot. To his left, he saw the hill where he and his brother, Tom, had played years ago. Ahead, he saw the creek where he once fished and swam. To his great relief, it seemed as if nothing in the lush North Carolina *landscape* had changed in two years.

Jacob, now fifteen, remembered that terrifying evening long ago when he and his family left this beautiful spot. The year had been 1864, and Jacob had felt that the world had been turned upside down. Friends were fighting friends, and families were torn apart by the Civil War. That night, Father had awakened Jacob from a deep sleep. Jacob fumbled to pull on his clothes and then sleepily climbed into the family's wagon. In an instant, his family was on the road.

In the days before Jacob's family left, they had heard rumors about soldiers sweeping the countryside, sometimes burning houses, sometimes taking prisoners. Jacob's family knew that they might have to flee from the violence.

To prepare for this possibility, Jacob had protected the thing he loved most— a small wooden chest given to him by his grandmother. Inside the chest were a letter from her and two gold coins, which Jacob planned to use to start his own farm someday. Jacob buried the chest under a huge oak tree two miles from his home.

Now, as he spotted the same oak tree in the distance, his heart began to pound. He had thought about this moment many times during the past two years. He had seen himself lifting the chest from the earth and slowly opening it. He prayed that the chest would still be there.

Jacob cried out when he saw a pile of dirt at the base of the tree. The chest had been discovered! Jacob leapt from his horse and knelt by the tree. He dug into the moist earth, searching in vain for his lost treasure.

Wiping tears from his eyes, Jacob mounted his horse and turned toward the farm. If the chest was gone, what had happened to his home? Jacob felt numb. The beautiful hills, tall trees, and even the songs of birds seemed far away.

A short while later, Jacob's horse crossed a small stream, and Jacob steadied himself in the saddle. He knew that he would be able to see his family's farm from the top of the next hill. At the crest of the hill, Jacob closed his eyes.

When he opened them, he gasped. Except for the weeds that had grown up in the garden, his house looked just as it had the day they had left. His father's chair sat on the front porch, and Tom's fishing pole stood next to the front door. Jacob almost expected his mother to wave at him from the window.

Jacob tied his horse to the fence and climbed the steps. He didn't give his lost chest a single thought as he opened the door and went inside.

---

19. **The author organized this story by —**

A listing a series of people and events

B presenting causes and effects

C comparing and contrasting the major events

D describing events in the order in which they happened

20. **Jacob's family left the farm because they —**

F wanted to move to a better place

G wanted to live with Jacob's grandmother

H had heard rumors that soldiers were coming

J had purchased another farm

21. **What did Jacob find under the oak tree?**

A A pile of dirt

B Tom's fishing pole

C The chest

D A wagon

22. **When Jacob reaches the hill above his house, he feels —**

F surprised

G happy

H scared

J annoyed

23. **Which question *best* summarizes Jacob's *main* problem in the story?**

A Where is the wooden chest?

B Who took the gold coins and the letter?

C Will the things I left behind still be there?

D Why did we have to move away?

GO ON

Reading and Literary Analysis

24. North Carolina is the story's —

   F plot

   G setting

   H main character

   J resolution

25. In this story the word *landscape* means —

   A farm

   B state

   C scene

   D home

26. "Something of Value" and "The Wooden Chest" were both written to —

   F persuade the reader

   G explain something to the reader

   H entertain the reader

   J instruct the reader

27. Both "Something of Value" and "The Wooden Chest" are told from the —

   A first-person point of view

   B first-person and third-person points of view

   C third-person point of view

   D second-person point of view

28. "Something of Value" and "The Wooden Chest" both deal with —

   F the meaning of friendship

   G how difficult it is to be brave

   H money versus other values

   J the value of independence

29. The truth about life that the writer reveals is the story's —

   A theme

   B characterization

   C setting

   D plot

GO ON

Reading and Literary Analysis

A Small Thing

1   Jenna burst out the door of the vacation cabin, letting the screen door slam behind her. She followed the dirt trail to a grassy field, running all the way across the field until she reached the pier. Walking to the end of the pier, Jenna caught her breath and gazed at the water. Her face still burned with anger.

2   Jenna and her cousin, Mack, had been playing a game of cards. She should have known better—Mack would win. For years, he had won every game or contest with Jenna. It's not that he gloated over winning or tried to make Jenna feel bad; it was just that Jenna had had enough of losing.

3   She became aware of the air on her cheeks and of the gentle lapping of water against the lakeshore. She heard the faint whisper of the breeze through the grass. When she focused her eyes, she could see tall shapes of pine trees across the lake, standing like silent guards.

4   Looking up, Jenna studied the sky. The clouds were scattered over a blue cloak, and the sun shone on the still water. Jenna felt a sense of smallness that did not diminish her. She also felt her anger slipping away.

5   After a few minutes, Jenna dove deep into the water and began swimming toward a platform in the middle of the lake. Between the platform and shore, she rolled over and floated on her back. Suspended between earth and space, she was a cloud drifting in the sky. In fact, in the face of the immense sky and the peaceful lake, she was beginning to feel that the world was a wonderful place and that losing a game of cards was the most unimportant event imaginable.

6   As she reached the platform, Jenna became aware of a chorus of croaking bullfrogs and chirping crickets. She clung to the ladder on one side of the platform, letting the concert sink into her ears for a few minutes. Then she used her feet to launch herself away from the platform and paddled slowly back toward the shore, composing an apology as she swam.

Reading and Literary Analysis

30. One theme of this story is that —

    F winning isn't everything
    G losers shouldn't complain
    H winners have a right to brag
    J vacations are a time to relax

31. Jenna's change of mood is foreshadowed by the —

    A slamming screen door
    B cool air on her hot face
    C chorus of bullfrogs and crickets
    D tall shapes of the pine trees

32. Another theme of this story is that —

    F cousins often disagree
    G anger always lasts a short while
    H nature can have a calming effect
    J running is the best exercise

33. Jenna was angry because —

    A Mack made fun of her
    B Mack did not want to play cards
    C she was tired of losing to Mack
    D she could not go outdoors

34. Which word *best* describes Jenna at the beginning of the story?

    F Anxious
    G Bored
    H Excited
    J Furious

35. By the end of the story, what does Jenna think about what happened in the card game with Mack?

    A She is angry at Mack.
    B She decides that being a good loser is important, too.
    C She resolves to be a better card player.
    D She hopes Mack will apologize.

36. What part of the setting is established in paragraph 1?

    F The time is late at night.
    G The weather is warm.
    H Tall pine trees stand across the lake.
    J The story takes place at a vacation cabin near water.

37. When Jenna returns to the cabin, she will probably —

    A read a book
    B go to bed
    C apologize to Mack
    D watch a movie

38. "Pine trees across the lake, standing like silent guards" is an example of —

    F a simile
    G an analogy
    H a metaphor
    J an idiom

GO ON

Reading and Literary Analysis

Let's Listen to Mozart

Read this article, which appeared on the editorial page of the school newspaper of Lindale Middle School.

The members of the PTA collected four thousand dollars at Fall Fest, the fund-raiser held last week. Now they are trying to decide what to do with the money. I would like to propose that the money be used to install a sound system throughout the school and to purchase CDs of classical music to play during school hours. This music would be heard in the halls, lunchroom, courtyard, and gym.

Most readers are probably familiar with studies that have shown that listening to classical music improves a baby's ability to learn. In fact, a state program in Georgia gives parents of newborns classical music CDs. Scientists have shown that listening to classical music improves learning in older children and adults as well. For example, a study at the University of California showed that listening to ten minutes of Mozart improved the spatial reasoning skills of college students.

I believe that listening to classical music is one of the best ways to spend one's time. Imagine visiting a school where the students' work is inspired by the music of Mozart, Handel, Bach, and others. It seems to me that the changes would be many. For example, classical music in the lunchroom might help reduce the earsplitting noise and encourage meaningful conversation. Having classical music in the halls between classes might calm students, leading to more relaxed class discussions and, as a result, more learning.

Other people have different ideas about how the money should be spent. These ideas include a new scoreboard for the football field and new benches for the locker room. I think that these things can wait. The scoreboard, although difficult to read, still works. The benches in the locker room are sturdy and serviceable.

People who are not fans of classical music may also object to the idea. If so, we could play other kinds of music at certain times and on certain *informal* occasions, such as at the end of each school day and on game days.

I hope that you will support my plan. I'm doing further research into the benefits that classical music may have in improving learning skills. I plan to present my findings at a meeting in the school library on Tuesday morning at 9:00 A.M. If you, too, would like to read with Rachmaninoff and stroll with Stravinsky, please join me.

39. **Who is the audience for this article?**

   A Musicians in the Lindale City Orchestra

   B Students at Lindale Middle School

   C Lindale City Council members

   D Readers of the Lindale city newspaper

40. **The purpose of this essay is to —**

   F entertain

   G describe

   H instruct

   J persuade

41. **Which of these is *not* given as support for the writer's argument?**

   A Classical music helps babies learn.

   B Classical music has survived the ages.

   C Classical music has a calming effect on listeners.

   D Listening to classical music improves spatial reasoning.

42. **The author points out that some people want to spend the money on a new scoreboard. This is an example of —**

   F the author's conclusion

   G an opinion

   H a statistic

   J a counterargument

43. **Which statement *cannot* be proven?**

   A Listening to classical music is one of the best ways to spend one's time.

   B A state program in Georgia gives parents of newborns classical music CDs and cassettes.

   C Listening to ten minutes of Mozart improved the spatial reasoning skills of college students.

   D The scoreboard, although admittedly difficult to read, still works.

44. **With which statement would the author *most* likely agree?**

   F Every type of music helps students learn.

   G Listening to classical music can be inspirational.

   H Students should only listen to music in the hall.

   J Teachers should learn more about classical music.

45. **In this editorial, the word *informal* means —**

   A traditional

   B relaxed

   C new

   D seasonal

GO ON

Vocabulary

DIRECTIONS: Choose the word or group of words that means the same, or about the same, as the underlined word. Then, mark the space for the answer you have chosen.

SAMPLE   A

The <u>industrious</u> beavers built a sturdy dam in half a day.

A   destructive
B   hard-working
C   cooperative
D   clever

---

46.   Through their <u>dialogue</u>, Chris and Lee discovered many common interests.

F   expressions
G   disappointment
H   conversation
J   activities

47.   Only a <u>remnant</u> of her paper remained after her computer crashed.

A   paragraph
B   copy
C   answer
D   part

48.   They danced slowly in time to the <u>melancholy</u> music.

F   sad
G   fast
H   rhythmic
J   lighthearted

49.   The <u>humid</u> air made Jill's hair curlier than usual.

A   brisk
B   damp
C   windy
D   dusty

50.   She <u>confronted</u> the man who gave false statements to the newspaper.

F   looked for
G   invited
H   reasoned with
J   challenged

STOP

Holt Assessment: Literature, Reading, and Vocabulary

Entry-Level Test

Answer Sheet

Sample

A   Ⓐ   Ⓑ   Ⓒ   Ⓓ

B   Ⓕ   Ⓖ   Ⓗ   Ⓙ

1. Ⓐ Ⓑ Ⓒ Ⓓ
2. Ⓕ Ⓖ Ⓗ Ⓙ
3. Ⓐ Ⓑ Ⓒ Ⓓ
4. Ⓕ Ⓖ Ⓗ Ⓙ
5. Ⓐ Ⓑ Ⓒ Ⓓ
6. Ⓕ Ⓖ Ⓗ Ⓙ
7. Ⓐ Ⓑ Ⓒ Ⓓ
8. Ⓕ Ⓖ Ⓗ Ⓙ
9. Ⓐ Ⓑ Ⓒ Ⓓ
10. Ⓕ Ⓖ Ⓗ Ⓙ
11. Ⓐ Ⓑ Ⓒ Ⓓ
12. Ⓕ Ⓖ Ⓗ Ⓙ
13. Ⓐ Ⓑ Ⓒ Ⓓ
14. Ⓕ Ⓖ Ⓗ Ⓙ
15. Ⓐ Ⓑ Ⓒ Ⓓ
16. Ⓕ Ⓖ Ⓗ Ⓙ
17. Ⓐ Ⓑ Ⓒ Ⓓ
18. Ⓕ Ⓖ Ⓗ Ⓙ
19. Ⓐ Ⓑ Ⓒ Ⓓ
20. Ⓕ Ⓖ Ⓗ Ⓙ
21. Ⓐ Ⓑ Ⓒ Ⓓ
22. Ⓕ Ⓖ Ⓗ Ⓙ
23. Ⓐ Ⓑ Ⓒ Ⓓ
24. Ⓕ Ⓖ Ⓗ Ⓙ
25. Ⓐ Ⓑ Ⓒ Ⓓ
26. Ⓕ Ⓖ Ⓗ Ⓙ

27. Ⓐ Ⓑ Ⓒ Ⓓ
28. Ⓕ Ⓖ Ⓗ Ⓙ
29. Ⓐ Ⓑ Ⓒ Ⓓ
30. Ⓕ Ⓖ Ⓗ Ⓙ
31. Ⓐ Ⓑ Ⓒ Ⓓ
32. Ⓕ Ⓖ Ⓗ Ⓙ
33. Ⓐ Ⓑ Ⓒ Ⓓ
34. Ⓕ Ⓖ Ⓗ Ⓙ
35. Ⓐ Ⓑ Ⓒ Ⓓ
36. Ⓕ Ⓖ Ⓗ Ⓙ
37. Ⓐ Ⓑ Ⓒ Ⓓ
38. Ⓕ Ⓖ Ⓗ Ⓙ
39. Ⓐ Ⓑ Ⓒ Ⓓ
40. Ⓕ Ⓖ Ⓗ Ⓙ

Sample A

Ⓐ   Ⓑ   Ⓒ   Ⓓ

41. Ⓐ Ⓑ Ⓒ Ⓓ
42. Ⓕ Ⓖ Ⓗ Ⓙ
43. Ⓐ Ⓑ Ⓒ Ⓓ
44. Ⓕ Ⓖ Ⓗ Ⓙ
45. Ⓐ Ⓑ Ⓒ Ⓓ
46. Ⓕ Ⓖ Ⓗ Ⓙ

Sample B

Ⓐ   Ⓑ   Ⓒ   Ⓓ

47. Ⓐ Ⓑ Ⓒ Ⓓ
48. Ⓕ Ⓖ Ⓗ Ⓙ
49. Ⓐ Ⓑ Ⓒ Ⓓ
50. Ⓕ Ⓖ Ⓗ Ⓙ

Answer Sheet

End-of-Year Test

Answer Sheet

Sample

A Ⓐ Ⓑ Ⓒ Ⓓ

B Ⓕ Ⓖ Ⓗ Ⓙ

1. Ⓐ Ⓑ Ⓒ Ⓓ
2. Ⓕ Ⓖ Ⓗ Ⓙ
3. Ⓐ Ⓑ Ⓒ Ⓓ
4. Ⓕ Ⓖ Ⓗ Ⓙ
5. Ⓐ Ⓑ Ⓒ Ⓓ
6. Ⓕ Ⓖ Ⓗ Ⓙ
7. Ⓐ Ⓑ Ⓒ Ⓓ
8. Ⓕ Ⓖ Ⓗ Ⓙ
9. Ⓐ Ⓑ Ⓒ Ⓓ
10. Ⓕ Ⓖ Ⓗ Ⓙ
11. Ⓐ Ⓑ Ⓒ Ⓓ
12. Ⓕ Ⓖ Ⓗ Ⓙ
13. Ⓐ Ⓑ Ⓒ Ⓓ
14. Ⓕ Ⓖ Ⓗ Ⓙ
15. Ⓐ Ⓑ Ⓒ Ⓓ
16. Ⓕ Ⓖ Ⓗ Ⓙ
17. Ⓐ Ⓑ Ⓒ Ⓓ
18. Ⓕ Ⓖ Ⓗ Ⓙ
19. Ⓐ Ⓑ Ⓒ Ⓓ
20. Ⓕ Ⓖ Ⓗ Ⓙ
21. Ⓐ Ⓑ Ⓒ Ⓓ
22. Ⓕ Ⓖ Ⓗ Ⓙ
23. Ⓐ Ⓑ Ⓒ Ⓓ
24. Ⓕ Ⓖ Ⓗ Ⓙ

25. Ⓐ Ⓑ Ⓒ Ⓓ
26. Ⓕ Ⓖ Ⓗ Ⓙ
27. Ⓐ Ⓑ Ⓒ Ⓓ
28. Ⓕ Ⓖ Ⓗ Ⓙ
29. Ⓐ Ⓑ Ⓒ Ⓓ
30. Ⓕ Ⓖ Ⓗ Ⓙ
31. Ⓐ Ⓑ Ⓒ Ⓓ
32. Ⓕ Ⓖ Ⓗ Ⓙ
33. Ⓐ Ⓑ Ⓒ Ⓓ
34. Ⓕ Ⓖ Ⓗ Ⓙ
35. Ⓐ Ⓑ Ⓒ Ⓓ
36. Ⓕ Ⓖ Ⓗ Ⓙ
37. Ⓐ Ⓑ Ⓒ Ⓓ
38. Ⓕ Ⓖ Ⓗ Ⓙ
39. Ⓐ Ⓑ Ⓒ Ⓓ
40. Ⓕ Ⓖ Ⓗ Ⓙ
41. Ⓐ Ⓑ Ⓒ Ⓓ
42. Ⓕ Ⓖ Ⓗ Ⓙ
43. Ⓐ Ⓑ Ⓒ Ⓓ
44. Ⓕ Ⓖ Ⓗ Ⓙ
45. Ⓐ Ⓑ Ⓒ Ⓓ

Sample A

Ⓐ Ⓑ Ⓒ Ⓓ

46. Ⓕ Ⓖ Ⓗ Ⓙ
47. Ⓐ Ⓑ Ⓒ Ⓓ
48. Ⓕ Ⓖ Ⓗ Ⓙ
49. Ⓐ Ⓑ Ⓒ Ⓓ
50. Ⓕ Ⓖ Ⓗ Ⓙ

Answer Sheet

Answer Key

Answer Key

Entry-Level Test,
page 1
Reading and Literary Analysis

Sample A C	20. J
Sample B G	21. A
1. C	22. G
2. G	23. C
3. C	24. F
4. F	25. C
5. D	26. G
6. F	27. D
7. D	28. H
8. G	29. C
9. D	30. F
10. H	31. A
11. A	32. J
12. H	33. A
13. C	34. J
14. H	35. A
15. A	36. G
16. J	37. A
17. A	38. J
18. G	39. A
19. A	40. H

Vocabulary

Sample A A	46. G
41. B	Sample B D
42. J	47. C
43. D	48. G
44. H	49. D
45. A	50. G

Collection 1

Collection 1 Diagnostic Test
Literature, Informational Text, Vocabulary, *page 15*

1. A	6. J
2. H	7. B
3. B	8. F
4. J	9. C
5. D	10. G

Rikki-tikki-tavi
by Rudyard Kipling
Selection Test, *page 17*
Comprehension

1. B	6. F
2. H	7. B
3. A	8. G
4. H	9. C
5. A	10. G

Literary Focus

11. D
12. F
13. D
14. F

Vocabulary Development

15. b
16. e
17. a
18. c
19. d

Holt Assessment: Literature, Reading, and Vocabulary

Answer Key

Constructed Response

20. Students' responses will vary. A sample response follows:

From the beginning of the story, Rikki-tikki protects his human family through his courage and cleverness. When Nagaina threatens to kill Teddy, Rikki-tikki uses the cobra's egg to distract her. This diversion gives Teddy's father a chance to pull Teddy out of Nagaina's reach. This last egg represents the survival of Nagaina's family. Rikki-tikki realizes that he and his human family will never be safe until Nagaina and her eggs are destroyed. When Nagaina flees down a hole with her egg, Rikki-tikki chases after her. Rikki-tikki drags himself out of the hole, the winner of the final battle.

from People, Places, and Change
Selection Test, *page 20*
Comprehension

1. C	**6.** J
2. F	**7.** B
3. B	**8.** H
4. H	**9.** A
5. A	**10.** F

Three Skeleton Key
by George G. Toudouze
Selection Test, *page 22*
Comprehension

1. A	**6.** H
2. H	**7.** B
3. B	**8.** G
4. F	**9.** B
5. A	**10.** H

Literary Focus

11. A
12. F
13. B
14. H

Vocabulary Development

15. c
16. d
17. e
18. a
19. b

Constructed Response

20. Students' responses will vary. A sample response follows:

The *Flying Dutchman* is a fabled Dutch ghost ship whose captain is said to be condemned to sail the seas until Judgment Day. Le Gleo is afraid of seeing this mythic ship because it will supposedly bring bad luck. The men's discussion of this ship foreshadows the ghostly absence of humans on the ship and the bad luck that the men will soon experience.

Eeking Out a Life
by Matt Surman
Selection Test, *page 25*
Comprehension

1. B
2. J
3. D
4. H
5. A

Vocabulary Development

6. marauding
7. extolling
8. voracious
9. diminutive
10. docile

Answer Key

The Monsters Are Due on Maple Street
by Rod Serling

Selection Test, *page 27*

Comprehension

1. D
2. G
3. C
4. F
5. C
6. F
7. C
8. G
9. D
10. G

Literary Focus

11. D
12. F
13. B
14. H

Vocabulary Development

15. transfixed, assent
16. explicit, menace
17. intimidated, defiant
18. converging, intelligible
19. variations, idiosyncrasy

Constructed Response

20. Students' responses will vary. A sample response follows:

   Les Goodman tries to reason with his neighbors, but they let their fear take over and refuse to listen. They start to act as a violent mob instead of as thinking individuals. And so begins the nightmare! First, they turn against Les. Then, they turn against Steve and question the fact that he has a ham radio. Next, violence breaks out. When a figure appears out of the darkness, Charlie picks up a shotgun and shoots. Only instead of shooting a space alien, he kills his neighbor Pete Van Horn. Then, the mob turns on Charlie. The nightmare continues. Lights start to go on and off, and suspicion moves from one person to another. No one is safe as panic spreads throughout the town. What started as a little incident with the power going off turns into a nightmarish state of anger and violence.

Cellular Telephone Owner's Manual

Selection Test, *page 31*

Comprehension

1. C
2. F
3. B
4. F
5. C
6. H
7. A
8. G
9. B
10. F

Collection 1 Summative Test,
page 33

Vocabulary Skills

1. D
2. F
3. D
4. J
5. B

Comprehension

6. G
7. A
8. F
9. B
10. H

Reading Skills and Strategies: Constructed Response

Making Inferences

11. The best answer is D. Students' responses will vary, but effective responses will mention that Victor's positive feelings about seventh grade are tied to his new relationships with Teresa and Mr. Bueller. Students may give examples such as Teresa's request that Victor help her with French and Mr. Bueller's decision not to expose Victor's limited knowledge of French.

Holt Assessment: Literature, Reading, and Vocabulary

Answer Key

Retelling

12. Students' responses will vary. A sample response follows:

> Victor meets Teresa, who indicates that she is impressed that he knows French. Victor worries that Mr. Bueller will reveal the truth, but Mr. Bueller remembers what it is like to want to impress a girl and doesn't say anything. Teresa asks Victor to tutor her in French. After school, Victor goes to the library and checks out three French textbooks.

Making Predictions

13. Students' responses will vary. A sample response follows:

> There is a good chance that Teresa will become Victor's girlfriend. It is obvious that she already likes him, since she asks him to tutor her. In addition, Victor likes her and wants to please her. In fact, he goes to the library to find books so that he can study and learn French. These actions will only help him and Teresa get closer.

Literary Focus: Constructed Response

14. Students' responses will vary. A sample response follows:

Description of Conflict

> Victor is having an internal conflict. He is struggling with the fear that Mr. Bueller or someone else will reveal that he pretended to know French. If the truth had been disclosed to Teresa, she probably would not have been interested in Victor.

Resolution

> Victor's secret is not revealed by Mr. Bueller or by anyone else. Teresa is impressed by Victor's "knowledge." He decides to check out books on French from the library so that he can impress Teresa even more.

Collection 2

Collection 2 Diagnostic Test

Literature, Informational Text, Vocabulary, *page 39*

1. C	**6.** G
2. F	**7.** D
3. D	**8.** F
4. J	**9.** B
5. B	**10.** H

Mother and Daughter
by Gary Soto

Selection Test, *page 41*

Comprehension

1. C	**6.** H
2. J	**7.** D
3. A	**8.** J
4. G	**9.** A
5. B	**10.** G

Literary Focus

11. B

12. J

13. C

14. H

Vocabulary Development

15. matinees

16. antics

17. sophisticated

18. meager

19. tirade

Constructed Response

20. Students' responses will vary. A sample response follows:

> Mrs. Moreno is a realistic character because she has both admirable and annoying traits, as real people do. Mrs. Moreno is affectionate, loving, and kind toward her daughter. She encourages Yollie's school career and tries hard to

Answer Key

provide for her daughter despite the family's poverty. When she sees that having a new outfit means a great deal to Yollie, Mrs. Moreno dips into her savings to provide the clothes. This act shows that she is generous and sensitive to her daughter's needs. On the other hand, some people in the neighborhood are amused by Mrs. Moreno's odd clothing and sense of humor. She is not skilled in home projects, as shown by her rock-hard candy apples and the disastrous job she did dyeing Yollie's dress. Gary Soto made Mrs. Moreno into a lifelike character by showing both her positive and negative traits.

The Smallest Dragonboy
by Anne McCaffrey
Selection Test, *page 44*

Comprehension

1. A	**6.** G
2. H	**7.** A
3. B	**8.** H
4. J	**9.** D
5. D	**10.** H

Literary Focus

11. C

12. F

13. C

14. J

Vocabulary Development

15. goaded

16. imminent

17. perturbed

18. alleviate

19. confrontation

Constructed Response

20. Students' responses will vary. A sample response follows:

Keevan faces several obstacles in his quest to become a dragonboy. First, he is very young and small. As a result, he is often taunted by older and larger boys. Keevan overcomes this obstacle by being determined and brave. These character traits enable him to withstand the maltreatment he receives. Second, Keevan is at a disadvantage because he is badly injured. His skull is fractured and he has a broken leg. Keevan overcomes these obstacles by strength of will. He forces himself to get to the Impression, even though he suffers great physical pain. The author shows us that Keevan's willpower and determination allow him to come out on top.

Here Be Dragons
by Flo Ota De Lange
Selection Test, *page 47*

Comprehension

1. A

2. H

3. D

4. J

5. C

Vocabulary Development

6. c

7. e

8. b

9. a

10. d

A Rice Sandwich
by Sandra Cisneros
Selection Test, *page 49*

Comprehension

1. A	**6.** F
2. G	**7.** D
3. C	**8.** J
4. H	**9.** B
5. B	**10.** H

Answer Key

Literary Focus

11. A

12. J

13. D

14. G

Vocabulary Development

15. d

16. e

17. a

18. b

19. c

Constructed Response

20. Students' responses will vary. A sample response follows:

Esperanza would be a good friend because she is smart, brave, and funny. She is smart because she knows what she wants and how to go about getting it—in this case, eating lunch in the canteen. In addition, she is very aware of her surroundings, realizing that other kids have perceived privileges that she doesn't. Esperanza bravely embraces new experiences (in this instance, eating lunch in school), which suggests that she would be a stimulating, exciting friend. Finally, she has a great sense of humor. This is shown by the excuses she presents to her mother to wear her down.

On the other hand, some might find Esperanza too persistent. Even though she is shy, she manages to get her way but realizes it isn't what she expected. Some may feel that she should be content with what she has.

Antaeus
by Borden Deal
Selection Test, *page 52*

Comprehension

1. B

2. H

3. A

4. J

5. D

6. F

7. C

8. H

9. A

10. G

Literary Focus

11. D

12. H

13. B

14. F

Vocabulary Development

15. c

16. e

17. b

18. d

19. a

Constructed Response

20. Students' responses will vary. A sample response follows:

The owner of the building resembles Hercules because he is stronger than T. J. and the other boys, and he has the power to destroy the garden. T. J. and the rest of the boys are like Antaeus, gathering strength from the earth, because planting the garden gives them a sense of purpose and accomplishment. In T. J.'s case the garden gives him additional strength because it brings him happiness by connecting him to the South. It also brings him respect among the other boys. All the boys, like Antaeus, are beaten at the end of the story. T. J. tries to run away, and the other boys never return to the roof.

In a Mix of Cultures, an Olio of Plantings
by Anne Raver
Selection Test, *page 55*

Comprehension

1. C

2. J

3. B

4. F

5. C

6. J

7. A

8. G

9. B

10. H

Answer Key

Collection 2 Summative Test,
page 57

Vocabulary Skills

1. A

2. H

3. C

4. J

5. B

Comprehension

6. J

7. D

8. G

9. C

10. F

Reading Skills and Strategies: Constructed Response

Making Inferences

11. B. Students' responses will vary. A sample response follows:

Aesop makes readers aware that others (such as Mercury) might have complicated reasons that we cannot fully understand, so honesty is always the best policy. In addition, the truthful Woodman wins in the end when Mercury gives him all the axes, showing that honesty brings rewards. In contrast, the dishonest Woodmen think they are being clever when they attempt to trick Mercury, but Mercury knows better.

Understanding Motivation

12. Students' responses will vary. A sample response follows:

The other Woodmen are motivated by greed and arrogance. They greedily want to get Mercury to give them golden axes, as he had to the first Woodman. They are also motivated by conceit, because they believe they are more intelligent than Mercury and so will be able to trick him. Of course, they are mistaken and suffer greatly for their presumption. The Woodmen's actions reveal that they are devious and over-confident.

Literary Focus: Constructed Response

13. Students' responses will vary. A sample response follows:

Character	Trait	Example
The Poor Woodman	hard-working	"It was late in the day and the Woodman was tired. He had been working since sunrise. . . ."
	honest	He accepts only his own axe, not the gold or silver one from Mercury.
	grateful	"The poor Woodman was very glad that his axe had been found and he could not thank the kind god enough."
Mercury	kind	When the Woodman told Mercury about his axe, Mercury dived into the pool immediately.
	tricky	He surfaced from the pool with a wonderful golden axe and asked the Woodman if it was his axe.
The Other Woodmen	arrogant	They actually believed that they could trick a god.
	dishonest	The Woodsmen went into the woods, hid their axes, and pretended they had lost them. Then they called on Mercury to help them.

Holt Assessment: Literature, Reading, and Vocabulary

Answer Key

Collection 3

Collection 3 Diagnostic Test
Literature, Informational Text, Vocabulary, *page 62*

1. B	**6.** H
2. H	**7.** C
3. A	**8.** G
4. J	**9.** D
5. A	**10.** F

The Highwayman
by Alfred Noyes

Selection Test, *page 64*

Comprehension

1. B	**6.** J
2. H	**7.** C
3. D	**8.** G
4. F	**9.** D
5. C	**10.** J

Literary Focus

11. B

12. J

13. D

14. F

Constructed Response

15. Students' responses will vary. A sample response follows:

Alfred Noyes uses plot to convey his theme about love and sacrifice. Noyes sets up the plot by showing readers that Bess and the highwayman are deeply in love. The plot develops as we see that Tim the ostler also loves Bess and is very disturbed by her love for the highwayman. His jealousy suggests that he will betray Bess, which sets the plot in motion. After his betrayal, the plot builds to its climax: Bess's suicide to warn her lover that he is riding into a trap.

Gentlemen of the Road
by Mara Rockliff

Selection Test, *page 67*

Comprehension

1. C	**6.** G
2. J	**7.** B
3. A	**8.** F
4. G	**9.** D
5. D	**10.** H

Annabel Lee
by Edgar Allan Poe

Selection Test, *page 69*

Comprehension

1. B	**6.** F
2. J	**7.** A
3. C	**8.** J
4. H	**9.** D
5. D	**10.** G

Literary Focus

11. A

12. J

13. B

14. G

Constructed Response

15. Students' responses will vary. A sample response follows:

The narrator becomes mentally unbalanced by the death of Annabel Lee. His thoughts and actions, if taken literally, are clearly not rational. His references to jealous angels and demons suggest that he has lost touch with reality. His constant preoccupation with Annabel Lee has an obsessive quality. The narrator's excessive reaction to Annabel Lee's death reinforces the poem's theme of grief and loss. His grief shows how some people have a great deal of difficulty dealing with the death of

Answer Key

a loved one, even though many years have passed. The narrator torments himself with this loss for the rest of his life.

The Fall of the House of Poe?
by Mara Rockliff
Selection Test, *page 72*

Comprehension

1. D
2. F
3. C
4. J
5. A

Vocabulary Development

6. absorbed
7. representatives
8. circulated
9. petitions
10. demolish

User Friendly
by T. Ernesto Bethancourt
Selection Test, *page 74*

Comprehension

1. C
2. F
3. B
4. H
5. A
6. H
7. B
8. G
9. D
10. J

Literary Focus

11. A
12. J
13. C
14. G

Vocabulary Development

15. c
16. d
17. a
18. e
19. b

Constructed Response

20. Students' responses will vary. A sample response follows:

Both Louis and Kevin are caring and thoughtful toward one another. Their friendship is shown as Louis tries to protect Kevin's feelings by causing trouble for Ginny and Chuck. Kevin feels so bad about Louis's actions that he decides that he must disconnect Louis to prevent him from causing further harm. However, Louis and Kevin are also very different. Louis is vindictive and cruel. He makes upsetting crank calls to Ginny, causes Chuck to be arrested by the Secret Service, triggers junk mail deliveries, and prompts an IRS audit. In contrast, Kevin does not plan any revenge to punish Ginny for her cruelty, even though she wounds his feelings. He does not even respond to her insults; rather, he just quietly gets off the bus.

It Just Keeps Going and Going . . .
by Joan Burditt
Selection Test, *page 77*

Comprehension

1. A
2. H
3. D
4. G
5. B
6. G
7. A
8. F
9. C
10. J

Echo and Narcissus
retold by Roger Lancelyn Green
Selection Test, *page 79*

Comprehension

1. B
2. H
3. B
4. F
5. A
6. G
7. C
8. F
9. B
10. J

Holt Assessment: Literature, Reading, and Vocabulary

Answer Key

Literary Focus

11. C

12. J

13. A

14. H

Vocabulary Development

15. vainly

16. detain

17. parched

18. intently

19. unrequited

Constructed Response

20. Students' responses will vary. A sample response follows:

Hera and Aphrodite have different attitudes toward Echo. Hera is angry at Echo. As a result, she punishes the nymph harshly by limiting Echo's speech to copying what other people say. This limitation affects Echo's fate because she is not able to tell Narcissus how she feels about him. This sets off a chain of misunderstandings. Aphrodite, in contrast, is sympathetic toward Echo. Therefore, she grants Echo's wish to die after she is rejected by Narcissus. Echo dies quietly and painlessly; and her voice lives on as an echo. This act of kindness makes Echo immortal because her voice lingers among the rocks whenever someone speaks.

Collection 3 SummativeTest,

page 82

Vocabulary Skills

1. D

2. G

3. C

4. F

5. A

Comprehension

6. H

7. A

8. J

9. C

10. G

Reading Skills and Strategies: Constructed Response

Understanding Cause and Effect

11. Brer Tiger falls for Anansi's trick because he is foolish and vain. He is too concerned with stopping a rumor to pay attention to what Anansi is doing. He also ignores Anansi's reputation as a trickster.

12. As a result of the trick, Brer Tiger runs off and leaves the field clear for Anansi to court Linda. Another effect of the trick is that Anansi comes across as someone who commands respect for being able to make the great tiger, the king of the jungle, his servant.

13. Linda believes the rumor that Brer Tiger was Anansi's horse because she sees Anansi riding on top of Brer Tiger. She was too foolish to question whether or not she was being tricked.

Literary Focus: Constructed Response

14. Students' responses will vary. A sample response follows:

Story Clues: Title—"Anansi's Riding Horse"; *Inference About Theme*—The theme will concern Anansi and a horse.

Story Clues: Linda's Character—"For Linda there was nothing whatsoever to think about. Anansi was puny and weak, and not at all good-looking…Linda laughed at him… Tiger was strong and handsome with brilliant burning eyes…. Linda was in love with him." *Inference About Theme*—Linda is shallow and places appearance above character. She will be easy to trick.

Story Clues: Plot—"But then the forest began to buzz with a most peculiar rumor: Anansi claimed that Brer Tiger was his riding

Answer Key

horse." *Inference About Theme*—Anansi is clever; he starts a rumor to humiliate his rival.

Story Clues: Plot—"Anansi jerked the rein back, shouting gleefully as he dismounted, 'See, gal, didn't I tell ya he was my riding horse!'" *Inference About Theme*—Anansi tricks Brer Tiger and Linda. Anansi banishes his rival.

Theme: Brains win out over brawn.

Collection 4

Collection 4 Diagnostic Test
Literature, Informational Text, Vocabulary, *page 88*

1. B	**6.** G
2. F	**7.** A
3. C	**8.** H
4. H	**9.** D
5. B	**10.** J

After Twenty Years
by O. Henry
Selection Test, *page 90*
Comprehension

1. D	**6.** F
2. F	**7.** A
3. B	**8.** G
4. H	**9.** C
5. B	**10.** J

Literary Focus

11. C

12. F

13. A

14. J

Vocabulary Development

15. d	**18.** c
16. b	**19.** a
17. e	

Constructed Response

20. Students' responses will vary. A sample response follows:

Most responses will agree with the statement. Jimmy and Bob are enemies because Jimmy is a police officer and Bob is a wanted criminal. They are also enemies because Jimmy has Bob arrested. Even though he doesn't do it himself, Jimmy turns Bob in. However, Jimmy and Bob are friends because they both keep their appointment after twenty years. They hold each other in high regard, even though Bob has become a criminal. Jim cannot deal with arresting a friend so he asks another officer to arrest Bob. The author uses the omniscient point of view to show the relationship between the men from each side.

What's *Really* in a Name?
by Joan Burditt
Selection Test, *page 93*
Comprehension

1. C	**6.** H
2. G	**7.** B
3. A	**8.** G
4. J	**9.** C
5. A	**10.** F

Bargain
by A. B. Guthrie
Selection Test, *page 95*
Comprehension

1. A	**6.** F
2. G	**7.** C
3. B	**8.** H
4. J	**9.** A
5. C	**10.** J

Answer Key

Literary Focus

11. B

12. F

13. C

14. F

Constructed Response

15. Students' responses will vary. A sample response follows:

Readers can infer from the story's outcome that the author believes that justice is a valid course of action, while revenge is not. If Mr. Baumer had killed Slade just because Slade did not pay his bill, that would be seeking revenge. However, Slade had been tormenting and physically assaulting Mr. Baumer. Further, there was no other way that Mr. Baumer could safeguard his life. The law was not a recourse at that time in the West, and no one was willing to stop Slade. Therefore, Mr. Baumer sought justice by having Slade destroy himself through his own weaknesses—not being able to read and greed. By using the first-person point of view, the writer is able to reinforce this distinction. In the first-person point of view, readers identify with Al and through him, with Mr. Baumer.

Yeh-Shen
retold by Ai-Ling Louie
Selection Test, *page 98*

Comprehension

1. C	**6.** H
2. J	**7.** A
3. A	**8.** F
4. G	**9.** D
5. D	**10.** G

Literary Focus

11. A

12. J

13. C

14. F

Constructed Response

15. Students' responses will vary. A sample response follows:

"Yeh-Shen" is told from the omniscient point of view. In this point of view, the narrator is all-knowing. As a result, the narrator can tell you everything, past and present, about all the characters, even their most private thoughts. If "Yeh-Shen" had been told from the first-person point of view, for example, readers would see events through the eyes of one character only. Readers would not have known many plot events. For example, we would not have known why the stepmother killed the fish and that she cooked it for dinner.

Mirror, Mirror, on the Wall, Do I See Myself As Others Do?
by Joan Burditt
Selection Test, *page 101*

Comprehension

1. C	**6.** H
2. F	**7.** C
3. D	**8.** G
4. G	**9.** B
5. A	**10.** J

Names/Nombres
by Julia Alvarez
Selection Test, *page 103*

Comprehension

1. D	**6.** H
2. H	**7.** A
3. C	**8.** G
4. G	**9.** C
5. A	**10.** J

Answer Key

Literary Focus

11. D
12. F
13. A
14. G

Vocabulary Development

15. b
16. a
17. e
18. c
19. d

Constructed Response

20. Students' responses will vary. A sample response follows:

"Names/Nombres" is told from the first-person point of view. This point of view helps make the essay very personal and subjective. Since Julia is telling her own story, she is naturally very involved in it. The author's theme—the importance of adapting to a new culture while keeping your heritage—is also very personal and subjective. Julia is able to reinforce her theme by relating her personal experiences. For example, she writes about how people mispronounced her family's name throughout her childhood. As time changed, so did the attitudes of other people in embracing other cultures.

An Unforgettable Journey
by Maijue Xiong

Selection Test, *page 106*

Comprehension

1. B	**6.** J
2. J	**7.** D
3. A	**8.** H
4. H	**9.** B
5. C	**10.** F

Literary Focus

11. C
12. J
13. A
14. H

Vocabulary Development

15. c
16. d
17. a
18. e
19. b

Constructed Response

20. Students' responses will vary. A sample response follows:

The writer uses a subjective point of view. She wants to express her opinions and feelings about her experience. By choosing this point of view, the writer is able to evoke the fear and terror of her displacement like a private snapshot of her life. For example, she gives in-depth details of the journey through the jungle and life in the refugee camp. Most likely, she did not choose an objective point of view because she did not want to present merely facts and figures. She wanted the reader to experience her life firsthand.

Exile Eyes
by Agate Nesaule

Selection Test, *page 109*

Comprehension

1. C	**6.** H
2. J	**7.** D
3. A	**8.** F
4. G	**9.** C
5. B	**10.** J

Holt Assessment: Literature, Reading, and Vocabulary

Answer Key

Elizabeth I
by Milton Meltzer
Selection Test, *page 111*

Comprehension

1. D
2. G
3. A
4. J
5. B
6. H
7. C
8. F
9. C
10. J

Literary Focus

11. B
12. J
13. A
14. H

Vocabulary Development

15. b
16. a
17. e
18. c
19. d

Constructed Response

20. Students' responses will vary. A sample response follows:

    If the biography were written in the first-person point of view rather than from the omniscient point of view, readers would get a subjective view of events rather than an objective view. It would become autobiographical and all events would be filtered through Elizabeth's eyes. We would only get her interpretation of events. Since there are many facts that she could not know (such as her lasting reputation and enduring legacy), these would not be included. The main idea would change from an objective assessment of Elizabeth and her reign to a biased view of a narrow slice of time.

Collection 4 Summative Test,
page 114

Vocabulary Skills

1. D
2. G
3. C
4. F
5. A

Comprehension

6. G
7. A
8. J
9. B
10. H

Reading Skills and Strategies: Constructed Response

Making Predictions

11. Students' responses will vary. A sample response follows:

    At the end of the story, the narrator and the other girls will probably be kind to the new girl. When the narrator says hello to the new girl at the end of the story, she is welcoming the new girl into their group. The narrator is sensitive to the new girl's situation. Since the narrator is clearly the leader, it is logical to predict that the other girls will follow her lead.

Answer Key

Determining the Main Idea

12. Students' responses will vary. A sample response follows:

C. It is very difficult to make new friends. The narrator describes the new girl by saying, "She is standing in the doorway, stocky terrier stance contradicted by a hesitant, scared expression." Her fear shows that it is hard to make friends. "She is an outsider, an outcast," as the narrator realizes. The new girl "can't and won't make the first move because she's the newcomer and it's up to us, and she knows this."

Possible response A: The girls are aware that the newcomer might be frightened by her new school, yet they want to test her instead of welcoming her. When the new girl gives them a lofty look, the others think she has overstepped her bounds. They are eager for a confrontation, which never happens.

Distinguishing Facts from Opinions

13. A. fact

B. opinion

C. opinion

D. fact

E. opinion

Literary Focus: Constructed Response

14. Students' responses will vary. A sample response follows:

At recess, the girls pour out the side door, and Andrea and Christine gather into a circle with the other girls, Janine, Flo, and Margaret. "Look," giggles Flo, pointing over to the paved area. The girls see the new girl, bouncing a ball against the wall, catching it, sometimes kicking it hard and having it leap high. They know she is watching them furtively without seeming to look—she can't and won't make the first move because she's the newcomer and it's up to the girls, and she knows this. The change from a first-person point of view to an omniscient point of view gives an objec-

tive account of events. In the first-person point of view, the readers only see events through the eyes of one character. It is often a more subjective account of a story.

Collection 5

Collection 5 Diagnostic Test
Literature, Informational Text, Vocabulary, *page 119*

1. C	**6.** J
2. H	**7.** B
3. A	**8.** H
4. G	**9.** A
5. B	**10.** J

Amigo Brothers
by Piri Thomas
Selection Test, *page 121*
Comprehension

1. C	**6.** G
2. F	**7.** A
3. D	**8.** G
4. J	**9.** D
5. C	**10.** F

Literary Focus

11. D

12. H

13. C

14. F

Vocabulary Development

15. pensively

16. barrage

17. torrent

18. dispelled

19. frenzied

Constructed Response

20. Students' responses will vary. A sample response follows:

"Amigo Brothers" is a short story, a brief

Answer Key

work of fiction. Since short stories have only a few characters, they are well suited to self-contained stories. "Amigo Brothers" tells the simple story of two best friends who find themselves fighting each other in a boxing match. In addition, short stories have a strong plot that leads to a climax and a resolution. "Amigo Brothers" reaches its climax during the boxing match. The resolution takes place when Felix and Antonio walk off together, their friendship intact.

Right Hook—Left Hook: The Boxing Controversy
by Joan Burditt
Selection Test, *page 124*

Comprehension

1. C	**6.** G
2. F	**7.** C
3. D	**8.** J
4. H	**9.** A
5. B	**10.** H

from Barrio Boy
by Ernesto Galarza
Selection Test, *page 126*

Comprehension

1. A	**6.** H
2. G	**7.** D
3. B	**8.** F
4. J	**9.** A
5. C	**10.** J

Literary Focus

11. A

12. H

13. C

14. J

Vocabulary Development

15. formidable

16. contraption

17. assured

18. reassuring

19. contraption

Constructed Response

20. Students' responses will vary. A sample response follows:

Ernesto Galarza probably tells his life story as an autobiography because he wants to present the facts of his life from his own point of view. He wants to include the facts and details from his life in chronological order, as he remembers them. Since he wants to tell the truth about his life, he has to use nonfiction. Both short stories and novels are forms of fiction, so they would not suit his purpose. Essays are nonfiction, but they present facts about a topic or an issue, not an account of the writer's own life.

Song of the Trees
by Mildred D. Taylor
Selection Test, *page 129*

Comprehension

1. C	**6.** H
2. H	**7.** B
3. A	**8.** G
4. J	**9.** D
5. C	**10.** J

Literary Focus

11. A

12. F

13. D

14. G

Vocabulary Development

15. c

16. e

17. a

18. d

19. b

Answer Key

Constructed Response

20. Students' responses will vary. A sample response follows:

"Song of the Trees" is a novella because it is longer than a short story. Both a novella and a short story are works of fiction. Both are written to entertain, not instruct. Both have just one main plotline, one or two main characters, one important conflict, and one main theme. A short story can be read in one sitting. A novella is longer, and cannot usually be read in one sitting.

Fish Cheeks
by Amy Tan
Selection Test, *page 132*

Comprehension

1. A	**6.** H
2. G	**7.** A
3. D	**8.** J
4. H	**9.** C
5. B	**10.** F

Literary Focus

11. C

12. G

13. A

14. J

Vocabulary Development

15. clamor

16. rumpled

17. muster

18. appalling

19. wedges

Constructed Response

20. Students' responses will vary. A sample response follows:

When different cultures come together, funny situations often arise, especially around the holidays. Amy Tan shows us the humor in a Christmas dinner, when Chinese and American traditions clash.

First, there is the menu. We can't help but laugh in anticipation of the reaction of the minister's family when, instead of the traditional turkey dinner, they have placed before them "slimy rock cod with bulging fish eyes," tofu that looks like "rubbery white sponges," and squid with "their backs crisscrossed with knife markings so they resembled bicycle tires." Then, there is the behavior at the table. We can picture the chaos as the Chinese family reaches with their chopsticks across the table and the father burps at the end of the meal. How funny it is when the minister "musters up a quiet burp" to try to show his appreciation! Finally, there is the reaction of the narrator. We sympathize with her when, to her great embarrassment, her father offers her the fish cheek. We can just imagine how she looks at the boy she has a crush on and how she wants to crawl under the table. This is a person's worst nightmare come to life. However, the essay also has a serious purpose. Although it is funny to see these cultures clash, we recognize the truth of the mother's words, "You must be proud you are different. Your only shame is to have shame." We can laugh about cultural differences, but it is important to take pride in your heritage.

A Mason-Dixon Memory
by Clifton Davis
Selection Test, *page 135*

Comprehension

1. D

2. G

3. A

4. H

5. B

Answer Key

Vocabulary Development

6. d

7. e

8. b

9. a

10. c

Buddies Bare Their Affection for Ill Classmate
Austin American-Statesman

Selection Test, *page 137*

Comprehension

1. A	**6.** F
2. H	**7.** B
3. D	**8.** J
4. G	**9.** A
5. C	**10.** H

I'm Nobody!
by Emily Dickinson

Selection Test, *page 139*

Comprehension

1. C	**6.** F
2. G	**7.** C
3. D	**8.** G
4. H	**9.** C
5. A	**10.** J

Literary Focus

11. D

12. F

13. B

14. H

Constructed Response

15. Students' responses will vary. A sample response follows:

> Fame should not be important in your life. In fact, it can be more of a burden than a blessing. Fame means that you are always in the public eye. It means that the people who call themselves your friends may be just hangers-on. It means that you may become self-centered and vain.
>
> The short form of the poem fits the poet's ideas of fame perfectly. It is modest—it does not demand center stage. It is not loud or boastful. Through vivid figures of speech and compressed language, it makes its point quietly but strongly.

I Like to See It Lap the Miles
by Emily Dickinson

Selection Test, *page 142*

Comprehension

1. C	**6.** G
2. H	**7.** C
3. D	**8.** G
4. F	**9.** A
5. B	**10.** J

Literary Focus

11. C

12. J

13. C

14. F

Constructed Response

15. Students' responses will vary. A sample response follows:

> Emily Dickinson develops the train's personality by giving the train the characteristics of a proud, irritable, high-spirited horse. When she describes how the train peers in a "supercilious" manner in line 6, she creates the image of a horse that feels superior to its surroundings. In line 11, she compares the train to a "complaining" horse that dislikes inconvenience and discomfort. She gives the train a horse's playful qualities by describing how it chases "itself down Hill" in line 13.

Answer Key

I Am of the Earth
by Anna Lee Walters
Early Song
by Gogisgi/Carroll Arnett
Selection Test, *page 145*

Comprehension

1. C
2. G
3. D
4. F
5. A
6. H
7. D
8. G
9. C
10. J

Literary Focus

11. A
12. G
13. B
14. H

Constructed Response

15. Students' responses will vary. A sample response follows:

Both poems describe the joy, celebration, and connection the speakers feel toward the earth. They both show a love of nature, too. In "I Am of the Earth," the speaker describes how the earth nourishes people. The poem also describes how thankful the speaker feels to be a part of the earth, and her connection to her "brothers and sisters," also living on the earth. In "Early Song," the speaker uses the images of the "good brown earth" and "dark blood" to show the pleasure the earth brings.

Madam and the Rent Man
by Langston Hughes
Selection Test, *page 148*

Comprehension

1. B
2. F
3. D
4. J
5. A
6. H
7. B
8. G
9. A
10. H

Literary Focus

11. C
12. F
13. B
14. J

Constructed Response

15. Students' responses will vary. A sample response follows:

All poetry contains rhythm, as this poem shows. This poem has a strong beat, which carries it along. Further, all poems present an image or situation in compressed language, as shown in "Madam and the Rent Man." The speaker describes a complete situation—a rent man passing the buck when he did not make promised repairs—in just thirty lines.

Harlem Night Song *and* Winter Moon
by Langston Hughes
Selection Test, *page 151*

Comprehension

1. B
2. G
3. C
4. J
5. C
6. F
7. A
8. H
9. D
10. F

Literary Focus

11. A
12. J
13. D
14. G

Constructed Response

15. Students' responses will vary. A sample response follows:

Hughes uses clear and specific imagery in the two poems to help the reader see and hear what he is describing. By describing the moon as shining over the Harlem rooftops in "Harlem Night Song," Hughes creates a vivid image to help his reader

Holt Assessment: Literature, Reading, and Vocabulary

Answer Key

quickly see and understand the setting of the poem. In the lines "Down the street / A band is playing," he enables the reader to hear that the night is filled with music. In "Winter Moon," Hughes carefully builds his description to create a vivid image of a crescent moon. For example, he calls the moon "thin" and "slim" to stress how small it is, and he calls it "sharp" to help the reader see the pointy ends of the crescent.

I Ask My Mother to Sing
by Li-Young Lee
Selection Test, *page 154*

Comprehension

1. B		**6.** F	
2. J		**7.** A	
3. A		**8.** H	
4. G		**9.** D	
5. B		**10.** G	

Literary Focus

11. C

12. H

13. D

14. F

Constructed Response

15. Students' responses will vary. A sample response follows:

The speaker enjoys hearing the song. As the title of the poem indicates, he encourages his mother to sing the song and states, "I love to hear it sung." The speaker's mother and grandmother also seem to enjoy the song. The speaker compares the women to young girls when they sing, which conveys an image of happiness. Also, the women continue to sing at the end of the poem. However, the song makes the women sad as well, and they cry at the end of the poem. The reader can infer that the song is associated with experiences and places from their past when they were younger. For the women the song is about

happy memories, but it is also about loss. Since the song is not about the speaker's own experiences, it does not make him sad.

Ode to Family Photographs
by Gary Soto
Selection Test, *page 157*

Comprehension

1. D		**6.** G	
2. J		**7.** D	
3. B		**8.** J	
4. H		**9.** B	
5. A		**10.** F	

Literary Focus

11. A

12. F

13. C

14. H

Constructed Response

15. Students' responses will vary. A sample response follows:

Soto's family photographs make his family seem ordinary because the subjects of the pictures, such as a pond, a car's bumper, and a boy with chocolate on his face, are common ones. The family members are depicted as having warm feelings for each other. For example, no one was critical of the mother even though she didn't take good photographs. In fact, the family members seemed to enjoy one another's company. They had fun when the mother photographed them, and the pictures show them "laughing hard." For Soto, these photographs capture the bonds and happy times his family shared.

Answer Key

Father William
by Lewis Carroll
Sarah Cynthia Sylvia Stout Would Not Take the Garbage Out
by Shel Silverstein

Selection Test, *page 160*

Comprehension

1. C	**6.** G
2. H	**7.** B
3. D	**8.** H
4. G	**9.** D
5. A	**10.** F

Literary Focus

11. A

12. J

13. B

14. G

Constructed Response

15. Students' responses will vary. A sample response follows:

   Both poets use humor and exaggeration to make a serious point. Carroll uses exaggeration to make the son's questions sound ridiculous. For example, when the son asks if it is all right for the father to stand on his head, Father William replies that it's perfectly safe to do because he's sure that he doesn't have a brain. The father's silly answer shows that he thinks his son's question is foolish. Carroll is pointing out that young people shouldn't assume that older people are weak and limited in their abilities. Silverstein uses exaggeration throughout his poem to describe the pile of garbage and Sarah's fate. The pile of garbage grew so large that "it touched the sky" and spread across the country, and Sarah apparently died because she did not take the garbage out. At the end of the poem, when the speaker reminds the audience to take the garbage out, he or she is really saying: If you don't fulfill your responsibilities, you may face negative consequences.

The Runaway
by Robert Frost

Selection Test, *page 163*

Comprehension

1. A	**6.** J
2. H	**7.** A
3. C	**8.** G
4. H	**9.** C
5. D	**10.** F

Literary Focus

11. C

12. J

13. A

14. H

Constructed Response

15. Students' responses will vary. A sample response follows:

   In "The Runaway," the speaker tells about seeing a young colt in a field during a snowfall. He seems to address some of his comments about the colt to the person with whom he is walking in the woods. Through his comments, we learn that he is a sensitive and caring human being who is concerned about the colt. We see how he interprets the colt's behavior. In fact, he tells his companion, "I think the little fellow's afraid of the snow." In addition, the speaker helps us to see the deeper meaning of the poem: "I doubt if even his mother could tell him, 'Sakes' / It's only weather.' He'd think she didn't know." Through his words, we come to understand that young people, like the colt, have to learn for themselves. However, there ought to be someone "to come and take [them] in."

Holt Assessment: Literature, Reading, and Vocabulary

Answer Key

The Pasture *and* A Minor Bird
by Robert Frost

Selection Test, *page 166*

Comprehension

1. B	**6.** H
2. J	**7.** A
3. D	**8.** F
4. G	**9.** B
5. C	**10.** H

Literary Focus

11. C

12. G

13. C

14. F

Constructed Response

15. Students' responses will vary. A sample response follows:

Both poems discuss small, ordinary elements of nature, such as a calf and a bird. The speaker in "The Pasture" seems to appreciate these aspects of nature, and therefore he invites an unseen person to join him as he goes to clean out a spring and fetch a calf. In contrast, the speaker in "A Minor Bird" does not appreciate the bird that is singing near his house. The bird's sad-sounding song annoys him, and he tries to make it fly away. However, at the end of the poem, the speaker realizes that the fault lies within himself, not the bird. He develops more respect for the bird, and he understands that every living thing has a right to express itself.

Names of Horses
by Donald Hall

Selection Test, *page 169*

Comprehension

1. B	**4.** J
2. H	**5.** C
3. A	**6.** J

7. B	**9.** D
8. G	**10.** F

Literary Focus

11. C

12. H

13. A

14. F

Constructed Response

15. Students' responses will vary. A sample response follows:

The poem is an elegy because the speaker mourns the loss of the horses that used to work on farms. The speaker respects the horses for their strength and endurance. He or she emphasizes that the horses performed hard labor that made their shoulders strain, for example. They worked "all winter" and "all summer," even in the hot sun, and the labor that they performed was essential to the running of the farms. For example, they hauled wood for stoves and helped make hay. By exclaiming "O" and naming the horses in the last line of the poem, the speaker gives the horses individual identities and expresses sadness over the loss of these loyal workers.

maggie and milly and molly and may
by E. E. Cummings

Selection Test, *page 172*

Comprehension

1. C	**6.** H
2. G	**7.** A
3. D	**8.** G
4. J	**9.** C
5. B	**10.** F

Literary Focus

11. C

12. F

13. B

14. H

Answer Key

Constructed Response

15. Students' responses will vary. A sample response follows:

As with all the other poetry in this collection, "maggie and milly and molly and may" has rhythm and figures of speech. For example, Cummings uses the simile "may came home with a smooth round stone / as small as a world and as large as alone." It also has personification: "and maggie discovered a shell that sang / so sweetly she couldn't remember her troubles." The poem also contains some exact rhymes (may/day) and some slant ones (milly/molly). Unlike most other poets, however, Cummings experiments with capitalization and punctuation. This poem, unlike the other poems in this collection, does not use any capitalization.

All in green went my love riding
by E. E. Cummings
Selection Test, *page 175*

Comprehension

1. A	**6.** J
2. G	**7.** C
3. D	**8.** G
4. F	**9.** A
5. D	**10.** H

Literary Focus

11. B

12. J

13. B

14. F

Constructed Response

15. Students' responses will vary. A sample response follows:

Through the poet's use of alliteration, repetition, and rhyme, words and lines flow together to create a sense of movement in the poem. For example, in the fifth stanza, *horn* and *hip* are linked through alliteration (line 11). The repetition of the word *riding*

links lines 11 and 12, and the use of slant rhyme (*down* and *dawn*) links lines 12 and 13. These repeated sounds make the words and lines in the stanza roll together, and they help to drive the reader forward. This sense of forward motion reflects the actions of the hunter who is chasing after the deer. The use of repetition, in particular the repetition of the line "four lean hounds crouched low and smiling," also builds tension in the poem and creates a sense of suspense about what will happen during the hunt.

Arithmetic
by Carl Sandburg
Selection Test, *page 178*

Comprehension

1. C	**6.** F
2. G	**7.** C
3. A	**8.** G
4. H	**9.** B
5. D	**10.** J

Literary Focus

11. C

12. F

13. D

14. F

Constructed Response

15. Students' responses will vary. A sample response follows:

Carl Sandburg uses a number of traditional poetic elements in "Arithmetic." He uses imagery that appeals to the sense of sight when he describes pigeons flying into your head and the striped zebra. He uses repetition to present his observations. For example, he begins most of the stanzas with the phrase "Arithmetic is where" or "If you." He also uses internal rhyme and alliteration. In stanza 3, the words *six* and *sticks* rhyme, and in stanza 4, Sandburg uses alliteration in *head* and *hand* and *pencil* and *paper.*

Holt Assessment: Literature, Reading, and Vocabulary

Answer Key

For Poets
by Al Young
Selection Test, *page 181*

Comprehension

1. C   4. J

2. F   5. B

3. A   6. H

Literary Focus

7. C

8. J

9. A

10. G

Constructed Response

11. Students' responses will vary. A sample response follows:

   The theme of the poem can be expressed as "Poets need to experience the world first-hand." When the speaker tells poets not to stay underground, he is using figurative language to tell poets not to remove themselves from the world. They shouldn't be like moles, which live in the dark ground, or like unfeeling stones. Instead, the speaker thinks that poets should inter-act with other living things. For example, speaking figuratively, he tells poets, "Commune with snakes." As the speaker explains in the third stanza, poets who are living like moles should come out of their holes and explore the world around them.

Collection 5 Summative Test,

page 183

Vocabulary Skills

1. D

2. G

3. B

4. J

5. C

Comprehension

6. J

7. D

8. G

9. C

10. F

Reading Skills and Strategies: Constructed Response

Identifying Personification

11. Students' responses will vary. A sample response follows:

   The writer personifies fire in the last two lines of the poem to make it come alive. Fire cannot "sleep"; that ability is reserved for living creatures. By making the fire seem human, the poet intensifies the emotion. This makes his love for his grandmother seem even stronger.

Making Generalizations

12. Students' responses will vary. A sample response follows:

   Based on "grandmother," poetry presents a feeling or emotion in compressed lan-guage. Here, the feeling is love for the speaker's grandmother. In addition, poetry uses figurative language to express its emo-tion. The poet here uses a simile to show his love for his grandmother: "and her words / would flow inside me / like the light / of someone / stirring ashes / from a sleeping fire / at night." Linking fire and love shows the depth of his emotion.

Describing Mental Images: Appealing to the Senses

13. Students' responses will vary. A sample response follows:

   C. Smell is the strongest sense, creating the most vivid mental image.

Answer Key

Literary Focus: Constructed Response

14. Students' responses will vary. A sample response follows:

Prose: novels—made-up stories; lots of characters; subplots; many themes; many conflicts; long.

Prose: novellas—made-up stories; one or two characters; no subplots; one theme; one conflict; about 100 pages.

Prose: short stories—made-up stories; one or two characters; no subplots; one theme; one conflict; under 100 pages.

Poetry: poems—images; figures of speech; sound devices; stanzas; compressed language; specific forms.

Collection 6

Collection 6 Diagnostic Test
Literature, Informational Text, Vocabulary, *page 188*

1. B	**6.** H
2. J	**7.** B
3. A	**8.** G
4. F	**9.** C
5. D	**10.** J

The Origin of the Seasons
retold by Olivia Coolidge

Selection Test, *page 190*

Comprehension

1. C	**6.** H
2. G	**7.** C
3. D	**8.** J
4. F	**9.** B
5. A	**10.** J

Literary Focus

11. B
12. F
13. D
14. G

Constructed Response

15. Students' responses will vary. A sample response follows:

While taking care of Demophoon, Demeter acts like both a human mother and a punishing goddess. Demeter feels great grief over the loss of her daughter, and taking care of Demophoon provides her with some relief from her sorrow. She takes care of the baby as if he were her own child, rocking him and singing to him, for example. Like a human mother, she also makes plans for the baby's future. However, since Demeter is a goddess, these plans involve making Demophoon immortal so that she can keep him forever. She also uses her power as a goddess to take away Demophoon's chance of becoming immortal. Angered by Metaneira's interference, she vows that Demophoon will become a hero but will have to die.

Orpheus, the Great Musician
retold by Olivia Coolidge

Selection Test, *page 193*

Comprehension

1. B	**6.** H
2. H	**7.** A
3. D	**8.** F
4. F	**9.** D
5. C	**10.** H

Literary Focus

11. B
12. G
13. A
14. J

Vocabulary Development

15. ghastly
16. reluctance
17. ascended
18. inconsolable

Holt Assessment: Literature, Reading, and Vocabulary

Answer Key

Constructed Response

19. Students' responses will vary. A sample response follows:

Hades is usually characterized as a hard-hearted god. In this myth he is described as "grim," with a "pitiless form" and "rigid cheeks." The author says that Hades does not care if people are miserable. However, Hades cries when he hears the love and longing in Orpheus's song. He is so touched by the powerful music that he does something uncharacteristic: He gives Orpheus a chance to get Eurydice back.

The Power of Music
by Nadja Salerno-Sonnenberg
Selection Test, *page 196*

Comprehension

1. D	**6.** H
2. G	**7.** B
3. A	**8.** F
4. J	**9.** A
5. D	**10.** F

The Flight of Icarus
retold by Sally Benson
Selection Test, *page 198*

Comprehension

1. B	**6.** F
2. J	**7.** B
3. A	**8.** J
4. G	**9.** D
5. C	**10.** J

Literary Focus

11. C

12. H

13. B

14. F

Constructed Response

15. Students' responses will vary. A sample response follows:

The flight of Icarus and the situation of a teenager driving the family car are similar in several ways. The parents of teenagers often warn their children to follow the rules of the road, and they worry about their children's safety. Like a typical parent, Daedalus gives his son careful instructions—warning him not to fly too low or too high—so that he will remain safe. For many teenagers, driving represents freedom. For Icarus, flying provides him with a sense of freedom as well. He is so attracted to the feeling of freedom that he behaves carelessly and ignores his father's warnings. He behaves irresponsibly, as some teenagers do, which has extreme consequences in his case.

King Midas and the Golden Touch
retold by Pamela Oldfield
Selection Test, *page 201*

Comprehension

1. A	**6.** G
2. H	**7.** B
3. D	**8.** F
4. F	**9.** C
5. B	**10.** H

Literary Focus

11. A

12. J

13. C

14. J

Constructed Response

15. Students' responses will vary. A sample response follows:

King Midas learns that having enormous wealth does not matter if you lose your health and your family. In the beginning of

Answer Key

the myth, Midas is greedy. He wants to be envied for his power. However, when he discovers that his gift prevents him from eating and drinking, he realizes that he has made a terrible mistake and decides to ask Dionysus to take back the gift. But then the situation gets even worse. When he accidentally turns his daughter into gold, he is overcome with grief. The reader knows that King Midas's views have definitely changed because he is willing to do anything to save his daughter, and he begs Dionysus for forgiveness. His great happiness when his daughter is brought back to life is further proof that he has learned what is truly important in life. He says, "I have learned my lesson . . . and I am content."

The Funeral Banquet of King Midas
by John Fleischman
Selection Test, *page 204*
Comprehension

1. B
2. H
3. D
4. J
5. A
6. G

Vocabulary Development

7. interior
8. avalanche
9. excavating
10. archaeologists

Oni and the Great Bird
retold by Abayomi Fuja
Selection Test, *page 206*
Comprehension

1. A
2. J
3. C
4. H
5. B
6. J
7. A
8. G
9. C
10. H

Literary Focus

11. D
12. H
13. B
14. F

Vocabulary Development

15. imposter
16. commenced
17. implored
18. hovered
19. invincible

Constructed Response

20. Students' responses will vary. A sample response follows:

"Oni and the Great Bird" contains many motifs that have appeared in other stories. Oni himself represents the motif of the superhero who is born with unusual gifts. This motif is found in the *Superman* comics and in the myth of Hercules, for example. The character of Anodo represents the typical human-eating monster, similar to the Minotaur in Greek mythology and the Big, Bad Wolf in the Grimm fairy tale. For the most part, I was not surprised by these motifs, because they are the types of characters that I expect to find in folk tales and myths. However, I was somewhat surprised to read about a magical boot that fits only its owner's foot. The boot reminded me of Cinderella's glass slipper. It was interesting to realize that the boot is a motif connecting stories from different cultures.

Master Frog
retold by Lynette Dyer Vuong
Selection Test, *page 209*
Comprehension

1. A
2. G
3. C
4. G
5. C
6. F
7. B
8. H
9. B
10. H

Holt Assessment: Literature, Reading, and Vocabulary

Answer Key

Literary Focus

11. D

12. J

13. A

14. F

Vocabulary Development

15. charade

16. presumptuous

17. admonished

18. cowered

19. entreaties

Constructed Response

20. Students' responses will vary. A sample response follows:

Kien Tien understands the meaning of the saying "Beauty is only skin-deep." When Master Frog first appears in the palace, she does not react in disgust, as her sisters do, but instead she offers to marry him. She does so primarily to prevent him from harming the kingdom. However, she also sees some good in the ugly frog when she recognizes that he is not cruel. Once they are married, Kien Tien discovers that her husband is smart and pleasant, and her attachment to him deepens. Although she is happy when he turns into a prince, it is clear that she would have loved him had he remained a frog.

The Crane Wife
told by Sumiko Yagawa
Selection Test, *page 212*

Comprehension

1. A		**6.** H
2. H		**7.** D
3. A		**8.** G
4. J		**9.** C
5. A		**10.** F

Literary Focus

11. B

12. H

13. D

14. F

Constructed Response

15. Students' responses will vary. A sample response follows:

In the beginning of the folk tale, Yohei is a simple, kindhearted man who rescues an injured crane from death. Although his marriage brings him happiness, Yohei becomes increasingly concerned about money. With his wife's assistance, he earns more money, and when his neighbor plants the idea in his head that he could become even wealthier, Yohei wants to become rich. The desire for wealth leads to a change in his character, causing Yohei to become an ambitious, calculating person. Instead of following his wife's warning, as he once did, Yohei allows his curiosity and greed to get the best of him, resulting in the breaking of a taboo and the loss of his wife.

Aunty Misery
by Judith Ortiz Cofer
Selection Test, *page 215*

Comprehension

1. C		**6.** H
2. F		**7.** A
3. A		**8.** G
4. J		**9.** C
5. B		**10.** F

Literary Focus

11. B

12. J

13. C

14. H

Constructed Response

15. Students' responses will vary. A sample response follows:

Aunty Misery's wish has more positive consequences than even she might have

Answer Key

expected. To protect her fruit, she wishes that the children will become stuck in her pear tree. This wish later proves useful in another way: It enables her to prevent Death from taking her with him. However, her wish then leads to negative consequences. Death remains in the tree for many years, and the lack of deaths in the world makes people suffer and lose money. Aunty Misery remedies this situation by granting Death his freedom. She does so, however, under the condition that he never come for her again. In this way, Aunty Misery eliminates the negative consequences caused by her wish and ends up gaining an unexpected benefit, immortality.

The Hummingbird King
retold by Argentina Palacios
Selection Test, *page 218*

Comprehension

1. C
2. G
3. B
4. J
5. D
6. F
7. A
8. J
9. B
10. H

Literary Focus

11. B
12. H
13. B
14. F

Constructed Response

15. Students' responses will vary. A sample response follows:

   Like "The Hummingbird King," "Oni and the Great Bird" contains a superhero, but the fates of the main characters in these two folk tales differ greatly. Like Kukul in the beginning of "The Hummingbird King," Oni cannot be killed in battle. Oni's power is part of him, and he survives at the end of the tale and gains control over half a kingdom. Kukul's power, however, is not

part of him. Instead, he can resist death only when he is protected by the feather. Once the feather is stolen, he is no longer a superhero, and he is killed.

The Search Goes On
by Carolyn Meyer and Charles Gallenkamp
Selection Test, *page 221*

Comprehension

1. D
2. H
3. B
4. F
5. A

Vocabulary Development

6. unscrupulous
7. ransacked
8. artifacts
9. connoisseurs
10. decipher

Collection 6 Summative Test,
page 223

Vocabulary Skills

1. B
2. J
3. A
4. H
5. D

Comprehension

6. H
7. B
8. F
9. D
10. H

Holt Assessment: Literature, Reading, and Vocabulary

Answer Key

Reading Skills and Strategies: Constructed Response

Summarizing

11. Students' responses will vary. A sample response follows:

After the Frogs ask Jupiter for a king, the god responds by placing a large log in the water. At first the Frogs are scared because they think the log is a giant. Then they realize that their new king makes no effort to rule them. Dissatisfied, the Frogs complain to Jupiter again. This time, to teach the Frogs a lesson, Jupiter sends a hungry, frog-eating Crane to be the king. When the Frogs beg Jupiter to take the Crane away, Jupiter tells them they are responsible for their own bad luck. The Frogs are stuck with their fate.

Understanding Cause and Effect

12. Students' responses will vary. A sample response follows:

Jupiter sends the Crane to Frogland because he thinks the Frogs have been foolish for requesting a king and need to be taught a lesson. As a result of Jupiter's action, many Frogs lose their lives and the surviving Frogs beg Jupiter to remove the Crane before more bloodshed occurs. However, Jupiter refuses to help the Frogs because he believes they should suffer the consequences of their poor judgment.

Literary Focus: Constructed Response

13. Students' responses will vary. A sample response follows:

In "The Frogs Who Wished for a King," Aesop is warning readers to appreciate what they have. Although people might think that change will improve their lives, it may not lead to greater happiness. He conveys this moral by showing how the Frogs cause their own destruction by not appreciating the freedom that they originally had. This moral still applies to life today. People are often dissatisfied with their lives, and therefore they try to better their situation.

For example, they might buy a bigger house or try to get more power in their jobs. However, instead of making them happier, these changes often make people more unhappy.

Collection 7

Collection 7 Diagnostic Test
Literature, Informational Text, Vocabulary, *page 227*

1. A	**6.** H
2. H	**7.** B
3. C	**8.** J
4. F	**9.** D
5. B	**10.** G

King Arthur: The Sword in the Stone
retold by Hudson Talbott

Selection Test, *page 229*
Comprehension

1. B	**6.** J
2. H	**7.** B
3. A	**8.** J
4. H	**9.** D
5. D	**10.** G

Literary Focus

11. A

12. H

13. D

14. G

Vocabulary Development

Students' responses will vary.

15. wild, disorderly

16. dishonesty

17. gathering

18. series of contests

19. calm

Answer Key

Constructed Response

20. Students' responses will vary. A sample response follows:

The theme of "King Arthur: The Sword in the Stone" can be stated as "true greatness will always be revealed." The dramatic story of Arthur's assuming his birthright as King of England and going on to unite his country resonates even today. We like to believe that people will be able to see our own special traits and appreciate us for the seeds of greatness that we possess.

Three Responses to Literature

Selection Test, *page 232*

Comprehension

1. D	**6.** G
2. H	**7.** B
3. C	**8.** H
4. G	**9.** D
5. C	**10.** F

Literary Focus

11. C

12. G

13. C

14. F

Constructed Response

15. Students' responses will vary. A sample response follows:

For an essay to be successful, it is essential that the writer answer the question so that the essay makes a point. Essay 3, for example, is not successful because the writer fails to address the question. The reader of this essay gets detailed information about the plot of the story, but never learns the writer's views of whether Arthur has the potential for greatness. A successful essay must also contain support to convince the reader that the writer's points are valid. For example, Essay 1 is a strong response to the question because the writer provides concrete details about Arthur's personal

traits and actions, as well as quotations, to back up the main ideas in the essay.

He's No King

Selection Test, *page 235*

Comprehension

1. B	**6.** G
2. G	**7.** C
3. A	**8.** J
4. J	**9.** B
5. B	**10.** F

Merlin and the Dragons
by Jane Yolen

Selection Test, *page 237*

Comprehension

1. C	**6.** J
2. H	**7.** A
3. B	**8.** F
4. G	**9.** A
5. D	**10.** J

Literary Focus

11. D

12. G

13. A

14. G

Vocabulary Development

15. b

16. d *or* c

17. e

18. a

19. c *or* d

Constructed Response

20. Students' responses will vary. A sample response follows:

The frame story serves to reinforce the story's theme. The frame story describes the early life of Emrys, the so-called "demon's son" from Wales. As he grows up, Emrys learns that he has magical powers. These

Holt Assessment: Literature, Reading, and Vocabulary

Answer Key

range from the mundane—predicting rain—to the extraordinary—predicting the future. When he helps defeat the evil Vortigern, young Emrys allows the reign of Uther Pendragon, who will father Arthur. Through this story, Arthur comes to understand that he was destined to rule England. As Arthur realizes, "Then I am king by right and not just because I pulled a sword from a stone." This statement reinforces the story's theme: Some people are destined for greatness, but they must be ready to accept their destiny.

Sir Gawain and the Loathly Lady
retold by Betsy Hearne

Selection Test, *page 240*

Comprehension

1. D
2. J
3. C
4. F
5. B
6. H
7. D
8. G
9. C
10. F

Literary Focus

11. A
12. H
13. B
14. J

Vocabulary Development

Students' responses will vary.

15. code that governed knights
16. charming, delightful
17. disgusting
18. face
19. lack of control

Constructed Response

20. Students' responses will vary. A sample response follows:

   The author makes Sir Gawain an appealing character through indirect characterization. By seeing how Sir Gawain acts, what he says, and how other people respond to

him, readers get a full picture of a chivalrous knight. When King Arthur needs help solving the riddle, Sir Gawain springs into action. He directs Arthur to ride one way and promises to help: "I will ride another way, and every man and woman's answer I will write in a book." All the women gladly give their answers, so readers can infer that he is polite. He even agrees to marry the loathly lady to help his king: "For you are my king and I am your friend," he says. "It is my part to save your life, or else I am a false knight and a great coward." Finally, Sir Gawain gives Dame Ragnell the right to choose her own fate, revealing that he is fair.

Collection 7 Summative Test, *page 243*

Vocabulary Skills

1. A
2. J
3. C
4. G
5. B

Comprehension

6. G
7. A
8. J
9. C
10. H

Literary Focus: Constructed Response

11. Students' responses will vary. A sample response follows:

   Objectivity: Method of Evaluating—find textual support. *Proof*—"Saturday in October, a balmy afternoon." "The wind came up suddenly...."

   Primary sources: Method of Evaluating—almanacs, newspapers, personal interviews. *Proof*—"It was over in three or four minutes." "No one was killed." "Roads were cut off, a bridge buckled."

Answer Key

Collection 8 Diagnostic Test
Informational Text, *page 247*

1. D	**6.** G
2. F	**7.** A
3. B	**8.** H
4. G	**9.** D
5. B	**10.** J

Analyzing Information in Public Documents
Selection Test, *page 249*

Comprehension

1. A	**6.** G
2. H	**7.** B
3. C	**8.** J
4. F	**9.** D
5. D	**10.** H

Analyzing Information in Workplace Documents
Selection Test, *page 251*

Comprehension

1. B	**6.** G
2. G	**7.** A
3. C	**8.** J
4. J	**9.** C
5. D	**10.** H

Analyzing Information in Consumer Documents
Selection Test, *page 253*

Comprehension

1. D	**6.** G
2. G	**7.** A
3. C	**8.** J
4. H	**9.** A
5. A	**10.** H

Following Technical Directions
Selection Test, *page 255*

Comprehension

1. B	**6.** G
2. J	**7.** D
3. C	**8.** H
4. H	**9.** A
5. A	**10.** G

Collection 8 Summative Test,
page 257

Vocabulary Skills

1. disoriented

2. apprehension

3. itinerary

4. hazardous

5. solitary

Comprehension

6. F	**11.** B
7. D	**12.** J
8. G	**13.** A
9. C	**14.** H
10. H	**15.** B

Informational Focus: Constructed Response

16. Students' responses will vary. A sample response follows:

Weather: Warning—"Sudden changes in weather catch many unaware." *Safety Measures*—"Be prepared for all weather conditions." "Be over passes and away from high open areas by noon." "During a storm, stay away from peaks…, ridges, caves…."

High water: Warning—During early spring and summer, high water levels and swift currents are common. *Safety Measures*—"Cross in a wide, shallow spot." "Unbuckle waist straps, use a long stick…and face upstream." "Don't tie yourself in to 'safety ropes.'"

Answer Key

Tick-borne diseases: Warning—"Two known diseases [are] carried by ticks in this area." *Safety Measures*—"If you are bitten by a tick and later experience flulike symptoms, contact your doctor."

Giardia lamblia: Warning—Boil all water or melted snow for at least five minutes. *Safety Measures*—See your doctor if you are infected.

Safety hints: Warning—Stay alert. Be careful. *Safety Measures*—"Stay on the trail!!!"

End-of-Year Test, *page 262*
Reading and Literary Analysis

Sample A A	**23.** C
Sample B J	**24.** G
1. A	**25.** C
2. J	**26.** H
3. B	**27.** C
4. J	**28.** H
5. A	**29.** A
6. G	**30.** F
7. C	**31.** B
8. G	**32.** H
9. A	**33.** C
10. J	**34.** J
11. B	**35.** B
12. J	**36.** J
13. A	**37.** C
14. J	**38.** H
15. B	**39.** B
16. G	**40.** J
17. C	**41.** B
18. F	**42.** J
19. D	**43.** A
20. H	**44.** G
21. A	**45.** B
22. H	

Vocabulary

Sample A B

46. H
47. D
48. F
49. B
50. J

Skills Profile

SKILLS PROFILE

STUDENT'S NAME_____ GRADE _____

TEACHER'S NAME _____ DATE _____

For each skill, write the date the observation is made and any comments that explain the student's development toward skills mastery.

SKILL	NOT OBSERVED	EMERGING	PROFICIENT
Literature			
Understand the characteristics of different forms of prose, such as the novel, novella, short story, and essay.			
Identify events that advance the plot, and determine how each event explains past or present actions or foreshadows future actions.			
Analyze the methods writers use to reveal character.			
Identify and analyze recurring themes across works.			
Contrast different points of view, and explain how they affect the overall theme of a work.			
Determine how literary elements in a work elicit a range of responses to that work.			
Informational Text			
Analyze the structure and purpose of various types of informational texts.			
Locate information by using consumer, workplace, and public documents.			
Analyze texts that show cause-and-effect relationships.			
Analyze an author's argument, point of view, or perspective.			
Follow technical instructions in order to understand the use of a simple mechanical device.			
Assess the quality of the author's evidence to support claims, noting instances of bias and stereotyping.			

Holt Assessment: Literature, Reading, and Vocabulary

STUDENT'S NAME_____ GRADE _____

TEACHER'S NAME _____ DATE _____

SKILL	NOT OBSERVED	EMERGING	PROFICIENT
Vocabulary			
Identify idioms, analogies, metaphors, and similes.			
Use Greek, Latin, and Anglo-Saxon roots and affixes to understand vocabulary from various content areas.			
Clarify word meanings by using definitions, examples, restatements, and contrasts.			

Skills Profile